Editing Keys	Key	Action
Controlling the cursor	←	Moves cursor left one character
	→	Moves cursor right one character
	↑	Moves cursor up one line
	↓	Moves cursor down one line
	Ctrl +←	Moves cursor left one word
	Ctrl +→	Moves cursor right one word
	Home	Moves cursor to beginning of line
	End	Moves cursor to end of line
	Ctrl +Home	Moves cursor to beginning of module/procedure
	Ctrl +End	Moves cursor to end of module/procedure
Inserting and deleting text	Ins	Toggles between insert and typeover mode
	Del	Deletes character at cursor
	Backspace	Deletes character to left of cursor
	Ctrl +T	Deletes word
	Ctrl +Y	Deletes line
Working with selected text	Shift +cursor-control keys	Selects text
	Shift +Del	Cuts selected text to clipboard
	Del	Cuts selected text without saving to clipboard
	Ctrl +Ins	Copies selected text to clipboard
	Shift +Ins	Inserts text from clipboard
Working with windows	F6	Makes next window active
	Shift +F6	Makes previous window active
	Alt +Plus	Increases window size one line
	Alt +Minus	Decreases window size one line
	Ctrl +F10	Toggles between active window and full screen
	Ctrl +↑	Scrolls one line up
	Ctrl +↓	Scrolls one line down
	PgUp	Scrolls one full screen up
	PgDn	Scrolls one full screen down
	Split command (from View menu)	Divides the View window horizontally
	Esc	Clears help screens and dialog boxes

Mastering QuickBASIC

Mastering QuickBASIC

Rita Belserene

SYBEX ®

San Francisco • Paris • Düsseldorf • London

Acquisitions Editor: Dianne King
Editor: Alan Hislop
Technical Editor: Maryann Brown
Word Processors: Chris Mockel and Scott Campbell
Series Designer: Julie Bilski
Chapter Art and Layout: Charlotte Carter
Technical Art: Jeffrey James Giese
Screen Graphics: Delia Brown
Typesetter: Winnie Kelly
Proofreader: Patsy Owens
Cover Designer: Thomas Ingalls + Associates
Cover Photographer: David Bishop
Screen Reproductions produced by XenoFont

CGA (Color Graphics Adapter), EGA (Enhanced Graphics Adapter), MCGA (Multicolor Graphics Array), VGA (Video Graphics Array), and IBM PC are trademarks of International Business Machines Corporation.
Hercules Graphics Adapter is a trademark of Hercules Computer Technology.
MS-DOS and QuickBASIC are trademarks of Microsoft Corporation.
WordStar is a trademark of WordStar International.
XenoFont is a trademark of XenoSoft.

SYBEX is a registered trademark of SYBEX, Inc.

TRADEMARKS: SYBEX has attempted throughout this book to distinguish proprietary trademarks from descriptive terms by following the capitalization style used by the manufacturer.

SYBEX is not affiliated with any manufacturer.

Every effort has been made to supply complete and accurate information. However, SYBEX assumes no responsibility for its use, nor for any infringement of the intellectual property rights of third parties which would result from such use.

Library of Congress Card Number: 89-63413
ISBN 0-89588-589-1
Manufactured in the United States of America
10 9 8 7 6 5 4 3 2 1

This book is dedicated to
Emilia Pisani Belserene, astronomer;
and to every woman who has used education
to redefine her universe.

ACKNOWLEDGMENTS

I would like to thank the many people who provided support and assistance throughout the writing of this book. Tanya VanDam at Microsoft Corporation responded with lightning speed to my request for materials. At Sybex, Dianne King got this project in motion and Barbara Gordon kept it moving. Alan Hislop repaired my choppy prose and corrected the dozens of "whiches" that should have been "thats," for which I am very grateful. Maryann Brown assisted with her encouraging words, as well as with her technical review of the manuscript.

At the Berkeley Adult School, my colleagues John Levy and Rie Kimbara were generous with their ideas and support, while Atsushi Maki, our resident computer wizard, answered each of my questions without ever making me feel foolish for asking them. I am particularly grateful to Matthew Newman, who put considerable time and careful thought into this project and made enormously helpful comments.

On a personal note, I would like to thank all the friends whose homes and computers I used while my own home became a construction zone. I am especially indebted to Karen Platt. Without her generosity and flexibility this project could never have been completed.

Finally, I thank my husband, Don, for loving me through all the trying times.

CONTENTS AT A GLANCE ━━━

TABLE OF CONTENTS ———————————

INTRODUCTION

Mastering QuickBASIC is a tutorial introduction to QuickBASIC, Version 4.5. QuickBASIC is one of a new generation of BASIC programming languages. Like those variations on BASIC that have preceded it, QuickBASIC is easy to learn and to use, making it an ideal choice for beginners. But this flexible new BASIC has also grown sophisticated and powerful enough for professional use.

Regardless of your programming experience, you should find QuickBASIC remarkably easy to get along with. In addition to the programming language itself, QuickBASIC offers program development features designed to help you create and modify your programs quickly and easily. These features include extensive online help, an editor smart enough to catch many errors for you, and debugging devices that help you locate programming mistakes as quickly and efficiently as possible.

To get started, you will need QuickBASIC Version 4.5 software and an IBM Personal Computer or an IBM-compatible computer with at least 384K of available memory (640K of memory is recommended for best performance). QuickBASIC is designed to be installed and used on a hard drive, but it is also possible, although far less convenient, to use QuickBASIC on a dual floppy-drive system.

ABOUT THIS BOOK

As you read this book, you will be building skills in three areas:

- *Thinking like a programmer*: This book will help you develop general programming skills that you can apply to programs written in any language.

- *Speaking the language*: You will learn how to use the statements and commands that make up the QuickBASIC language.

• *Understanding the QuickBASIC environment*: Developing programs is a dynamic process. Throughout the book you will learn editing and debugging techniques that will speed this process and minimize frustration.

Well-written computer programs are carefully structured. Among other things, this means dividing large tasks into smaller tasks of manageable size. Computers do not require this kind of division of tasks, but it is a style that works well for people. I use the same approach in presenting information in this book. Each new technique is first introduced in very short sample programs designed to help you learn the language quickly. These samples illustrate exactly what a command does and provide the details you need to know in order to master it. More realistic programs follow that will help you think like a programmer by showing you how to put your skills to practical use.

WHO SHOULD READ THIS BOOK

This book is written for anyone new to QuickBASIC. Some readers will bring prior programming experience to their study of Quick-BASIC, but such experience is not necessary, and this book makes no assumptions about what you already know about BASIC or other programming languages.

It *is* assumed, however, that readers of this book have some computer experience and are familiar with a computer keyboard. You should also have some knowledge of the DOS operating system, particularly commands used for copying disks or files and for working with disk directories.

IF YOU ARE NEW TO PROGRAMMING

At its best, computer programming can be a delightful experience. It is problem solving in one of its purest forms, a marvelous variety of solitaire that draws you in, sometimes at the expense of time you might have spent with friends and associates. At its worst programming can be a source of terrible frustration, plunging you into a sullen irritability that your poor friends and associates must also suffer through.

This book is designed to help you enjoy programming. Programming examples are carefully chosen to introduce you to new ideas progressively, giving you an opportunity to master each skill with a minimum of confusion. A full range of topics is covered to put as many tools as possible at your disposal. With these new skills, and some old standbys like patience and concentration, you will be delighted with what you can accomplish.

IF YOU HAVE PROGRAMMING EXPERIENCE

Whatever your prior programming experience, you will probably find some aspects of QuickBASIC to be a pleasant surprise. For example, the QuickBASIC editor offers you a variety of WordStar-style editing options that make writing and updating programs easy to do from within QuickBASIC. Like interpreted programming languages, QuickBASIC allows you to run programs as you develop them, with your code still on screen. If a bug interrupts a program's execution, you are returned to your program code at the point where the error occurred. You can then correct it immediately and continue program execution from that point, rather than having to restart your program after each correction. If you are used to a programming language that requires you to wait through a time-consuming compiling process after each revision, you will enjoy the speed and simplicity of QuickBASIC's dynamic debugging. Once completed, programs can be compiled into stand-alone executable files. This feature, plus greatly improved running speed, will please programmers whose previous experience has been with interpreted versions of BASIC such as BASICA and GWBASIC.

QuickBASIC enhanced language features provide many programming options that make it far more powerful than the BASIC you may know now. Among these are

- SUB and FUNCTION procedures, which make it easy to develop well-structured programs and to reuse completed procedures when you write new programs.

- The SELECT CASE statement, which helps simplify control of program flow.

- The use of flexible, user-defined data-types to facilitate reading and writing data to files.

- The availability of long integers for greater precision with improved speed.

This book is designed to help you get up and running in Quick-BASIC. A variety of programming examples demonstrates how to use the QuickBASIC language, and each chapter demonstrates new techniques to help you take advantage of the program development features available in the QuickBASIC environment.

HOW THIS BOOK IS ORGANIZED

Chapters 1–14 provide you with a step-by-step introduction to programming with QuickBASIC. These chapters introduce new ideas progressively, and incorporate a wide variety of programming examples that demonstrate these ideas. The final two chapters of the book are organized as reference chapters. These chapters are not written in a tutorial format, but are designed instead to provide you with handy reference information to use, both as you work through the exercises in this book, and again later, as you develop your own programs.

If you are a beginner, you will want to work through this book progressively, although it is not necessary to cover all of the detailed information in each chapter before proceeding to the next.

Experienced programmers may prefer to skim through much of the material, making use of the two reference chapters to fill in details.

CHAPTER 1: A QUICKBASIC OVERVIEW

Gives you a chance to sample each of QuickBASIC's key features. Step-by-step exercises show you how to work with the QuickBASIC menus as you create, edit, save, print, and compile a short program.

CHAPTER 2: UNDERSTANDING THE QUICKBASIC ENVIRONMENT

Hands-on exercises guide you through QuickBASIC's extensive online help features and introduce you to essential QuickBASIC editing features.

CHAPTER 3: MAKING THE COMPUTER WORK FOR YOU: VARIABLES AND CALCULATIONS

Introduces you to simple input and output techniques and the fundamentals of performing calculations. Explains how to work with the four BASIC data-types and describes the use of both numeric and string variables.

CHAPTER 4: COMMUNICATING EFFECTIVELY: INPUT AND OUTPUT TECHNIQUES

Discusses a variety of input and output techniques that will help you develop clear, easy-to-use programs. Methods used for formatting numeric output are included here. Editing procedures for working with blocks of material and conducting word search operations are also covered.

CHAPTER 5: DOING IT AGAIN: PROGRAM LOOPS

Introduces two methods used to control repetitive operations, FOR...NEXT and DO...LOOP structures. Editing techniques that simplify work with indented material are included here. This chapter also introduces debugging tools that allow you to examine program execution step-by-step, watching what happens to the values of program variables as you go.

CHAPTER 6: MAKING DECISIONS: PROGRAM BRANCHING

Shows decision making with IF...THEN and SELECT...CASE statements. Logical expressions used in decision statements are explained and the use of Boolean variables is introduced. Debugging techniques useful for working with logical expressions are included here.

CHAPTER 7: DIVIDE AND CONQUER: DEVELOPING SUB PROCEDURES

Discusses the advantages of a modular approach to programming and demonstrates the use of QuickBASIC SUB procedures. Different methods for passing variable values between the main program and SUB procedures are covered in detail. Introduces the use of QuickBASIC Full Menus, which offer expanded command options that will be used from this chapter on.

CHAPTER 8: GETTING FANCY: MORE ABOUT INPUT AND OUTPUT

Shows you a variety of additional methods for getting data and displaying the results in ways that will make your programs eye-catching and easier to use. Covers how to store data within your program and access it, using DATA and READ statements.

CHAPTER 9: USING QUICKBASIC FUNCTIONS

Explains how functions operate and shows you how to use functions in your programs. You will learn the functions that are part of the QuickBASIC language and also how to create your own function procedures. Demonstrates functions used for handling both character strings and numeric values.

CHAPTER 10: MANAGING ARRAYS

Illustrates the use of subscripted variables to manipulate quantities of data. Programming techniques for sorting and searching data are introduced here.

CHAPTER 11: WORKING
WITH SEQUENTIAL DATA FILES

Introduces programming methods used for storing and retrieving data on disk files. Steps for creating, writing to, and reading from sequential files are described and demonstrated.

CHAPTER 12: WORKING
WITH RANDOM-ACCESS DATA FILES

Continues the study of data files, introducing techniques for creating and using data stored in structured, random-access data files. A short programming application is used to demonstrate each of the steps involved in working with random-access files. This is followed by a longer application that introduces the use of indexing techniques.

CHAPTER 13: EXPLORING
QUICKBASIC GRAPHICS

Discusses hardware considerations that affect the use of graphics commands and introduces techniques that can be used to produce useful and visually exciting screen displays.

CHAPTER 14: REFINING
YOUR PROGRAMMING TECHNIQUE

Introduces techniques to make your programming more professional. You will learn how to use program modules and libraries to facilitate program development. Error-trapping techniques are also explained that help protect users of your programs from confusing run-time errors.

CHAPTER 15: THE QUICKBASIC ENVIRONMENT:
A MENU COMMAND SUMMARY

This summary covers each of the program development features available with QuickBASIC Full Menus.

CHAPTER 16: THE BASIC LANGUAGE: A COMMAND SUMMARY

Includes syntax and a brief description for each of the BASIC statements and functions covered in this book.

ICONS USED IN THIS BOOK

Three visual icons are used in this book:

The Note icon indicates a note that augments the material in the text.

The Tip icon represents a practical hint or special technique.

When you see the Warning icon pay particular attention—it represents an alert or warning about a possible problem or offers a way to avoid the problem.

A QuickBASIC Overview

1

CHAPTER 1

THE QUICKBASIC SOFTWARE YOU ARE ABOUT TO explore provides you with a powerful variety of tools for developing computer programs. This chapter is organized into a series of exercises to help get you started with QuickBASIC and give you a comfortable familiarity with what it can do. As you follow the step-by-step instructions, you will explore the QuickBASIC menus, create and edit a short program, run and print your program, and then create a free-standing version of the program, which you will run from the operating system. When you have completed this chapter you will have a strong overall framework to rely on as you develop your QuickBASIC programming technique. Before getting started, lets look at a few fundamentals to ensure that we are speaking a common language.

A computer program is a series of instructions written according to a carefully constructed set of rules called program *code*. The form this code takes depends on the programming language being used. At its core, QuickBASIC is an enhanced version of the popular BASIC programming language. One crucial function of QuickBASIC software is to convert the BASIC code that you create, known as *source code*, into the code that the computer actually uses to carry out program instructions, known as *machine language*.

WordStar-style editing commands make editing particularly easy for programmers who are already familiar with that word processing package.

In addition to providing this translation service, QuickBASIC includes supporting features that help make writing and modifying programs easier. For tasks such as inserting, deleting, or moving parts of a program, QuickBASIC provides you with a built-in editor. Additional support features are available for finding and correcting programming errors, a process known as *debugging*. QuickBASIC debugging tools are designed to help you accomplish this sometimes frustrating task as efficiently as possible. These support features collectively make up what is known as the QuickBASIC *environment*.

To become an effective QuickBASIC programmer, you will want to have a thorough understanding of both the BASIC programming language and the QuickBASIC environment.

GETTING STARTED

Although you can use QuickBASIC with a either a hard-disk or a floppy-disk system, it is somewhat slow and awkward on a floppy-disk system. Instructions given here are for installation and setup on a hard-disk system. Information about using QuickBASIC with a floppy-disk system is provided in Appendix B.

The file named PACKING.LST on the Utilities 2 disk gives a complete list describing the files provided with your QuickBASIC distribution disks. Use the command TYPE PACKING.LST > PRN to get a printed copy of this list.

INSTALLING QUICKBASIC ON YOUR HARD DISK

You can install QuickBASIC using the Setup program provided with your software. Place the disk labeled "Setup/Microsoft QB Express" in your disk drive, and at the A:\> type

```
setup
```

and press ◄─┘. (In this book the ◄─┘ symbol is used to indicate the Enter key.) Installation instructions will appear on your monitor. Select the highlighted choices for an *Easy Setup*. When you have completed the installation process, follow directions to return to the operating system.

The Setup program creates a QB45 directory on your disk and copies all necessary files to this directory. Two subdirectories to the QB45 directory are also created, and a variety of sample Quick-BASIC programs are copied to these directories. You can work from within the QB45 directory, or you can change the search path in your AUTOEXEC.BAT file to include this directory. This will allow you to run QuickBASIC from any directory on your disk.

To start QuickBASIC, type

```
qb
```

at the DOS prompt and press ◄─┘. Your monitor should display the Welcome screen shown in Figure 1.1. If the **qb** command fails to load the program, check to be sure you are in the QB45 directory. Or, if you altered your AUTOEXEC.BAT file, check that you have run the altered batch file or restarted your system using the modified file.

Figure 1.1: The QuickBASIC Welcome screen

THE WELCOME SCREEN

If your Quick-BASIC software is not newly installed, it might bypass the QuickBASIC Welcome screen and move you directly to the Work screen shown in Figure 1.2.

The Welcome screen in Figure 1.1 is an example of a QuickBASIC dialog box. Dialog boxes give you a choice of options and often ask you to provide additional information as well. In this case, you have two choices: to take an introductory tour of QuickBASIC or to clear the box and get right to work in QuickBASIC. For now, press the Esc key to clear the screen and go directly to QuickBASIC's Work screen, shown in Figure 1.2. (Later you might want to return to the Welcome screen and explore the QuickBASIC Survival Guide. To do so, start QuickBASIC again and press ◄─┘ when the Welcome screen appears.)

EXPLORING THE QUICKBASIC MENUS

The Menu bar at the top of the Work screen contains headings that provide entry into the QuickBASIC menus. A menu is a list of command choices. To execute a command you open a menu and then select one of the items on the list. The following exercises demonstrate different techniques for opening and closing menus.

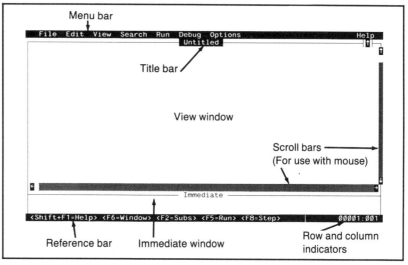

Figure 1.2: The QuickBASIC Work screen

OPENING AND CLOSING
MENUS USING QUICK KEYS

QuickBASIC menus are displayed on screen only when you are ready to use them. There are two different techniques for opening menus using your keyboard, both of which use the Alt key to activate the Menu bar. The quickest way to open a menu once the menu bar is activated is to press the first letter of that menu heading. Here are the steps:

1. Press the Alt key. The first letter of each menu name should be highlighted. Pressing that highlighted letter selects that menu choice.

2. Press F to open the File menu (see Figure 1.3.). A pull-down menu that lists several choices for file-related activities appears below the word *File*. For the moment, however, we won't proceed any further.

3. Press the key labeled Esc to close the menu.

Practice opening and closing each of the menus using this technique. It is not necessary to hold the Alt key down while you press a letter to

In ths book, letter keys will be identified using uppercase letters, as they appear on the keyboard. Pressing either F or f will open the File menu, however.

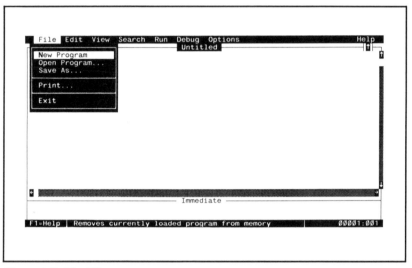

Figure 1.3: The File menu

If you want to de-activate the Menu bar without selecting a menu, you can do so by pressing the Alt key a second time or by pressing Esc.

select a menu. The Alt key acts as a switch to activate the Menu bar. While it is active, pressing a highlighted letter will open a menu.

BROWSING THE MENUS USING THE CURSOR-CONTROL KEYS

You can also select menus using the cursor-control keys—those keys marked with arrows: ↑, ↓, →, and ←. This method takes a bit more time, but provides you with some helpful information along the way. To try it, take the following steps:

1. Press the Alt key to activate the Menu bar. In addition to highlighting the first letter of each heading, this action causes one heading—File—to change appearance. Notice that there has also been a change in the message that appears in the Reference bar at the bottom of your screen.

2. Press the → key. This action selects the Edit menu heading.

3. Press ↵ to open the Edit Menu. Press the ↑ and ↓ keys to highlight different choices within this menu. As you move up and down, read the message in the Reference bar, which changes as you make selections, displaying a short summary of the action produced by each menu choice.

4. Press the → key. The View menu to the right opens, and the Edit menu closes.

5. Continue to browse the menus by using the cursor-control keys and reading the Reference bar to learn more about the choices in each menu.

6. Press Esc to close the menus and return to the Work screen.

USING A MOUSE TO MAKE MENU SELECTIONS

If your system includes a desktop mouse, you have the option of using it to speed up cursor movement and menu selection. Quick-BASIC completely supports the use of any mouse that is compatible with a Microsoft Mouse. Microsoft provides you with a mouse driver named MOUSE.COM on the Utilities 2 disk, and to use a mouse you must install this program before you start QuickBASIC. Do this by starting with a disk or directory that contains the MOUSE.COM file and typing **MOUSE** at the DOS prompt.

When you start QuickBASIC with the mouse driver installed, there are two cursors. The smaller keyboard cursor is initially positioned in the View window, while the mouse cursor is tucked away in the upper left-hand corner of your screen. Slide the mouse over your work surface to move the box-shaped mouse cursor into view.

Choices made from the keyboard by pressing the Alt key and choosing a highlighted key can also be made with a mouse by moving the mouse cursor to the desired choice and clicking the *left* mouse button. To open a menu using the mouse, position the mouse cursor anywhere on a menu heading and click the left mouse button. Close a menu by moving the cursor to any location outside the menu box and clicking the left mouse button.

To install the mouse driver automatically each time you start up your system, place MOUSE.COM in a directory that is in your search path and include the MOUSE command in your AUTOEXEC-.BAT file. You can remove the driver from memory at any time by typing MOUSE OFF at the DOS prompt.

SELECTING FULL MENUS AND EASY MENUS

QuickBASIC offers you two alternative sets of menus. The shorter Easy Menus are designed with beginners in mind. They simplify choices to help avoid confusion and frustration. Full Menus offer a greater range of selections to use as you develop your skills and begin to create more complex programs.

When it is first installed, QuickBASIC is preset to use the Easy Menus. In the next exercise you will use QuickBASIC commands to change to Full Menus and then back again to Easy Menus.

1. Press Alt and then O to open the Options menu.

2. Press ↓ twice to highlight the Full Menus choice. Your screen should now match Figure 1.4.

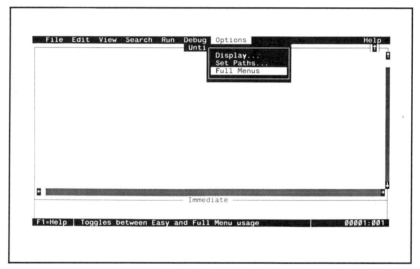

Figure 1.4: Selecting Full Menus

3. Press ◄— to select Full Menus. The Options menu will close and you will be returned to the Work screen. An additional menu, Calls, has appeared on the Menu bar between Debug and Options.

4. Browse the expanded menus by pressing Alt, then ◄—, and using the ◄— and —► keys to move through each of the menus. Each menu includes many new options. Figure 1.5 shows the expanded File menu.

5. Open the Options Menu.

6. The Full Menus command toggles you back and forth between Easy and Full Menus. Selecting this choice now will return you to the Easy Menus. You can do this in a single keystroke by

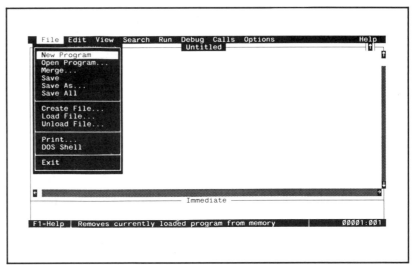

Figure 1.5: The expanded File menu using Full Menus

pressing F (the highlighted letter). You will be returned to the Work screen as it appeared originally. (Figure 1.2)

This book uses Easy Menus through Chapter 6. Chapter 7 introduces you to the Full Menus, and these expanded options are used from that point on. When you change menu levels, QuickBASIC "remembers" your choice between sessions and always returns you to the most recently selected menu level. Your choice of menu level is stored in a disk file called QB.INI. If you have selected Full Menus, the Welcome screen that you saw earlier will no longer be displayed when you enter QuickBASIC.

CREATING YOUR FIRST QUICKBASIC PROGRAM

The View window that occupies most of the Work screen is used to type and edit program code. The cursor in the upper left-hand corner of the View window indicates that you can start typing material at that location. In the next exercises you will type a program into the View window, run the program, edit it, and then print and save the finished product.

ENTERING THE SALESTAX PROGRAM

Figure 1.6 shows a short program designed to calculate sales tax. When this program runs, the computer will ask you to enter the price of an item. The program should then calculate a 7% sales tax based on that price. The computer uses this calculated value to display the amount of the tax and the total price with tax included. An error has been built into the program to give you a chance to try your hand at editing later.

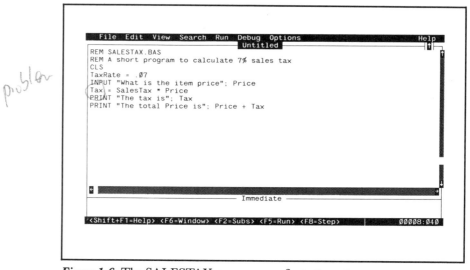

Figure 1.6: The SALESTAX program—a first attempt

As you type the program, pay particular attention to punctuation marks.

Use the row indicator to locate program lines identified by number in the text.

Type the program *exactly* as it appears in Figure 1.6. If you make typing errors, you can use the backspace key to go back and correct them. Press ◄─┘ at the end of each line to begin the next line. As you move from one line to the next, QuickBASIC translates each statement into a form the computer can understand so that the program is ready to run as soon as you have typed the last line. While you type, notice that the row and column indicators in the lower right-hand corner of your screen change to reflect the position of your cursor.

ELEMENTS OF A QUICKBASIC PROGRAM

Take a few minutes to study the design of the SALESTAX program. It consists of eight program lines. QuickBASIC program statements are delineated when you press ◄─┘ at the end of each line. Blank lines and indentations are frequently used in longer programs to make them easier to read; they do not affect a program's performance. In many BASIC programs, statements on each line are preceded with a line number. QuickBASIC can execute BASIC programs that include line numbers, but they are not an essential part of a program and will not be used in this book. When you run a Quick-BASIC program, statements are executed in the order they appear on screen. Execution stops after the last program line or where an END statement is encountered.

Using a consistent style makes programs easier to read. Words that are part of the BASIC language (CLS, INPUT, and PRINT) are displayed in uppercase letters. Variables names (Price, TaxRate and Tax) are chosen by the programmer and are distinguished by uppercase letters for the first letter only, or, when several words are combined to form a single name, for the first letter of each word, as in TaxRate.

Each command used in this program will be introduced and explained in detail in later chapters, but a quick summary here will give you a general sense of how the program operates. The first two lines are remark statements, as indicated by the word REM. These provide helpful information to anyone reading the program listing. The computer takes no action when it sees a REM statement. The third line clears the monitor's Output screen (CLS). Line four assigns a value for the sales tax rate. The INPUT statement in line five sends a question to the Output screen and waits for the user's response. Line six performs a calculation. The PRINT statements in the last two lines display calculated results on the monitor screen. You will see these actions when you run the program in the next exercise.

RUNNING YOUR PROGRAM

When your screen matches Figure 1.6 exactly you are ready to run the program. You can start program execution by selecting the *Start* command in the Run menu. Follow these steps to run the SALES-TAX program:

1. Press Alt to activate the Menu bar.

2. Press R to open the Run Menu.

To run the program using a mouse, move the mouse cursor to Run, click the left button, and then move the cursor to Start and click again.

3. Press S to select Start. The Work screen, with your program code, will disappear and be replaced by a display screen called the Output screen. This screen has been cleared by the CLS command and now shows the following question, which it was instructed to display by your program's INPUT statement.

   What is the item price?

4. Respond to the question by typing **12** and pressing ⏎. The Output screen now looks like this:

   What is the item price? 12
   The tax is 0
   The total Price is 12

At the bottom of the screen is the message

Press any key to continue

The program ran, but the results are disappointing. The value for the tax should not be zero. Do we have a "computer" error here? Unfortunately, we do not. As a programmer you will learn to blame yourself for these errors. The computer did exactly what it was told to do, and therefore the error is in the program code. You will correct it in the next exercise.

Press any key and you will be returned to the Work screen and your program code.

EDITING THE SALESTAX PROGRAM

The problem with the SALESTAX program is that different parts of the program have used different names for the tax rate. Line four sets the tax rate equal to .07 using the variable **TaxRate**. Line six tries to calculate the amount of the tax using a variable called **SalesTax**. In the absence of any prior information about this latter variable, the computer sets SalesTax equal to zero and figures accordingly.

Changing line six is one way to correct the problem. The edited version is shown in Figure 1.7. Follow these directions to make the correction:

1. Find the cursor in your View window. It will be where it was before you ran the program—probably either at the end of the last line or at the beginning of the blank line underneath it.

2. You can move the cursor using the cursor-control keys. Move it to the *S* of SalesTax in line six.

3. The Del (or Delete) key erases the character or space at the cursor location. Press Del and the *S* will disappear. Press it four more times to erase *ales*.

4. Move the cursor to the blank space immediately following the edited word *Tax*. Anything you type will be inserted immediately to the left of the cursor, leaving the rest of the line intact. Type **Rate** and check to be sure that your edited program now matches Figure 1.7.

```
 File  Edit  View  Search  Run  Debug  Calls  Options                    Help
                               Untitled
REM SALESTAX.BAS
REM A short program to calculate 7% sales tax
CLS
TaxRate = .07
INPUT "What is the item price"; Price
Tax = TaxRate * Price
PRINT "The tax is"; Tax
PRINT "The total Price is"; Price + Tax




                               Immediate
 <Shift+F1=Help> <F6=Window> <F2=Subs> <F5=Run> <F8=Step>          00008:020
```

Figure 1.7: The edited SALESTAX program

The corrected version of the program should now work the way it was intended to. You could test it by running it again using the same technique you did before, but the next exercise shows a quicker way to run programs.

USING SHORTCUT KEYS

You will find that you return to many QuickBASIC commands over and over again. For these commands you are provided with shortcuts using the keyboard function keys labeled F1, F2, F3, etc.

Some commands are invoked by pressing one of these keys alone. Others require you to hold down "booster" keys (Shift, Alt, or Ctrl) while you press the appropriate function key. In this book, when you must hold one key down while pressing a second, a " + " is used to connect the names of the two keys. A shortcut written as Shift +F5 means to press the Shift key and, while you are still holding it down, press the F5 key.

Shift +F5 is the shortcut for running a program. Use this shortcut to run the SALESTAX program again. The program will run and you should see the question

What is the item price?

once again in the Output screen. Test the edited program by entering the value 12 one more time. The results should now look like this:

What is the item price? 12
The tax is .84
The total Price is 12.84

Run the program several times, using different values for the price each time. Practice both the menu method and the shortcut method for running the program until you feel comfortable with them both.

When shortcuts are available for a QuickBASIC command, they are indicated next to the menu listing for that command. Open the Run menu and notice that the shortcut Shift +F5 is written next to the Start command. Press Esc to close the menu. Your program is now working perfectly, and you are ready to save it as a file on your disk. To do this, you will need to understand how to work with QuickBASIC dialog boxes.

USING QUICKBASIC DIALOG BOXES

Many QuickBASIC commands require additional information before they can be completed. For instance, a new program needs to be given a file name the first time you save it. You might also want to indicate a particular directory or disk drive as the destination for the new file. When QuickBASIC requires such information, it displays a dialog box on screen. In addition to requesting information, dialog boxes also offer you a choice of further actions, such as proceeding with the command once all requested information has been supplied, cancelling the command, or displaying on-screen help to explain each item in the dialog box. In the next exercise you will save the SALESTAX program and, in the process, have an opportunity to become comfortable conducting these electronic dialogs with your computer.

SAVING THE SALESTAX PROGRAM

QuickBASIC programs can be saved as disk files using the *Save As* command in the File menu. Follow these steps to save the SALES-TAX program:

1. Open the File menu.

2. Use the ↓ key to select the *Save As* option. The Reference bar should read, "Saves current module with specified name and format."

3. Press ↵ to select this save option. Your screen will now display the Save As dialog box shown in Figure 1.8.

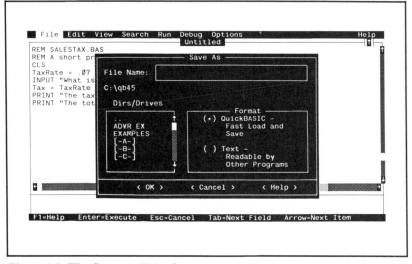

Figure 1.8: The Save As dialog box

Before continuing, take a few minutes to become familiar with the parts of the Save As box. There are three input areas and three actions to choose from. The File Name input area is where you enter a name for the file being saved. Beneath this is a disk and directory indicator that shows where the saved file will be located. If you wish to change drives or directories, you can do so by using the Dirs/Drives input area just beneath it. Format, the third input area, describes two different formats QuickBASIC can use when it saves a file and lets you choose between them. The default choice is for a quick save using a file format that is specific to QuickBASIC. The second choice produces files using a text format (ASCII) that can be read by other programs.

At the bottom of the dialog box are three action choices. The <OK> choice is highlighted by default. If you press ↵ while this choice is highlighted, the file save command will be executed using the information provided in the three input areas. You can change from this action choice to <Cancel>, which cancels the save operation and closes the box, or <Help>, which provides you with a bit more information about the Save As options.

There are two ways to move to an item in a QuickBASIC dialog box. You can use the Tab key to move from one box to the next (using Shift + Tab to move in the reverse direction). Or you can press the Alt key, which results in a highlighted letter for each item. To select the item, you hold the Alt key down while you press the highlighted letter. The next steps demonstrate both of these methods.

4. The cursor should be in the File Name input area. Type the name **SALESTAX**. You can enter the name in either upper-case or lowercase letters; once a file is saved, QuickBASIC will display the name using all uppercase letters. Limit your program file names to eight characters. A three letter .BAS extension, which is standard for BASIC language programs, will be added automatically.

5. Press Tab to move to the Dir/Drives item. If you want to save your files to the current directory, you do not need to make any changes here.

6. Press Tab to move to the Format area. The ↑ and ↓ keys move the choice indicator back and forth between these choices.

Whenever the <OK> action is highlighted, pressing ↵ closes a dialog box and executes the command. Don't press ↵ after typing the file name unless you are ready to procede with the save command.

Sometimes dialog box items can be selected by pressing and releasing Alt and then choosing a highlighted letter, but this will not work if your cursor is in the File Name input area. Item selection will always work properly if you hold the Alt key down while you make your selection.

Use the *Fast Load and Save* choice unless you want to save a file in ASCII format.

7. Press Alt to highlight letters for selecting items. While you are holding down the Alt key, press H to activate the Help box. Study the information that appears on screen. Close the Help box by pressing Esc (or ⏎).

8. Press Shift + Tab twice to select <OK>.

9. Press ⏎. This will save your file, close the dialog box, and return you to the Work screen. The name SALESTAX.BAS will replace the word 'Untitled' in the Title bar at the top of the View screen.

When you repeat the save command, the input you provided during your most recent save, including the file name, will be displayed when the dialog box reappears. This means that it's not necessary to retype the file name or specify disk drives or directories again when you save an updated version of your program.

Once you have saved a file to a disk, you can retrieve it at any time. You're ready now to clear the screen.

CLEARING THE WORK SCREEN

When you clear the Work screen, the program you are working with is also removed from memory. This leaves you free to retrieve a program from the disk or to start writing a new one.

- Clear your screen by opening the File menu and pressing N for New Program.

If you try to clear the screen without saving your most recent program changes, QuickBASIC displays the warning shown in Figure 1.9.

If you see this message and select <*Yes*>, QuickBASIC saves your file before clearing the screen. (If your program is untitled, a dialog box appears on screen as part of the save process.) Selecting <*No*> clears the screen and abandons the program. Choosing <*Cancel*> interrupts the command and returns you to your program. Choosing <*Help*> gives you an on-screen summary of these options.

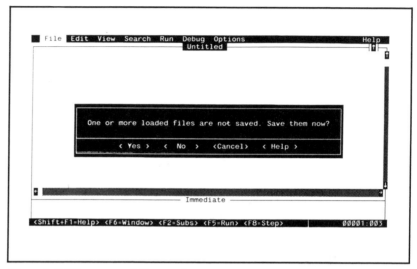

Figure 1.9: The unsaved file warning message

RETRIEVING A PROGRAM

Files that have been saved can be retrieved from disk storage and loaded into memory using the Open Program command in the File menu. Retrieve the SALESTAX program using these steps:

1. Open the File Menu and select *Open Program*. The Open Program Dialog box shown in Figure 1.10 appears on screen.

2. In order to select a program without typing in the file name, press Tab once to move to the list of file names. If you are working in the QB45 directory created by the QuickBASIC Setup program, there will be several sample program files on this list in addition to the SALESTAX program you just created.

File lists are always arranged in alphabetical order.

3. Press ↓ once to select the first file on the list. The selected file is highlighted and the name of that file appears automatically in the File Name input area. Continue pressing ↓ until the SALESTAX program is selected.

4. Press ←┘. The dialog box will close and the SALESTAX program will appear in the Work screen.

Now that you have retrieved your file, you are ready to print it.

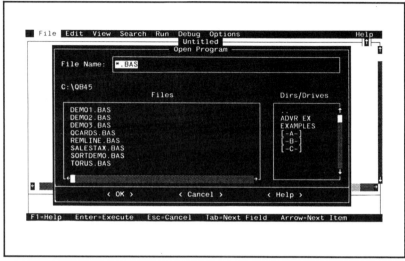

If you are using a mouse, you can open a program using the file list in the Open Program dialog box either by moving the mouse cursor directly to the name of the file and clicking twice or by clicking once on the file name and then moving the cursor to <OK> and clicking once again.

Figure 1.10: The Open Program dialog box

PRINTING A PROGRAM LISTING

Program listings can be printed by selecting the Print command from the File menu. To print the SALESTAX program follow these steps:

1. Open the File menu and select the *Print* command. The Print dialog box shown in Figure 1.11 will appear on screen. The third of the three choices, Current Module, has already been selected for you. This is the correct choice for printing an entire program. The other choices will be covered in future chapters.

With a mouse, clicking the left mouse button with the cursor on <OK> in a QuickBASIC dialog box will execute the command. This is equivalent to highlighting <OK> using the keyboard and then pressing ←.

2. Press ← to accept the default choice and execute the print command.

LEAVING QUICKBASIC

To return to the operating system, use the Exit command in the File menu.

- Open the File Menu and press X to activate the Exit option.

Figure 1.11: The print options

With certain mono-
chrome monitors,
QuickBASIC will alter
the appearance of the
cursor after you exit to
the operating system. To
return the cursor to its
normal appearance, use
the DOS command
MODE MONO at the
operating system prompt.

You have now used all of the commands in the easy File menu.
You should be fairly comfortable with the QuickBASIC menus, but
to get more practice you might want to explore the QuickBASIC
Survival Guide that is available to you from the Welcome screen
when you first load QuickBASIC. If you try this, return to the operating system when you are done so that you will be ready to start the
next exercise.

MAKING PROGRAMS THAT STAND ALONE

The SALESTAX program that you have created runs from within
the QuickBASIC environment. As it stands now, anyone who wants
to use it must know enough about QuickBASIC to be able to load
and run the program from within the QuickBASIC environment.
However, it is faster and more convenient for a user to be able to
work with stand-alone files. QuickBASIC enables you to create such
files, a procedure known as *compiling*, with just a few keystrokes. Any
stand-alone program you create will be given an .EXE file extension
that identifies it as an executable file that can be executed from DOS

simply by typing the base name (the part of the name before the period) and pressing ◄┘.

USING SALESTAX.BAS
TO CREATE SALESTAX.EXE

To create a stand-alone executable file, you must first return to the QuickBASIC Work screen and load the SALESTAX program using a QuickBASIC option that allows you to combine these two steps into a single command. At the operating system prompt, type

qb salestax

You should see your program in the View window and the file name SALESTAX.BAS in the Title bar. To compile a program, use the Make EXE File command in the Run menu. The following steps use this command to create a program file called SALESTAX.EXE that can be used directly from the operating system.

If you are using a floppy-disk system, you will need to use several disks to create an .EXE file. Refer to Appendix B for more information.

1. Open the Run menu.

2. Press X to select *Make EXE file*. The dialog box shown in Figure 1.12 will appear. The file name SALESTAX.EXE has already been entered for you.

3. Press ◄┘ to accept this name and the other default selections.

While the program is compiling you will see a series of messages that describe steps in the compiling process displayed on the screen. The process of compiling takes a while. You will know it is completed when your program reappears in the View window.

RUNNING THE STAND-ALONE PROGRAM

To run a stand-alone program, first leave QuickBASIC. At the DOS prompt, type the part of the file name that precedes the .EXE extension. Try this with the SALESTAX.EXE file.

• Open the File Menu and select Exit

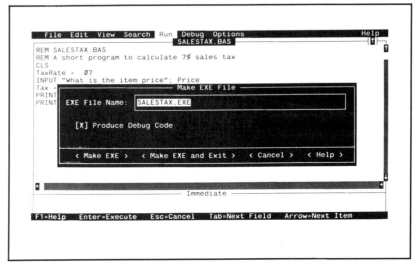

Figure 1.12: The Make EXE File dialog box

At the DOS prompt type

    salestax

and press ◄—┘. The SALESTAX program should run as it has before,
but without the displaying the message "Press any key to continue"
after the results have been displayed. Instead, you will be returned
directly to the DOS prompt with the program output still visible on
screen.

SUMMARY

QuickBASIC programs are developed within a programming
environment that provides many editing, debugging, and file management commands. This chapter has been an introduction to the
techniques you need to work within that environment.

The QuickBASIC environment uses pull-down menus to invoke
command options. These menus are displayed in a Menu bar that is
activated by pressing the Alt key. Menus can then be opened by
pressing a highlighted letter or by choosing a menu with the cursor-
control keys and then pressing ◄—┘. Within each menu, commands

are selected in the same manner. A mouse can also be used to work with QuickBASIC menus.

You have had an opportunity to try all of the commands in the File menu of QuickBASIC's Easy Menus. These commands are used for clearing the screen, opening programs that have been stored on disks, saving programs on disks, printing program listings, and leaving QuickBASIC to return to the operating system.

When QuickBASIC needs more information to execute a command, it displays a dialog box on screen. Items in a dialog box are used to enter additional information or to choose from among a list of available further actions.

This chapter gave you a small taste of the QuickBASIC editor. Chapter 2 will cover basic editing techniques in detail. It will also show you how to use QuickBASIC's online help to answer questions you may have about the BASIC programming language or the QuickBASIC program-development environment.

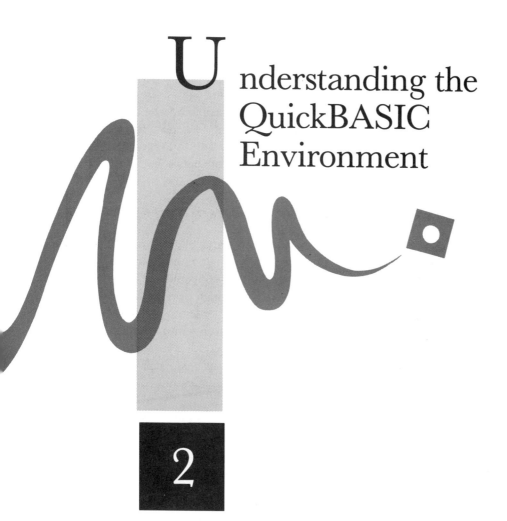

Understanding the QuickBASIC Environment

2

CHAPTER 2

THE QUICKBASIC ENVIRONMENT CONSISTS OF THE work screen and those features that are available through its menus to assist you in program development. These include editing and debugging tools and extensive online help. Understanding how to work with these features will make writing programs easier. This chapter shows you how to take full advantage of QuickBASIC's online help. You will also learn how to accomplish some basic editing tasks and learn about a few easy debugging features. You will learn how to use additional editing features and debugging tools throughout the book as you study programming concepts.

USING QUICKBASIC ONLINE HELP

If you are using QuickBASIC on a floppy-disk system, you will be prompted to change disks when you use online help.

An enormous amount of information about BASIC programming and about the QuickBASIC environment is available through QuickBASIC's online help. There are three avenues of approach to this information: context-sensitive help, which provides information about items displayed on screen; an alphabetically arranged index; and a table of contents that organizes help topics into main categories of related ideas.

You can use any one of these three approaches to call up a QuickBASIC Help screen. Each Help screen displays information about one aspect of QuickBASIC, and also includes several bracketed headings known as *hyperlinks*. Hyperlinks connect you quickly to additional Help screens, allowing you to explore your topic in more detail or to research additional subjects.

If you prefer to use a printed page for reference, it requires only a few keystrokes to get printed copies of QuickBASIC Help screens. The next exercises demonstrate these methods of using the online help.

GETTING INFORMATION INSTANTLY WITH CONTEXT-SENSITIVE HELP

Context-sensitive help can give you instant information about items in the QuickBASIC menus and also about elements of your program. The F1 key triggers this help feature. When QuickBASIC menus are activated, pressing F1 displays information about the currently selected menu item. If the menus are not active, pressing F1 displays information about the part of your program at the cursor position.

GETTING MORE INFORMATION ABOUT MENU ITEMS

Context-sensitive help for QuickBASIC menus is available for main headings, command choices, and dialog boxes. In this exercise you will display three different Help screens as you open the SALES-TAX program:

1. Press Alt. This activates the Menu bar and, at the same time, selects *File* from the choice of menus.

2. Press F1 to view the File Menu Help screen that is shown in Figure 2.1.

Figure 2.1: The File Menu Help screen

3. Press ⏎ (or Esc) to close the Help screen.

4. Press ⏎ to open the File menu and press ↓ once to select *Open Program*.

5. Press F1 to display a Help screen describing the Open Program command. This screen is shown in Figure 2.2.

Figure 2.2: The Open Program Command Help screen

6. Press ⏎ (or Esc) to close the Help screen and return to the File menu.

7. Press O to open the Open Program dialog box.

8. Press F1 to view a Help screen describing the items in this dialog box. This screen is shown in Figure 2.3. This is the same Help screen that you displayed in Chapter 1 by selecting <*Help*> in the dialog box. There are always several different methods of approaching information available through QuickBASIC's online help.

9. Press ⏎ (or Esc) to close the Help screen.

10. Select the SALESTAX program to open. You can do this either by typing SALESTAX into the File Name input area

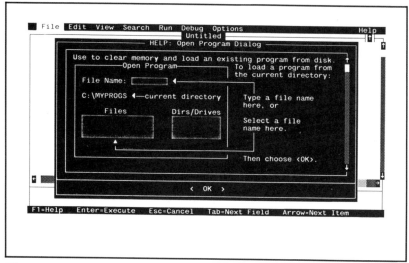

Figure 2.3: The Open Program Dialog Help screen

or by pressing Tab and then using the ↓ key to select SALES-TAX from the Files list.

11. Press ◄─┘ to open the program.

With the SALESTAX program in the View window, you are ready to use context-sensitive help in order to learn more about the program itself.

GETTING INFORMATION ABOUT YOUR PROGRAM In addition to offering assistance with QuickBASIC menus, online help also supplies information about all of the commands and statements that make up the BASIC programming language. Program-language Help screens are concise and thorough; they are excellent as reference, but are not designed to be an introduction to programming topics. If you have no prior programming experience, you may not find them very informative at this stage, but as you learn more about BASIC, you'll find them to be a valuable supplement to the material covered in this book.

To get information about an item in your program, position the cursor on that item and press F1. In this exercise you will use this

technique to learn more about the REM statement in the first line of
the SALESTAX program.

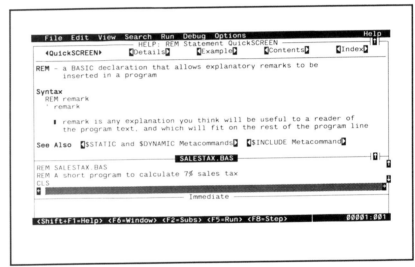

If you are using a
mouse, you can get
context-sensitive help by
positioning the mouse
cursor on an item in your
program and clicking the
right mouse button.

1. Position the cursor on any letter of the term REM in line 1.

2. Press F1 to display the REM Statement QuickSCREEN
    shown in Figure 2.4. This screen provides basic information
    about the REM statement.

Figure 2.4: The REM Statement QuickSCREEN

Before continuing, take a few minutes to examine the Work screen
as it appears in Figure 2.4. Three *windows* are visible, identified by
three different Title bars. The REM Statement QuickSCREEN
occupies the uppermost window. In this window, just under the title
bar, are five *hyperlinks* that you can use to call up additional online
Help screens. The rest of the QuickSCREEN contains information
about the REM statement. The next window is the View window,
which contains the SALESTAX program, only a few lines of which
are visible. Beneath the View window is the Immediate window,
which you will learn about in Chapter 3.

When more than one window is visible on the Work screen, the
window that contains the cursor is known as the *active* window. Only

one window is active at any one time, and it can be recognized quickly because the Title bar of the active window is highlighted. The View window is the active window when you use context-sensitive help to display a QuickSCREEN, and you will find the cursor in that window. Pressing F6 moves the cursor from one window to the next. (Pressing Shift + F6 moves it in the opposite direction.) To work within a QuickBASIC window, you must first be sure it is the active window.

In the next part of the exercise you will use the Details hyperlink to learn more about REM statements. The first step in this process is to make the Help screen the active window as follows:

3. Press F6. As a result, the title *Immediate* should be highlighted, indicating that this is now the active window.

4. Press F6 again so *HELP: REM Statement QuickSCREEN* is highlighted. Now that this Help screen is active, you can move the cursor to each of the hyperlinks by pressing the Tab key or by pressing the first letter of the hyperlink you want to select.

5. Practice moving the cursor through the hyperlinks and then return it to the *Details* hyperlink.

6. Press F1 (or ◄─┘) to view the REM Statement Details screen shown in Figure 2.5.

7. The REM Statement Details screen contains more information than can fit on screen at one time. Press Ctrl + ↓ and Ctrl + ↑ to move the information up and down through your field of view. These line-by-line scrolling commands work in any QuickBASIC window. You can also scroll screen-by-screen using PgUp-PgDn.

8. To get a printed copy of the complete contents of the Help screen, press Alt and then press F to open the File menu.

9. Press P to choose the *Print* command. The dialog box that appears indicates that the active window (the Help screen) has been selected for printing. Press ◄─┘ to accept this selection and proceed with the Print command.

10. Press Esc to close the Help screen.

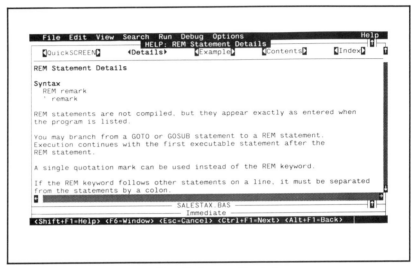

Figure 2.5: REM Statement Details from online help

If you are using a mouse, you can change the active window by positioning the mouse cursor anywhere in the window you want to activate and clicking the left button. To use a hyperlink, position the mouse cursor on the heading you want and click the right mouse button.

Context-sensitive help is useful when you want information about an item that is displayed somewhere on screen, but there will also be times when you want to retrieve information about something that is not on screen. To help you find information about any QuickBASIC topic as easily as possible, QuickBASIC offers two different reference listings, one arranged alphabetically, the other by topic.

UNDERSTANDING THE ONLINE REFERENCE LISTINGS

Sometimes you will have specific questions you want answered about a particular BASIC programming statement or command. At other times you may have only a general idea of what you want to accomplish, without knowing yet exactly which command or statement is involved. For these two kinds of research, QuickBASIC offers two kinds of reference listings, an index and a table of contents. Access to both of these listings is gained through the Help menu on the far right of the Menu bar.

USING ALPHABETICAL HELP LISTINGS The BASIC language is made up of commands and statements known as keywords. The index is an alphabetical list of BASIC keywords (and a few additional headings) that provides information about programming fundamentals. In the previous exercise, you used context-sensitive help to display the REM QuickSCREEN. In the next exercise you will use the index to call up this same screen.

1. Press Alt to activate the Menu bar.

2. Press H to open the Help menu.

3. Press I to display the help index. Information about how to use the index is displayed on the top of your screen.

4. Press R to view those topics that begin with the letter R; then use the cursor-control keys to position the cursor on *REM*.

5. Press F1 (or ◄──┘) to open the REM QuickSCREEN. This is the same screen you opened earlier using context-sensitive help, but this time you will look into the *Example* hyperlink.

6. Press E to move the cursor to the *Example* hyperlink.

When you use the index to open a Help screen, the Help screen immediately becomes the active window, so you can select a hyperlink or print the screen straightaway.

7. Press F1 (or ◄──┘) to select the *Example* hyperlink. This calls up a screen that shows you how to use the REM statement in a segment of program code. These examples will become increasingly useful to you as you learn more about programming in QuickBASIC.

8. Press Alt + F1. This command will show you the previous Help screen. Notice that this command remains in the Reference bar at the bottom of your screen while you work with online help.

9. Press Esc to close the Help screen.

USING HELP LISTINGS ARRANGED BY TOPIC The online table of contents lists areas of interest concerning both BASIC programming and the QuickBASIC environment. By beginning with one of the general categories listed, you can branch off into detailed information about the topic of your choice. In the next exercise you will use the table of contents to find and print a complete list of cursor-movement commands that will come in handy as you continue on to the editing section of this chapter.

1. Open the Help menu.

2. Press C to display the Table of Contents shown in Figure 2.6.

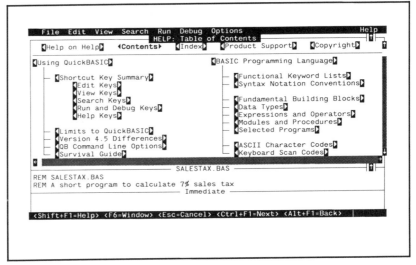

Figure 2.6: The Help Table of Contents

3. To select a topic in the Table of Contents you can move the cursor to that topic by using the cursor-control keys (these keys move the cursor one character at a time), the Tab key (which jumps you from one topic to the next), or by pressing the first letter of a bracketed item. Use any combination of these techniques to position the cursor on *Edit Keys*.

4. Press F1 (or ◄──┘) to display the information about editing keys shown in Figure 2.7.

5. Press C to move the cursor to *Cursor-movement keys*.

6. Press F1 to display a table of cursor-movement commands.

7. Print the list by opening the File Menu, selecting Print, and pressing ◄──┘ when you see the Print dialog box.

8. Press the Esc key to return to the Work screen.

```
┌────────────────────────────────────────────────────────────────────────┐
│ File  Edit  View  Search  Run  Debug  Options                      Help  │
│═══════════════════════════HELP: Editing Keys════════════════════════════ │
│  ◄Editing Keys►    ◄Contents►    ◄Index►                              ↑   │
│                                                                          │
│ Editing Keys                                                             │
│                                                                          │
│ The QuickBASIC smart editor recognizes key stroke combinations familiar to│
│ users of other Microsoft programs, such as Microsoft Word, as well as    │
│ WordStar key combinations. In the editing keys tables, the WordStar      │
│ equivalent keys are listed in the right column.                          │
│                                                                          │
│        ◄Cursor-movement keys►                                            │
│        ◄Text scrolling keys►                                             │
│        ◄Keys that select text to be changed by next command►            │
│        ◄Keys that insert and copy text►                                  │
│        ◄Keys that delete text►                                           │
│                                                                          │
│ ◄                                                             ↓          │
│────────────────────────── SALESTAX.BAS ─────────────────────────────────│
│ REM SALESTAX.BAS                                                         │
│ REM A short program to calculate 7% sales tax                            │
│────────────────────────────── Immediate ────────────────────────────────│
│                                                                          │
│ <Shift+F1=Help> <F6=Window> <Esc=Cancel> <Ctrl+F1=Next> <Alt+F1=Back>   │
└────────────────────────────────────────────────────────────────────────┘
```

Figure 2.7: The Editing Keys display from online help

The list you printed contains the most frequently used commands for moving the cursor around any QuickBASIC screen. These commands, and other editing techniques, are the subject of the next sections of this chapter.

EDITING YOUR QUICKBASIC PROGRAMS

If you printed the list of cursor-control commands in the previous exercise, you will have noticed that many commands can be executed with a choice of keystrokes. The second set of commands in this online summary will be familiar to readers who have done word processing with WordStar.

Writing programs almost invariably requires making changes to what has been written. To help you, QuickBASIC provides a full range of editing features that enable you to modify your program using standard word processing techniques for inserting, deleting, replacing, and moving text. Because you can make these modifications from within the QuickBASIC environment, you can alternate instantly between editing and running your program.

In addition to providing you with standard editing tools, QuickBASIC has a default feature known as the "smart editor" that will alert you when program lines are incorrectly written and will format each line to certain standardized conventions. The next exercises in this chapter give you an overview of basic editing techniques you need to write and modify QuickBASIC programs.

MOVING THE CURSOR

An assortment of cursor-control commands lets you move quickly and efficiently from one part of a program to another. Table 2.1 summarizes some of the most useful cursor-control keys.

Table 2.1: Cursor Movement Commands

MOVEMENT	CONTROL KEY(S)
Character left	Left Arrow ←
Character right	Right Arrow →
Line up	Up Arrow ↑
Line Down	Down Arrow ↓
Word right	Ctrl + →
Word left	Ctrl + ←
Beginning of line	Home
End of line	End
Beginning of next line	Ctrl + ↵
Beginning of program	Ctrl + Home
End of program	Ctrl + End

With the SALESTAX.BAS program in the Work screen, practice using the cursor controls in Table 2.1. When you feel comfortable with each of the commands, try the following:

1. Move to the beginning of the program with Ctrl + Home.

2. Press Ctrl + → several times. As you continue to move word by word to the right, you will eventually move the cursor to the beginning of the next line. Pressing Ctrl + ← repeatedly will eventually return the cursor to the previous line.

3. Press the → and ← keys repeatedly and notice that these keys do *not* cause the cursor to change lines when you reach the beginning or end of the current line.

4. Move to the end of the program with Ctrl + End. Press the ↓ key. The cursor has reached the end of its universe and will move no farther down.

When you feel confident with the cursor controls, you are ready to use QuickBASIC text-editing commands.

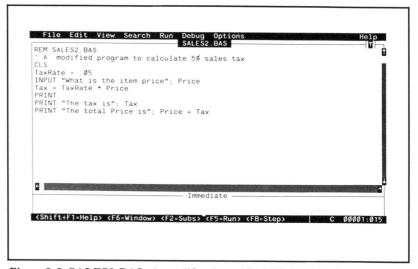

If you are using a mouse, you can move the editing cursor by positioning the mouse cursor anywhere in the program and clicking the left button. When you do this, the editing cursor will move to the mouse cursor position.

MODIFYING THE SALESTAX.BAS PROGRAM

Basic editing techniques include

- Inserting new material, either entire new program lines or new material within an existing line.

- Typing over parts of a program to replace existing text with new material.

- Deleting characters, words, or entire lines of text.

In the next exercises you will use these techniques to create a modified version of the SALESTAX.BAS program and save it as SALES2.BAS. The SALES2 program is shown in Figure 2.8.

```
 File  Edit  View  Search  Run  Debug  Options                    Help
                              SALES2.BAS
REM SALES2.BAS
' A  modified program to calculate 5% sales tax
CLS
TaxRate = .05
INPUT "What is the item price"; Price
Tax = TaxRate * Price
PRINT
PRINT "The tax is"; Tax
PRINT "The total Price is"; Price + Tax




                              Immediate
<Shift+F1=Help> <F6=Window> <F2=Subs> <F5=Run> <F8=Step>    C  00001:015
```

Figure 2.8: SALES2.BAS: A modification of SALESTAX.BAS

INSERTING MATERIAL WITHIN A LINE   When you first enter
the Work screen, QuickBASIC is in insert mode. In this mode
QuickBASIC adds any new material you type immediately to the left
of the current cursor position. The new material will not replace
material already on screen. The steps below add a word to the statement in line 2 of the SALESTAX program.

1. Move the cursor to the p of *program* in line 2.

2. Type the word *modified*. The rest of the line moves over to
   make room for this new addition.

3. Press the spacebar to separate the words.

Because this change is in a REM statement, it will have no effect
on the way the program runs. The next change you make will add a
new instruction to the program.

ADDING NEW PROGRAM LINES   Many program changes
require adding new program lines between already existing ones. The
next modification to the SALESTAX program is one that changes the
appearance of the program output. You will add a line that contains
only the word PRINT. This command instructs the computer to display a blank line in the Output screen. Placing this line above the two
PRINT statements that are already part of the program will result in
a separation between the question, "What is the item Price?" and
the two lines that display tax and total price.

1. Move the cursor to the first character of the PRINT statement in line 7.

2. Press ⬅ to create a blank line immediately above the cursor.

3. Press the ↑ key to move to this new blank line and type
   PRINT on this line. Check to be sure the change you made
   matches Figure 2.8.

Pressing ⬅ *always* creates a new program line. If the cursor is at
the beginning of a line, a new blank line will be created above the cursor. If the cursor is at the end of a line, a new blank line is created
below it. You may find that you occasionally press ⬅ inadvertently

when the cursor is in the middle of the line. When this happens, the line will be split in two. Try the following exercise to see this error and learn how to correct it.

1. Place the cursor in the middle of any line in the program.

2. Press ⏎. The statement is divided and the cursor is now on the first letter of the new line.

3. Without moving your cursor from this position, press the Backspace key to "erase" the ⏎ and return your program to its original appearance.

USING TYPEOVER MODE TO REPLACE EXISTING MATERIAL

The default setting for the QuickBASIC editor is insert mode. At times, you might find it more convenient to make corrections or modifications by typing directly over existing material, replacing it with new material as you type. By using the Insert key you can select to work in either insert or typeover mode. You will use typeover mode to change the SALESTAX program to calculate 5% rather than 7% tax.

1. Press the Insert key (labeled either Ins or Insert). Notice the change in the appearance of the cursor. The larger cursor indicates that you are in typeover mode.

2. Move the cursor to the 7 of *.07* in the fourth line and type 5. The 5 will replace the 7 and the modified program will use the new value to calculate sales tax.

3. The REM statement on line 2 should be updated to reflect this change. Move the cursor to line 2 and change 7% to 5% in the same way.

4. Press the Ins key to return to insert mode. The Ins key acts as a toggle, moving you back and forth between the insert mode and the typeover mode.

The final alterations to the SALESTAX program involve erasing material.

DELETING A WORD AT A TIME   In Chapter 1 you learned that individual characters can be erased by pressing the Del key. It is also possible to erase an entire word by placing the cursor on the first letter of the word and pressing Ctrl+T. The next change you'll make to the program will be to erase the keyword REM in line 2 and replace it with an apostrophe ('), which is another way to indicate remark statements.

1. Position the cursor on the first letter of *REM* on line 2.

2. Press Ctrl+T to erase *REM*.

3. Check the appearance of the cursor to be sure you are in insert mode and type in an apostrophe. (The apostrophe is located on the same key as the double quotation marks.)

4. Move the cursor to the s of *short* and press Ctrl+T to erase this word.

DELETING A LINE AT A TIME   You can erase an entire line of a program by pressing Ctrl+Y when the cursor is positioned anywhere on the line you want to erase. The last modification you will make to the SALESTAX program is to erase the first line of the program and replace it with a new remark statement, identifying the modified program as SALES2.BAS.

1. Move the cursor to any position in line 1.

2. Press Ctrl+Y to erase this line. The cursor will move to the first letter of the next line.

3. Without moving the cursor, press ↵ to create a blank line.

4. Move up to the blank line and type:

   REM SALES2.BAS

5. Press Shift+F5 to run the modified program. A sample output screen is shown here:

   What is the item price? 25

   The tax is 1.25
   The total Price is 26.25

When you want to erase a group of several lines, start with the top line of the group. Because the cursor moves down when you erase a line, it will be properly positioned each time to erase the next line in the group.

The basic editing commands used for inserting and deleting text are summarized in Table 2.2.

Table 2.2: Commands for Deleting Text

ACTION	CONTROL KEY(S)
Deleting	
Character (at cursor)	Del
Character (left of cursor)	Backspace
Word (to right of cursor)	Ctrl + T
Line (with cursor in any column)	Ctrl + Y
Inserting	
Insert mode on/off	Ins
Line (above line with cursor)	Home ◄─┘
Line (below line with cursor)	End ◄─┘

You have completed the editing changes, and your new program should now match Figure 2.8. The next exercise shows you how to save this program with its new name, leaving the original program unchanged on the disk.

SAVING THE MODIFIED PROGRAM UNDER A NEW NAME

By modifying an existing program, you were able to create a new sales tax program using just a few keystrokes. Making changes to one program in order to create a new one is a commonly used technique for speeding program development. When you want to keep both programs, it is a simple matter to save the modified program with a new name, leaving the original program unchanged on the disk. To save the modified sales tax program under the name SALES2.BAS, do the following:

1. Open the File menu.

2. Select the *Save As* option.

3. The Save As dialog box will appear with the name SALES-TAX in the File Name input area. Without moving the cursor from its position in this box, type

    sales2

    As soon as you start to type a new file name, the original file name disappears and is replaced by the new name.

4. With the new name in place, press ←┘. The modified program will be saved under the new name, you will be returned to the Work screen, and the new name, SALES2.BAS, will be displayed in the Title bar.

There may also be times when you *don't* want to save changes that you have made to a program. In the next section you will make changes to the SALES2.BAS program that are designed to demonstrate some important characteristics of the QuickBASIC editor. When you're done with the next section, you will learn how to exit to the operating system without saving these changes.

PROGRAMMING ERRORS AND THE QUICKBASIC SMART EDITOR

The term *syntax* refers to the details of organization and punctuation that must be adhered to when you write a line of program code. As soon as you move the cursor from one line of code to another, QuickBASIC will immediately check the line you are leaving to see if its syntax is correct. If there is an error on the line, a message describing the problem will appear on screen. This ability of the Quick-BASIC editor to find syntax errors is why it is described as a "smart" editor. With the smart editor at work, certain programming errors can be eliminated before you ever try to run a program. Some program errors do not result in immediate syntax error messages, but are discovered when QuickBASIC first tries to run your program. These compile-time errors also result in on-screen error messages. Many, many additional program errors are not caught by the editor, either when you write a line of code *or* when you try to run the program. This last kind of error may not prevent a program from running, but when the program runs the results are unsatisfactory. The

QuickBASIC editor cannot locate these errors because it is not quite smart enough to read your mind.

USING THE SMART EDITOR TO FIND SYNTAX ERRORS

The next exercises demonstrate the syntax-checking feature of the QuickBASIC smart editor. Methods for finding and correcting other kinds of programming errors are described throughout the chapters that follow. To test the smart editor:

1. Position the cursor on the semicolon (;) in the fifth line of the SALES2.BAS program. This semicolon is an essential part of the syntax of this INPUT statement.

2. Press Del to erase the semicolon.

3. Press the ↑ key to move the cursor up one line. Because of the syntax error you just created, you will see an error message telling you that the editor expects either a comma or semicolon on this line. The word *Price*, which is now located where the editor expected the comma or semicolon to be, has been highlighted. This message is shown in Figure 2.9.

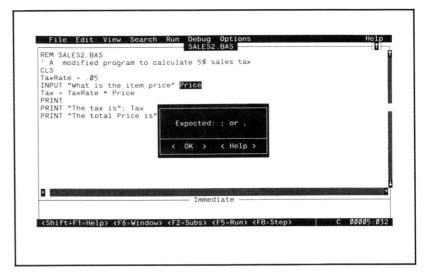

Figure 2.9: A syntax error message

4. Press Esc to close the error message and return to the Work screen.

5. Replace the semicolon and you will be allowed to move off this line without being scolded.

The error you just created resulted in a message on screen. The editor knew that something was wrong, but had to consult with you to know exactly what you wanted to do to fix it. The smart editor is also occasionally smart enough to make changes that affect your program's style without consulting you first. One of the conventions that make programs easier to read is the use of uppercase for all BASIC language keywords. In the SALES2.BAS program, these words are REM, CLS, INPUT and PRINT. The QuickBASIC editor is designed to convert such words to uppercase regardless of how you type them. To demonstrate, try the following:

1. Move to the end of line 9 and press ⬅ to add an additional line to the program.

2. On line 10, type the following exactly as it appears here:

    print "That's all folks

3. Press the ↑ key. Line 10 will change to read as follows:

    PRINT "That's all folks"

The smart editor is able to recognize BASIC language keywords (*print* in this example) and will convert all instances of these words to uppercase display. In addition to this change, the editor also added double quotation marks at the end of this PRINT statement because the syntax requires them.

EXITING QUICKBASIC WITHOUT SAVING YOUR WORK

The changes you just made to the SALES2 program were designed to demonstrate features of the QuickBASIC editor. There is no reason to save these changes. When you use the View screen to test out an idea and have no reason to keep the results, you can clear the screen without saving your work, as described in Chapter 1, or you may want to go directly to the operating system without keeping your work. To leave QuickBASIC without saving the changes you just made to your program, do the following:

1. Open the File menu.

2. Press X to exit QuickBASIC. A message appears on screen warning you that one or more files are not saved. You have a choice of saving your file now or proceeding with the exit command without saving it.

3. Press Tab to select <*No*>. This choice means that the file on disk will remain as it was the last time you saved it and that the changes you made since then will not be saved.

4. Press ◄┘ to proceed with the exit command. You will be returned to the operating system.

Because a warning message appears when you try to leave Quick-BASIC with an unsaved version of a program on screen, you are protected from inadvertently losing changes that you had meant to keep.

SUMMARY

The QuickBASIC environment provides you with a range of features designed to help you develop programs. This program development environment can be grouped into three parts: editing features, debugging features, and online help.

QuickBASIC online help provides you with a choice of context-sensitive information about items displayed on screen, an alphabetically arranged index to the BASIC programming language, and table of contents that you can use to learn more about both programming and the QuickBASIC environment. Context-sensitive information is triggered by using the F1 key. Access to the index and table of contents is through the Help menu. Help screens can be printed using the Print command from the File menu.

Basic editing tools include a variety of cursor-control commands, insert and typeover modes for modifying program statements, and commands that erase letters, words, or entire lines of text. These tools are summarized in Tables 2.1 and 2.2. When an existing program is modified to create a new one, the Save As command can be used to update the disk file or to give the revised program a new name, leaving the original disk file unchanged.

To make programs easier to read, BASIC language keywords are automatically capitalized by the QuickBASIC smart editor. The editor also checks each program line as soon as it is written and alerts you to any syntax errors.

The goal of this chapter has been to help you feel comfortable using the tools that are part of the QuickBASIC environment. With these tools at your disposal, you are ready to concentrate on writing programs. The remaining chapters of this book emphasize BASIC programming concepts, but also include many techniques that will help you extend your knowledge of the QuickBASIC environment as you develop your programming skills.

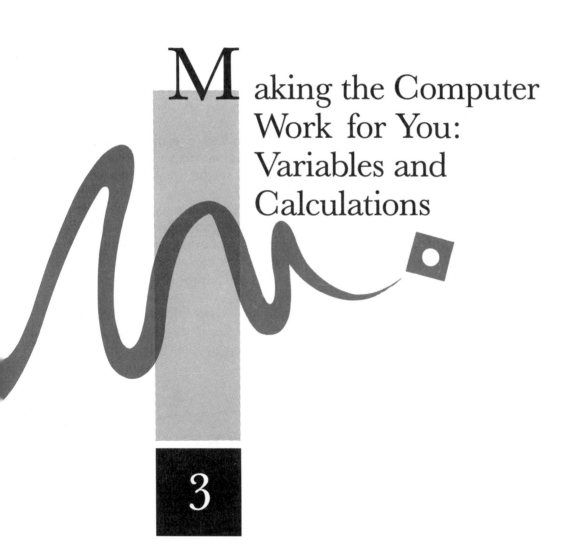

Making the Computer Work for You: Variables and Calculations

3

CHAPTER *3* _____

COMPUTERS CAN STORE ENORMOUS QUANTITIES OF information and perform mathematical computations with an astonishing degree of speed and accuracy. In this chapter you will learn how to program the computer to accomplish these feats of electronic wizardry. In order to perform calculations, a computer must have values to work with and a way of communicating the results of calculations to the individual using a program. *Input* operations supply the computer with data, and *output* operations deliver the results of the computer's activities. The first section of this chapter introduces a few basic input and output techniques.

Next you will learn how to instruct the computer to perform calculations and how to work with *variables* as a way of keeping track of information. A variable is a name given to a data value that is stored in the computer's memory. You will learn how to create and name variables and how to use them to store and retrieve both numeric and text information.

QuickBASIC uses four different data-types to describe numeric variables of different kinds. The final section of this chapter describes these data-types and explains how you can use them to help your programs run efficiently and accurately.

AN INTRODUCTION TO INPUT AND OUTPUT TECHNIQUES

A variety of input techniques can be used to enter data into a computer's memory. Computer programs use variables as one way of keeping track of this data. Some variables have values that are built into the program itself. For example, the variable **TaxRate** in the SALESTAX program is this kind of variable: **TaxRate** is used to store a value for the sales tax rate, which remains the same each time the program runs. A second method of providing input values for variables allows the person running the program to provide a different value for the variable each time the program runs. The variable **Price** in the SALESTAX program is used this way. Each time you run the program, you can enter a different value for this variable. Let's take a closer look at using variables in these two ways.

ASSIGNING VALUES TO VARIABLES

When you want to give a variable the same value each time a program runs, include an *assignment statement* that gives that value to the variable as part of the program. Such statements can be written with or without the BASIC keyword LET. The following two statements are equivalent ways to assign the value 10 to the variable called Joe:

```
Joe = 10
LET Joe = 10                              .
```

After executing either of the statements above, the computer will use the value 10 whenever the variable Joe is used in the program. If a subsequent assignment statement reads

```
Hilda = Joe + 7
```

the computer will add 10 + 7 and assign the resulting value, 17, to the variable named Hilda.

In an assignment statement the variable being assigned a value must always be placed to the left of the equal sign. Notice that the equal sign used in an assignment statement is not the same as an algebraic equality. Its role is to *set* the variable value on the left to a value equal to the expression on the right.

Variable values can be changed during the course of program execution. Look at the two program lines below. In the first line, the variable X is assigned the value 2. The second line redefines X using the earlier value as part of the expression used to calculate the new value. The end result of these two lines of code is to assign the value 3 to the variable X.

```
X = 2
X = X + 1
```

When the computer encounters a numeric variable whose value has not previously been defined, the value for that variable is set at zero.

DISPLAYING INFORMATION WITH A PRINT STATEMENT

Assignment statements affect the value of a variable in the computer's memory. When you want to see the value of a variable, *PRINT* statements can be used to display the value in the Output screen. Type the following short program into the View window and then run it to demonstrate the use of variables and the PRINT statement.

```
Sample = 1
PRINT Sample
Sample = Sample + 1
PRINT Sample
```

When you run this program you will see the following output:

```
1
2
```

The first PRINT statement displays the initial value of the variable Sample. The second PRINT statement displays the value of Sample after it is changed in line 3. After running the program, return to the Work screen and run the program again. The Output screen now shows the following:

```
1
2
1
2
```

The results of the first run of your program have remained on the Output screen. When you want to clear the results of previous output to the Output screen, you must include the statement CLS in your program. Try this by creating a new line above the first line of your program and typing CLS on this line. Your program now reads as follows:

```
CLS
Sample = 1
PRINT Sample
Sample = Sample + 1
PRINT Sample
```

When you run the modified program, the Output screen will be cleared before the program output is displayed. Use the New Program command to clear the View window without saving the program when you are ready to continue.

DEFINING FLEXIBLE VARIABLES USING THE INPUT STATEMENT

Programs that perform exactly the same task, using exactly the same numbers each time, are of limited value. What makes most programs useful is their ability to respond to data supplied by the individual at the keyboard. In BASIC programs, the INPUT statement enables the person running a program to change the value of program variables each time the program runs. An INPUT statement is always followed by a one or more variables that are used to store the data provided. When the computer encounters an input statement, a question mark appears on the Output screen, and execution of the program stops until a value has been typed in from the keyboard. The value typed in is then assigned to the variable named in the INPUT statement.

The next program employs the INPUT statement in its barest form. When you run this program, a question mark will appear on the Output screen indicating that the computer is waiting for input from the keyboard. When you type a number and press ↵, the variable named Value1 is set equal to that number. Then a second question mark appears, waiting for a value for Value2. Once the second number has been entered, the two values are added and stored using the variable named Sum. The PRINT statement then displays this figure.

```
CLS
INPUT Value1
INPUT Value2
Sum = Value1 + Value2
PRINT Sum
```

Type in the program and try running it several times, using different values each time. A sample Output screen is shown here:

```
? 3
? 4
7
```

Although this program can be used to perform addition, it is extremely cryptic. Only the person who wrote the program could possibly guess what to do when that first lonely question mark appears on the Output screen. There is nothing to tell the user what to do or what sort of result is being displayed.

To make INPUT and PRINT statements more helpful, you can add information in quotation marks to these statements. Anything between quotation marks is displayed on the Output screen exactly as it is written within the quotation marks. The modification of your program shown below uses this feature to make your addition program more "user-friendly," that is, comprehensible. Notice that REM statements have also been added to the program. If you plan on saving a program file, always include explanatory statements like these. It is a mistake to assume that what is clear as you write a program will remain clear when you return to it later. Edit your first version of the addition program so that it reads as follows:

When INPUT and PRINT statements contain more than one item, each item must be separated from the others by punctuation marks like the semicolons used in this example. You will learn more about how to use punctuation in Chapter 4.

```
REM SUM.BAS
'Adds two numbers. Demonstrates use of INPUT and PRINT
CLS
PRINT "This program adds any two numbers"
INPUT "What is your first number"; Value1
INPUT "What is your second number"; Value2
Sum = Value1 + Value2
PRINT "The sum of those two numbers is:";Sum
```

A sample Output screen from this program is shown here:

```
This program adds any two numbers
What is your first number? 5
What is your second number? 7
The sum of those two numbers is: 12
```

Run the program several times. When you feel comfortable with it, save it as SUM.BAS and clear the View window.

WORKING WITH NUMBERS

The SUM program adds numbers beautifully, but so does a dime-store calculator. Your computer is able to perform far more impressive calculations than this. In order to direct the computer to perform calculations, however, you will need to understand the notation that is used for arithmetic operations and the rules that determine which calculation is performed first when several operations are included in a single statement.

CALCULATION NOTATION

The symbols used in BASIC for common arithmetic operations are + for addition, − for subtraction, * for multiplication, / for division, and ^ for exponentiation. The next program uses each of these operations. It also demonstrates a new way of including remarks in your programs. Remark statements can be added to any line by using an apostrophe after you have typed the executable portion of that line. Anything following the apostrophe is ignored by the computer.

```
CLS
PRINT 12 + 3      'addition
PRINT 12 − 3      'subtraction
PRINT 12 * 3      'multiplication
PRINT 12 / 3      'division
PRINT 12 ^ 3      'exponentiation (12 ^ 3 = 12 × 12 × 12)
```

Type in the program. When you run it, the Output screen will display these results:

```
15
9
36
4
1728
```

Try changing values in the program to see how fractional and negative results are displayed. When you are satisfied that you know how to use the arithmetic symbols, clear the View window without saving the program.

ORDER OF OPERATIONS

You can combine many arithmetic operations within a single expression. When several operations are included in one long expression, BASIC uses standard rules of algebra to determine which operation to perform first and what order to use as it continues with each of the other operations. Exponentiation is performed first, then multiplication and division, and finally addition and subtraction. Where parentheses are present, expressions within the parentheses are performed first. The following program demonstrates several multi-operation statements. Predict the results of each line of the program and then run it to check your answers.

```
PRINT 4 + 5 * 3 ^ 2
PRINT 4 + (5 * 3) ^ 2
PRINT (4 + 5) * 3 ^ 2
```

In the first line the computer squares 3, multiplies the results by 5, and then adds 4 for a result of 49. In the second line the first operation is 5 times 3. The result is squared to give 225 and then 4 is added for a final result of 229. In the last line, the first operation, adding 4 + 5, gives nine. The next operation is squaring 3. The final result equals 9 times 9, or 81.

You can use parentheses even where they are not necessary in order to make your program easier to understand. Parentheses can also be nested within other parentheses. In this case the innermost operation is performed first.

INTEGER ARITHMETIC

The term *integer* refers to any number that has no fractional part. Two integer arithmetic operations are available in BASIC, integer division and the remainder operation. A backslash (\) is used to indicate integer division. In this operation, if the dividend and divisor are not integers, they are rounded by the computer to the nearest integer before division takes place. After the division operation, only the integer portion of the quotient is included in the resulting value. An example should make this clear. Type in and run the following short program:

```
Quotient = 10.7 \ 4.2
PRINT Quotient
```

When the computer performs the integer division in the first line, 10.7 is rounded to 11, and 4.2 is rounded to 4. When 11 is divided by 4 the result is 2.75. The fractional portion of this result is dropped, so that the resulting value for Quotient is 2.

A second arithmetic operation involving integers is known as the *modulo* operation. The syntax for this operation is

```
value1 MOD value2
```

The two values are included in the program statement as numbers or variables, and, as in integer division, they will be rounded to the nearest integer. The output of this operation is the whole number remainder when *value1* is divided by *value2*. The next program demonstrates this operation in combination with integer division. You can run it several times using different values for the dividend and divisor until you have a comfortable feel for these operations.

```
REM INTARITH.BAS
' Demonstrates integer arithmetic
INPUT "Dividend"; Dividend
INPUT "Divisor"; Divisor
PRINT
PRINT "Quotient  :"; Dividend \ Divisor
PRINT "Remainder :"; Dividend MOD Divisor
```

Sample output from this program is shown here:

```
Dividend? 13
Divisor? 5

Quotient  : 2
Remainder : 3
```

As you worked with these examples, you may have discovered that modifying a program with your own input and trying out your ideas is one of the best ways to understand programming concepts. Whatever your level of expertise, there will always be ideas that you will want to test and explore. As your programs get longer and more complex, however, it becomes cumbersome and risky to do your exploring by changing the program itself. One option you have is to save your program, clear the View window, and test your ideas there before returning to your program, but a much quicker option is also available: You can use the Immediate window located at the bottom of your screen.

USING THE IMMEDIATE WINDOW TO TEST IDEAS

Any line of program code that is typed into the Immediate window will be executed immediately as soon as you press ←. You can use this feature to test out ideas as you develop a program. To move the cursor from the View window to the Immediate window, press F6. You can enter up to ten lines of code in the Immediate window and execute these lines in any order you wish by moving the cursor to the line you want to execute and pressing ←.

The Immediate window initially occupies three lines in the Work screen. You can control the size of any QuickBASIC window by pressing Alt + Plus or Alt + Minus when that window is active. (Plus and Minus are used here to indicate the keys labelled + and − , respectively). Pressing Ctrl + F10 will expand the active window to occupy the entire Work screen. This key combination acts as a toggle, so that pressing Ctrl + F10 again will return the Work screen to its original appearance. When the View window is active, you can use this feature to close the Immediate window and thereby increase the amount of room available for your program. Try the following exercise to practice these techniques:

1. With the cursor anywhere in the QuickBASIC View window, press F6 to make the Immediate window the active window.

2. Practice changing the size of the Immediate window using Alt + Plus and Alt + Minus.

3. Press Ctrl + F10. The View window will disappear and the Immediate window will fill the screen. Repeat the command to return the screen to its previous appearance.

4. Press F6 to return the cursor to the View window; use Ctrl + F10 to expand the View window to occupy the full screen and then again to return the Immediate window to the screen.

When the Immediate window is active, you can use it to perform calculations and test out programming ideas. The next exercise shows you how to calculate the value of the following expression by using a BASIC statement in the Immediate window:

$$\frac{5\,(2+3)}{4+1} + 3$$

The BASIC statement that performs this calculation is

```
PRINT 5 * (2 + 3) / (4 + 1) + 3
```

1. Move the cursor to the Immediate window and type the statement as it appears above into the Immediate window

and then press ←. You will see the result, 8, displayed on the Output screen.

2. Press any key to return to the Immediate window and type **CLS** on the line just beneath the PRINT statement. Press ← to clear the Output screen.

Work done in the Immediate window is not saved with the program, but it is possible to copy lines from the Immediate window to the View window by using the Cut and Paste edit commands that you will learn in Chapter 4.

Use the following arithmetic expressions to practice calculations in the Immediate window. Use Alt + Plus to increase the window size if you need more room. All of the expressions equal 8, so if you've coded them correctly, you should get 8 in the Output screen each time. The correct BASIC statements for each of these expressions are shown in Figure 3.1. To clear the screen between trials, return the cursor to any position on the line that contains *CLS* and press ←.

$$2(3 + 1) \qquad 12 + \frac{4 + 5}{3} - 7 \qquad 5 + \frac{(5 - 2)^2}{10 - 7}$$

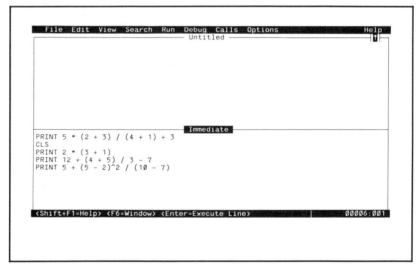

Figure 3.1: Performing calculations in the Immediate window

When you are done, return to the View window by pressing F6 and increase its size using Alt + Plus.

VARIABLES AND CONSTANTS

Variables are used in programs to store data values that may change during the course of program execution. You may also define

When a variable name appears in several places in your program, the Quick-BASIC smart editor will automatically adjust capitalization in all occurrences of the variable to match the capitalization you used most recently when entering that variable's name.

constants in a QuickBASIC program. Constants are used to store values that will remain unchanged throughout program execution. When you define variables and constants, choose names that will help make your program easy to read and understand. These names can be as long as 40 characters and can include a combination of letters, numbers, and the decimal point. BASIC keywords, like PRINT, are known as reserved words and cannot be used alone as variable names, but reserved words can be included as part of a longer variable name, such as PrintName or NameToPrint. Variables are generally written as shown here, using a combination of uppercase and lowercase letters. Constants are often distinguished from variables by the use of uppercase letters.

STRING VARIABLES

The variables you have worked with so far have been used to store numeric values, but variables can be used to store text as well. Variables used for this purpose are known as *string* variables and are identified by a dollar sign ($) placed at the end of the variable name. String variables can be defined with both assignment statements and INPUT statements and can be used to store any combination of letters, numbers, punctuation, and spaces. To define a string variable with an assignment statement you must place the text for that variable within double quotation marks. The following short program defines two string variables, FirstName$ and Address$, and then displays them using PRINT statements.

```
FirstName$ = "Don"
Address$ = "12 Elm St., Apt. 3B"
CLS
PRINT FirstName$
PRINT Address$
```

The output for this program is shown here:

```
Don
12 Elm St., Apt. 3B
```

INPUT statements can also be used to assign values to string variables when the variable in the INPUT statement is identified as a string variable. A modified version of the program you just created, which can accept different values for FirstName$ and Address$, is shown below. Edit your program and then run the modified program, experimenting with different values for the two string variables.

```
INPUT "What is your first name"; FirstName$
INPUT "What is your address"; Address$
CLS
PRINT FirstName$
PRINT Address$
```

When you are ready to continue, use the New Program command to clear the View window without saving the sample program.

Because commas are used in BASIC to separate data values, commas in a string such as an address will be misinterpreted. Avoid them for now; you will learn how to handle this problem in Chapter 4.

CONSTANTS

Constants are used to store values that will, as their name implies, remain constant throughout program execution. Constants can make your program easier to read because constant names are often more descriptive than the value they represent. They also make programs easier to update because you can change values used throughout your program by changing one easily located constant definition statement.

Constants are defined in a CONST statement, which can include one or several constants. Type in the following line to define two constants, *FIRST* and *SECOND*. Note the comma that separates the two parts of this statement.

```
CONST FIRST = 1, SECOND = 2
```

Once defined, these constants can be used in any expression as you would use a number. They cannot be reassigned. Try to add the following line to your program:

```
FIRST = FIRST + 1
```

This statement would present no difficulty if FIRST were a variable, but because it is a constant, the editor displays an error message when you try to move off this line. Press Esc to close the error message and erase both lines with Ctrl + Y.

The CIRCLE.BAS program in Figure 3.2 demonstrate a short application that calculates the area and circumference of a circle using a constant to store the value for π. The value of the radius is received as input during program execution. Remark statements throughout the program explain each line in detail. Notice that a blank line has been used in this program listing. Blank lines like this can make your program easier to read and have no effect on program execution.

```
REM CIRCLE.BAS
'   Calculates area and circumference of a circle
CONST PI = 3.14159              'Define constant to approximate pi
CLS                             'Clear the screen

INPUT "What is the radius of the circle"; Radius   'Get value for radius
Area = PI * Radius ^ 2                             'Calculate area
Circumference = 2 * PI * Radius                    'Calculate circumference

'Display a blank line and then the results
PRINT
PRINT "The area of the circle is"; Area
PRINT "The circumference of the circle is"; Circumference
```

Figure 3.2: The CIRCLE.BAS program

Sample output from the CIRCLE program is shown here:

```
What is the radius of the circle? 5
The area of the circle is 78.53975
The circumference of the circle is 31.4159
```

Experiment with the program by using a variety of values for the radius and then save it with the name CIRCLE.BAS. You will use this program again.

USING QUICKBASIC DATA-TYPES

You have seen that variables can be used to store both numeric and text information and that variables used to store text information are identified by using a $ as the last character of the variable. This is one of five possible suffixes you can use to define a variable's data-type; the others are used to distinguish between different types of numeric data. In the next sections you will learn more about selecting numeric data-types for the variables in your program.

NUMERIC DATA-TYPES

In order to improve speed and accuracy, QuickBASIC uses four different numeric data-types when it performs calculations, known as integers, long integers, single-precision numbers, and double-precision numbers. Each data-type is handled differently in the computer's memory. Understanding these four data-types will enable you to write programs that give accurate results as efficiently as possible. Information about QuickBASIC data-types is summarized in Table 3.1, and each data-type is explained in the material that follows.

Table 3.1: QuickBASIC Variable Types

VARIABLE TYPE	SUFFIX	DESCRIPTION	SIZE IN MEMORY (BYTES)
Integer	%	Integer values between − 32,768 and 32,767	2
Long Integer	&	Integer values between − 2,147,483,648 and 2,147,483,647	4
Single Precision	!	Floating-point numbers with 7-digit accuracy	4
Double Precision	#	Floating-point numbers with 15-digit accuracy	4
String Variables	$	A sequence of characters of variable length	4 + 1/char

SHORT AND LONG INTEGERS Numbers without fractional parts can be treated as integers. QuickBASIC recognizes two kinds of integers: Regular integers have values between − 32,768 and 32,767; long integers are numbers from approximately negative 2 billion to approximately 2 billion ($\pm 2 \times 10^9$). Integers are identified by the suffix %. An integer might be found in a program including a numbered list of items because integer variables are often used to keep track of numbered items. Such a variable could be called something like *Item-Number%*. If the list contained more than 32,767 items, however, it would require a long integer to number the items. The suffix for long integers is &. *ItemNumber&* is an example of a long-integer variable.

Integers are stored very efficiently in a computer's memory; each regular integer occupies 2 bytes of storage, and each long integer occupies 4 bytes. As a result, calculations using integer data-types can be performed more rapidly than calculations performed with equivalent single- or double-precision numbers. To get maximum speed and accuracy, it is good programming practice to use integer data-types wherever possible.

SINGLE-PRECISION NUMBERS Data values that have a decimal point are often referred to as *floating-point* numbers. QuickBASIC recognizes two kinds of floating-point numbers. Single-precision numbers are floating-point numbers with an accuracy of about seven digits. Examples of some single-precision numbers are:

```
3.456789
0.0000876
1.456E+9
```

The last example on the list is written in exponential form. The $E+9$ is a shorthand notation that means "multiply the preceding number by 10^9." Another way to think of $E+9$ is as an instruction to move the decimal point nine place values to the right, and thus the decimal equivalent for 1.456E+9 is 1456000000. Negative values of the exponent move the decimal to the left, so 2.345E -5 is equal to .00002345. You can input values of a number from the keyboard using either decimal or exponential notation.

The suffix for single-precision variables is !. Single-precision is also set as the default data-type, so that variables with no suffix are stored as single-precision data values. For example, in the CIRCLE.BAS program, Radius, Area, and Circumference are all single-precision variables that could be replaced by Radius!, Area!, and Circumference! without having any effect on the way the computer treats those three values.

When a variable is defined as single-precision, it cannot handle more than seven significant digits without losing accuracy. When greater accuracy is required, double-precision numbers can be used.

DOUBLE-PRECISION NUMBERS   Of the four available numeric data-types, double-precision numbers can handle the greatest range of data values with the greatest accuracy. These are floating-point numbers with an accuracy of 15 digits. Examples of values that could be accurately stored only as double-precision numbers are

```
999999999999999
10.23456789
1.563 D + 123
```

The first number is an integer that is too large to be stored as a long integer. The second number is a floating-point number with too many digits to be stored accurately as a single-precision number; it would be stored as 10.23457, rounding off at the seventh digit.

The third number in the list is written in exponential form. Double-precision numbers use a D rather than an E to indicate exponentiation. Although this number has only four significant digits, it could not be stored as a single-precision number because the exponent is too large. Single-precision numbers cannot exceed E + 38. Double-precision numbers are able to handle values as large as D + 308. Negative exponents can reach E − 45 for single-precision numbers and D − 324 for double-precision numbers.

Double-precision numbers occupy 8 bytes of space in memory—twice as much space as either single-precision numbers or long integers and four times as much as regular integers. For this reason they are generally used only when range or accuracy requirements preclude the use of some other data-type.

THE DATATYPE PROGRAM   The DATATYPE program, which you will create next, uses an interactive approach to help you understand the four numeric data-types. When you run the program, you will be prompted to enter values for four different variables. Each value is stored using a different variable type. The program immediately displays the value that has been stored for that variable. If the value you type exceeds the *range* limit that is determined by that variable's data-type, you will receive an *Overflow* error message. This message will be repeated until you enter a legal value. If the value you type exceeds the *accuracy* of that variable's data-type, it will be accepted as a legal value, but accuracy will be lost, and the program output immediately shows you how the value the computer stores differs from the value you entered.

Type in the DATATYPE program as it appears in Figure 3.3. Notice how suffixes are used to determine the data-type for each of the four variables in the program. Run the program several times, entering a variety of values for each data-type. Test for range by using very large and very small numbers. Test for accuracy by increasing the number of digits you use for each data-type. Try entering numbers using exponential form as well as decimal form. It is not necessary to enter a value for every line every time you run the program. Pressing ⏎ is a quick way to enter a zero.

Don't use commas when you enter large numbers; commas are used to separate data items, and in this context they will result in an error message.

```
'REM DATATYPE.BAS
'    Demonstrates how different data types are stored and displayed.

CLS

PRINT "Short Integers:"
INPUT "   What is the value"; si%
PRINT "   The computer stores"; si%
PRINT

PRINT "Long Integers:"
INPUT "   What is the value"; li&
PRINT "   The computer stores"; li&
PRINT

PRINT "Single-precision Numbers:"
INPUT "   What is the value"; sp!
PRINT "   The computer stores"; sp!
PRINT

PRINT "Double-Precision Numbers:"
INPUT "   What is the value"; dp#
PRINT "   The computer stores"; dp#
```

Figure 3.3: The DATATYPE program

A sample Output screen from the DATATYPE program is shown in Figure 3.4. The initial value entered was 32768, a number beyond the range of the integer variable (si%) in the first INPUT statement. The second entry for this variable, 32767, was found to be within the legal range. The value 56000.54 was entered next. Because this was stored as a long integer (li&), the number was rounded to the nearest whole number, and some accuracy was lost. When a 9-digit number was entered for the single-precision variable (sp!), it was rounded to the closest 7-digit value, and again some accuracy was lost. Finally, a large number with nine significant digits was entered to be stored as a double-precision variable (dp#). The resulting display is in exponential form and shows no loss of accuracy.

```
Short Integers:
   What is the value? 32768

Overflow
Redo from start
   What is the value? 32767
   The computer stores 32767

Long Integers:
   What is the value? 56000.54
   The computer stores 56001

Single-precision Numbers:
   What is the value? 12.3456789
   The computer stores 12.34568

Double-Precision Numbers:
   What is the value? 123456789000000000
   The computer stores 1.23456789D+17




Press any key to continue
```

Figure 3.4: Sample Output from the DATATYPE program

Save this program and clear the screen when you are ready to continue to the next section.

USING CONTEXT-SENSITIVE HELP TO DETERMINE DATA-TYPE   In Chapter 2 you used context-sensitive help to learn more about a QuickBASIC keyword that was part of your program. You can also use context-sensitive help to get information about variables and constants in your programs. To do this, position the cursor on any variable or constant in a program and press F1. The following instructions illustrate how to use this aspect of QuickBASIC's help features. First, open the CIRCLE.BAS program that you created earlier (Figure 3.2).

1. Move your cursor to the line in the CIRCLE program that reads *Area = PI * Radius ^ 2*.

2. Position the cursor on the variable *Area* and press F1. A Help window appears telling you that Area is a single-precision variable.

3. Press Esc to close the window.

4. Move the cursor to any occurrence of the constant *PI* and press F1. The Help window tells you that PI is a single-precision constant.

5. Next you will redefine PI as a double-precision value. To do this, change the CONST statement to read as follows:

   CONST PI = 3.14159265359#

6. Move the cursor to PI in one of the subsequent program lines and press F1. The Help window that opens reflects the change you just made to the data-type for PI.

By comparison to the human mind, computers have astonishingly fast and accurate recall of what they have been told. Remember to use context-sensitive help to take advantage of this recall as you develop longer programs that contain more information than you can successfully retain in your own memory.

CHANGING DEFAULT DATA-TYPES

You have now seen that you can specify the data-type of numbers in QuickBASIC programs by adding the appropriate suffix to variables, constants, or numeric values and that when no suffix is present, QuickBASIC uses single-precision as the default data-type. In the next section you will learn how to change the default definition of QuickBASIC data-types. Clear the View window when you are ready to proceed.

THE DEFTYPE STATEMENT   QuickBASIC provides five statements that can be used to change the data-type of some or all of the variables in your program. Each statement combines the letters DEF with a 3-letter data-type indentifier. This statement is followed by one or more letters of the alphabet. The effect of a DEFtype statement is to set all variables that begin with these letters to the designated data-type. For example,

DEFINT A–Z

changes the default definition of all variables in your program to the integer data-type. The *INT* here defines the data-type, and the letters A–Z refer to the first letters of the variables in your program. You can also specify just certain letters for variables defined in a DEFtype statement as shown here:

DEFDBLE m,n,p

This statement defines all variables starting with m, n, or p as double-precision values. Any combination of letters or letter ranges can be listed in a DEFtype statement. The letters and ranges you include in a DEFtype list must be separated by commas.

The five DEFtype statements that can be used this way are

STATEMENT	DATA-TYPE DEFINED
DEFINT	Integers
DEFLNG	Long Integers
DEFSNG	Single-precision
DEFDBL	Double-precision
DEFSTR	String

The next program will give you a sense of how these statements are used.

THE DEFDEMO PROGRAM   Computers are much more patient than people and make no complaints whatsoever when asked to perform pointless tasks. The short program that follows takes advantage of this desirable characteristic in order to give you a sense of the time required to perform the exact same series of calculations using the four different numeric data-types. You will use DEFtype statements to select the data-types.

This program introduces the TIME$ function, which returns the current time, measured in hours (from 0–24), minutes, and seconds. It also uses two paired statements, FOR and NEXT, to instruct the computer to repeat a task several times. This kind of repeating program structure is known as a *loop*. You will have an opportunity to explore program loops in detail in Chapter 5. This particular loop instructs the computer to add one to every whole number value for the variable x, starting with x = 1 and ending with x = 3000. Nothing is done with the resulting information; the loop is just a way to measure the length of time it takes your computer to perform 3000 addition operations. Type the program into your View window as it appears here:

```
REM DEFDEMO.BAS
PRINT TIME$
FOR X = 1 to 3000
  X = X + 1
NEXT X
PRINT TIME$
PRINT
```

When you run this program, the Output screen will show a starting and stopping time. The starting time is the time at which the computer reached the first 'PRINT TIME$' statement. The stopping time is displayed after the computer has completed its 3000 calculations and reaches the second 'PRINT TIME$' statement. You can use this output to see how much time was spent on this thankless task.

Because no data-type was specified, the variable X was defined as a single-precision number. Adding a DEFINT statement is one way to change X to a short integer. Change your program so that it reads as follows:

```
REM DEFDEMO.BAS
DEFINT a–z
PRINT TIME$
```

```
FOR X = 1 to 3000
   X = X + 1
NEXT X
PRINT TIME$
PRINT
```

If you have a fast system, try increasing the top value for X in the DEFDEMO program from 3000 to 30000 to get a better sense of the difference in time required to perform calculations using different data-types.

Run the program again. Because no CLS statement is included, you can now see and compare the results of the two different versions of the program. A sample Output screen might look like this:

```
14:45:35
14:45:42

14:49:05
14:49:06
```

In this example, the time elapsed for the first run was seven seconds. This dropped to only one second when the data-type was redefined. Specific times will depend on the time of day and the speed of your computer system. Try changing the default data-type to long integers and double-precision numbers and notice how these data-types affect program speed.

SUMMARY

QuickBASIC performs arithmetic operations using the symbols +, −, *, /, and ^ to represent addition, subtraction, multiplication, division, and exponentiation. When operations are combined in a single statement, they are performed in this order: expressions within parentheses first, exponentiation next, then multiplication or division, and finally addition or subtraction.

Variables are used to store data and can contain numeric or text information. Assignment statements are used to give a value to a variable within the program. INPUT statements are used to get values for variables from the keyboard. Constants are used to store values that will not change during program execution. Values for constants are assigned in a CONST statement.

Text is stored in string variables, which are identified by the symbol $ as the last character in the variable name. Numeric values are stored as one of four possible data-types—integer, long integer, single-precision, and double-precision—identified respectively by %, &, !, and #. Your choice of data-type will affect the range of values you can use, the degree of accuracy available, and the speed at which a program operates. Ordinarily, the default data-type is single-precision numbers, but you can control the default data-type for some or all variables by using DEFtype statements.

In addition to giving you a chance to work with variables and perform calculations, Chapter 3 introduced you to the use of the Immediate window as a way of seeing the results of a QuickBASIC statement immediately.

This chapter began with a brief introduction to techniques for controlling input and output. In Chapter 4, you will expand on these simple techniques. You will also learn how to use some new QuickBASIC editing features that will help speed up program development.

Communicating Effectively: Input and Output Techniques

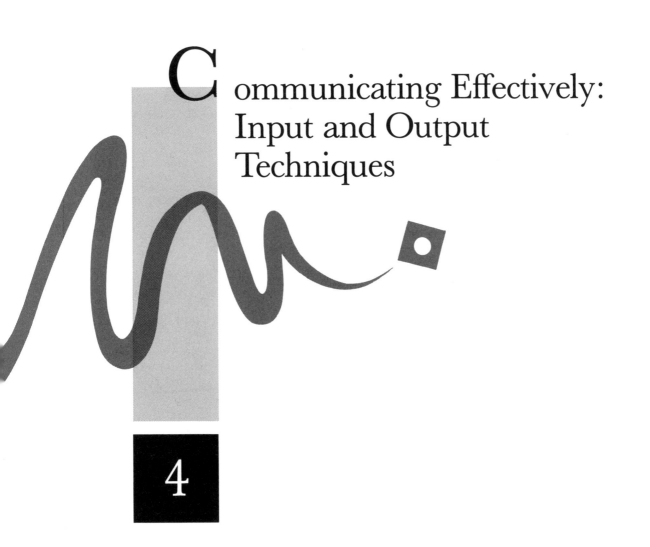

4

CHAPTER *4*

A COMPUTER PROGRAM IS A TOOL, AND, LIKE ANY good tool, it should perform its task without calling attention to itself. Part of your job as a programmer is to design programs so easy to use that they fade into the background and let the user concentrate on the task at hand. Careful input and output design are an essential part of this process. This chapter introduces you to techniques you can use to control the appearance of the screen when it requests data from the user, and again when it displays output information. You will also learn how to direct output to the printer.

Some time will also be spent with the QuickBASIC menus, concentrating here on the Edit and Search menus. Using the Edit commands, you will learn how to move, copy, or erase blocks of material. Using the Search commands, you will learn how to find particular words or expressions in your program and how to perform search-and-replace operations.

DESIGNING EASY-TO-READ OUTPUT

Good programs have effective output—well worded and easy to read. Although there are many advanced programming techniques used to achieve "state-of-the-art" screen displays, a beginner can achieve satisfactory results by concentrating on clarity and careful design.

POSITIONING OUTPUT ON THE SCREEN

The programs you have created so far all position output in the same way, placing each line directly beneath the one above it. In the next sections of this chapter, you will learn how to vary this positioning in order to create more effective displays.

PUNCTUATION IN PRINT STATEMENTS Two punctuation marks, the comma (,) and the semicolon (;), are used to control the spacing of items listed in PRINT statements. When items are separated by semicolons, each output item is displayed immediately following the previous item. The exact spacing depends on the kind of value being displayed. Positive numbers are separated by blank spaces in front and in back; negative numbers have a minus sign in front and a blank space in back; and character strings are displayed with no spaces between them. For wider spacing, you can separate items in a PRINT statement with commas. When commas are used, the items are spaced in even intervals, each 14 characters wide.

This short program demonstrates the effects of commas and semicolons in PRINT statements.

```
'Commas and semicolons in PRINT statements
A = 3
B = 17.5
C = -24
CLS
PRINT A; B; C
PRINT A, B, C
PRINT "A";"B";"C"
```

The output of this program is shown below. Look at the first two lines to compare the effect of semicolons and commas on an identical list of numbers. The last line shows the effect of semicolons on a list of three string values.

```
 3   17.5  -24
 3              17.5           -24
ABC
```

You can also put a comma or a semicolon at the end of a PRINT statement. When you do this, the output from the next PRINT statement in your program will continue on the current line, rather than using the one beneath it. The effect is the same as if you had used a single long PRINT statement.

WORKING WITH SPACES   When you are working with character strings in PRINT statements, you need to plan your spacing carefully. Run this short program to demonstrate the problem.

```
'Effect of semicolons in separating string variables
CLS
A$ = "Hi"
B$ = "There"
PRINT A$; B$
```

The output looks like this:

HiThere

The effect of the semicolon is to position the two words next to each other without including the space you would like to see between them. One way to correct this is to include a blank space as part of one of the strings. When string variables are stored, blank spaces are included, so "Hi" and "Hi " are not equivalent. Change line 3 so that it reads like this:

```
A$ = "Hi "
```

When you run the corrected program, the output will include the space you added to the A$ variable, as shown here:

Hi There

You can also incorporate spaces into string variables when you want to create designs in your program output. This is demonstrated by the program below, which displays a heart in the Output screen.

```
'HEART.BAS
'Heart shape
CLS
PRINT " ***    ***"
PRINT "*****  *****"
PRINT "***********"
PRINT "  *******"
PRINT "   ***"
PRINT "    *"
```

After you run this program, save it as HEART.BAS. You will use it again later in this chapter.

USING TAB AND SPC TO CONTROL OUTPUT Two BASIC functions, SPC and TAB, can be used within a PRINT statement to control the horizontal placement of material in a line of output. An example of the TAB function is shown here.

```
PRINT TAB(25); "HI"
```

The number in parentheses in the statement above is known as an *argument*. Arguments are data items that are included in BASIC commands and influence the results when the command is executed. The TAB function uses a numeric argument to position output the specified number of spaces from the left edge of your screen. In this example, the *H* of the word HI will be in column 25.

The SPC function also uses a numeric argument, but this function counts spaces from the end of the most recent output, rather than from the edge of the screen. The PRINT statement below displays the number 123 at the left edge of the screen, then ten blank spaces followed by 456:

```
PRINT 123; SPC(10); 456
```

Run the next program to get a sense of the difference between these two functions.

```
'Tab and space in print statements
CLS
PRINT TAB(20); "*"; TAB(30); "*"
PRINT SPC(20); "*"; SPC(30); "*"
```

The output screen will look like this:

```
                          *             *
                          *                                    *
```

In the first line, the TAB functions position the asterisks in columns 20 and 30. In the second line, the SPC functions result in 20 blank spaces before the first asterisk and 30 blank spaces between the first and second.

When you are planning output, find the best location by trying out your ideas using the Immediate window.

USING LOCATE TO POSITION SCREEN OUTPUT An additional statement—LOCATE—provides a flexible way to position screen output. Your monitor screen is a grid made up of 25 rows and 80 columns. LOCATE statements use coordinates within this grid to position output. The two coordinates specify row and column values, in that order. For example, *LOCATE 4,7* directs output to row 4, column 7.

Run the next program to see how LOCATE works.

```
'Using LOCATE
CLS
LOCATE 12, 40
PRINT "* (Row 12, Column 40)"
```

The output message appears in row 12, column 40—the center of the output screen. It is the initial character of the ouput string, in this case the *, that is placed in the position specified by the LOCATE statement.

Subsequent messages can be displayed anywhere on screen by using additional LOCATE statements; when no LOCATE statement is used, output continues beneath the most recent statement. Make the modifications to your program shown below to demonstrate this.

```
'Using LOCATE
CLS
LOCATE 12, 40
PRINT "* (Row 12, Column 40)"
PRINT "With no additional LOCATE, the next line is here."
LOCATE 1, 1
PRINT "Using LOCATE lets you display material anywhere."
```

FORMATTING WITH PRINT USING

You may have noticed that the SALESTAX program in Chapter 1 will frequently display total price in an awkward form. When you are working with dollars and cents you generally want to see exactly two decimal places, but in the default display of numeric output, the number of decimal places varies, including as many as are needed to show maximum accuracy. When you want to specify some other format for numeric output, you can use a PRINT USING statement. With it you can control features such as the location of the decimal point, the number of significant digits displayed, the placement of commas, and the display of symbols such as a dollar sign. Thus you can design your output so that a number like 10.7 is displayed as $10.70.

Look at this example to understand how a PRINT USING statement functions.

PRINT USING "###.##"; 34.6

The symbols within quotation marks are known as a *format string*. The numbers that follow will be displayed in a format that is defined by this string. In this example, 34.6 is formatted to fill six spaces, with a decimal point in the fourth position and two digits displayed after the decimal. As a result, 34.6 is displayed as 34.60.

Format strings are easiest to understand by looking at examples. Table 4.1 summarizes the symbols that can be used in format strings and includes examples of the effect of each of these symbols.

You can also use a variable as the format string in a PRINT USING statement. This technique is used in the next sample program to allow you to experiment with different number formats. Each time you run the program, you can input a format string and a number. The output shows you how the number is displayed using that format. A new kind of input statement is used in line 4; the LINE INPUT statement is necessary to allow input of commas in your format string. You'll learn more about LINE INPUT later in this chapter. A double-precision variable is used in line 5 to allow the greatest range of numeric values. Run this program several times, experimenting with different formatting symbols and a range of numeric values. The program and a sample Output screen are shown below. Save this program to use again later.

Table 4.1: Characters Used to Format Numbers

SYMBOL	EXPLANATION	VALUE	FORMAT STRING	RESULTING OUTPUT
#	Indicates number and position of digits.	7 34.6	##### #####	7 35
.	Indicates position of decimal point.	34.6 58.678	###.## ###.##	34.60 58.68
,	Prints commas every third digit. Placed left of the decimal.	34567.8 7654321	####,.## #######,	34,567.80 7,654,321
+	Indicates position of sign. Both + and − are displayed.	−92 92	##+ +##	92− +92
−	Places trailing sign for negative numbers only.	−76 76	##− ##−	76− 76
$$	Prints a dollar sign immediately in front of a number.	34	$$####	$34
$	Prints a left-justified dollar sign.	34	$#####	$ 34
**	Fills leading spaces with asterisks.	72 7200	**###.## **###.##	***72.00 *7200.00
**$	Fills leading spaces with asterisks, then a dollar sign.	65.135	**$##.##	**$65.14
^^^^	Prints numbers in exponential form. One digit position is used for the sign.	1289 −1289	##.##^^^^ ##.##^^^^	1.29E+03 −1.29E+03

```
REM FORMAT.BAS
'Demonstrates the PRINT USING statement
CLS
LINE INPUT "Type in a sample format string:   "; format$
INPUT "What number would you like to see"; value#
PRINT
PRINT "The resulting display is:";
PRINT USING format$; TAB(36); value#
```

Sample output from this program looks like this:

Type in a sample format string: * *$####,.##
What number would you like to see? 5681

The resulting display is: * *$5,681.00

You might want to eliminate the CLS statement; this will allow you to compare the results when you run the program using different values. If you do so, use a CLS statement in the Immediate window to clear the Output screen.

You can include several items in a PRINT USING statement. When a list of numeric values follows a format string, all the values will be displayed using that format; thus

PRINT USING "#######,"; 120000; 54321; 67

results in

120,000   54,321   67

Format strings can also be included within lines of text. You can use this feature to incorporate formatted numbers into your text output. For example,

PRINT USING "The value is $$##.##"; 3.2

results in

The value is $3.20

Using number formats and well-positioned output will help make your programs more effective and easier to use.

PRINTING ROWS OF REPEATED CHARACTERS

Another way to make your output easier to read is to use visual cues such as border lines to separate parts of the screen, which you can do easily with the STRING$ function. This function allows you to print any character a specified number of times. The syntax for this function is shown in the example below. The first item in the parentheses specifies the number of times a character is printed. The second item defines the character to be printed. A comma separates them.

```
PRINT STRING$(8, "*")
```

The output of this program line is a row of eight asterisks:

```
* * * * * * * *
```

There is a second way to choose the display character in a STRING$ function. Each display character is represented by a code number known as its ASCII code. When the second argument in a STRING$ function is a numeric value, it represents the ASCII code number for a display character. Thus you can select display characters that are not included on the keyboard, as well as those that are. You will learn more about ASCII codes in Chapter 8. In the example below, the code for an equal sign (61) is used in the second STRING$ function. Try running this program:

```
'Demonstrates STRING$
ShortLine$ = STRING$(10, "_")
LongLine$ = STRING$(80, 61)
CLS
PRINT ShortLine$
PRINT LongLine$
```

Its output will be a short single line followed by a double line made up of equal signs that fills the entire 80-character screen. The INVOICE program at the end of this chapter demonstrates a few practical applications for the STRING$ function.

CREATING HELPFUL PROMPTS FOR USER INPUT

A common experience among computer users is encountering an input prompt that seems to make no sense whatsoever. You have probably found yourself more than once trying all sorts of keys and getting more and more frustrated when none of them does what you want. As a programmer, always try to imagine what your program will look like to someone using it for the first time. Unless you are writing programs for your own use, you will probably concentrate increasingly on techniques that make your programs easier to interact with as you develop your skills as a programmer. The next sections of this chapter show you a few useful variations of the simple INPUT statement.

PUNCTUATION IN INPUT STATEMENTS

An INPUT statement—when used alone or with a semicolon between the prompt string and the variable—places a question mark automatically on screen. When you want a prompt to read as a statement rather than a question, use a comma instead of a semicolon. Compare the output of the following two lines:

```
INPUT "What is your name"; Name$
INPUT "Type your name please: ", Name$
```

A sample Output screen is shown here:

```
What is your name? Joe
Type your name please:  Joe
```

Notice that when you use a semicolon, the cursor will automatically move one space beyond the question mark before waiting for input. When you use a comma, however, you must place a trailing space within the prompt string to achieve the same effect.

It is possible to include several variables in a single INPUT statement. Commas are used to separate variable names in the INPUT statement, and again when values are typed from the keyboard. This kind of INPUT statement can make program writing a bit easier, but generally results in more confusing input prompts. The program below uses this form of input to average three numbers. To enter the numbers, you must type them all on one line, separated by commas. When you press ←, the program proceeds with the calculation and output display.

```
'Including several items in one INPUT statement
CLS
PRINT "This program averages three numbers."
PRINT "Enter them on one line separated by commas."
INPUT "Three values to average: ", A, B, C
PRINT
PRINT "The average is"; (A + B + C) / 3
```

A sample run looks like this:

```
This program averages three numbers.
Enter them on one line separated by commas.
Three values to average: 30,33,39

The average is 34
```

Commas used this way can separate string values as well as numeric values, but string values that might contain commas, such as addresses, will not be correctly read in. To handle these kinds of strings you can use the LINE INPUT statement explained in the next section.

THE LINE INPUT STATEMENT

In a simple INPUT statement, items are delineated by commas. In a LINE INPUT statement, items are delineated by a line feed: a string of characters is not assigned to a variable until ↵ is pressed. No question mark is added to the end of the prompt string. LINE INPUT statements can be used for string variables only, and can input only one variable at a time. Two similar input statements are shown below. If someone typed his full name as Donald J. Duprey, Esq., it would be correctly read by the LINE INPUT statement, but not the INPUT statement beneath it.

```
LINE INPUT "Type in your full name: "; FullName$
INPUT "Type in your full name: ", FullName$
```

Retrieve the FORMAT program you created earlier to see an example of the use of LINE INPUT. LINE INPUT was necessary in this program because the format strings you enter may contain a comma. Try changing the LINE INPUT statement to an INPUT statement, then enter a format string with a comma (such as ####,.##) to see the error statement that results.

USING A PRINTER FOR OUTPUT

The PRINT statement that you have been using sends output to the screen, rather than to a printer, and the word PRINT may therefore seem like an odd choice for this purpose. It is actually a vestige of BASIC's earliest days, before computers used monitors for input and output, when all output was directed to a printer. The BASIC command that sends output to a printer is LPRINT. LPRINT and LPRINT USING statements use the same syntax as PRINT and PRINT USING. The effects of punctuation, SPC, and TAB are the same on paper as they are on screen. However, LOCATE statements influence the position of on-screen output only. They are ignored when output is directed to the printer. The sample program below sends output both to the screen and to the printer. The role of the first INPUT statement is to suspend program execution until the user has determined that the printer is ready to receive instructions.

```
'Sending output to screen and printer
INPUT "Ready the printer, then press Enter", Ready$
PRINT
PRINT "PRINT statements direct output to the monitor."
LPRINT "LPRINT statements direct output to the printer."
```

Because screen display is faster than printed output and wastes no paper, it is often easiest to test output ideas on screen first and then convert your program so that it produces printed output. Quick-BASIC edit commands make it easy to convert PRINT statements to LPRINT statements. It is also possible to copy blocks of code when you want your program to produce both printed and on-screen output. These editing commands are covered in the next sections of this chapter.

WORKING WITH THE EDIT MENU

The QuickBASIC Edit menu includes commands for copying, moving, and deleting sections of your program. The copy command enables you to copy lines from one part of a program to another, from one program to another, or from the example programs that are included in QuickBASIC's online help to your own programs. The move command is useful when you want to change the order of statements in a program or move lines from one program to another. The delete command removes program lines, but stores them until the next deletion, allowing you to retrieve them if necessary. Commands in the Search menu allow you to search for words or phrases and replace them if necessary. You will use these techniques in the following exercises to modify the HEART.BAS program you've already created so that it prints a paper valentine in addition to creating an on-screen display.

CUTTING AND PASTING BLOCKS OF MATERIAL

When you want to copy, move, or delete a section of your program, you must first indicate which section you are working with by selecting a block of material. To do this in QuickBASIC, hold the Shift key down and simultaneously press a cursor-control key. As you move the cursor, the selected block will be highlighted.

After a block has been highlighted, *use cursor-control keys only*. If you press any other key, the selected block will be erased and replaced by that keyboard character. Material erased this way *cannot* be retrieved with the Paste command.

To delete a selected block, use the Cut command in the Edit menu or use the shortcut key combination Shift +Del. When a block is deleted in this way, it is placed in a memory storage area known as a *clipboard*. To retrieve material from the clipboard, use the Paste command in the Edit menu, or the shortcut key combination Shift +Ins. To move a block from one part of a program to another, use the Cut command to erase a block and move the material to the clipboard, select a new location using the cursor, and then retrieve the material with the Paste command.

Material remains in the clipboard until replaced or until you exit QuickBASIC. It can be replaced by material from another Cut command or by a line of text erased with Ctrl +Y. Material in the clipboard can be retrieved at any time into any program.

Selected blocks can also be deleted by pressing Del rather than Shift +Del. However, material erased this way is not sent to the clipboard and cannot be retrieved.

The next exercise uses the HEART.BAS program to demonstrate these commands.

1. Open the HEART program and place the cursor on the first character of the first line.

2. Hold the Shift key while you press ↓ three times. The first three lines of the program will be highlighted.

3. Press Shift + Del to erase the selected block and move it to the clipboard.

4. Without moving the cursor, retrieve the block by pressing Shift + Ins. If you had wanted to relocate this material, you could have done so by moving the cursor before pressing Shift + Ins.

When you delete or move a block, it is removed from its original location. When you want to duplicate material, leaving it in its original location, use the Copy command, which is explained in the next section.

COPYING BLOCKS OF MATERIAL

Copying blocks of material is similar to Cutting and Pasting. The steps used to copy blocks of material in QuickBASIC are summarized below and will be demonstrated in the exercise that follows.

- Select the block you want to copy by holding down the Shift key while using the cursor-control keys.

- Move a copy of the block to the clipboard by using the Copy command in the Edit menu, or by pressing Ctrl + Ins.

- Move the cursor to mark the location for the duplicate copy.

- Retrieve the material to the new location using the Paste command, or by pressing Shift + Ins.

You will use these steps to add a duplicate copy of all of the PRINT statements in the HEART program. Once you have copied these lines, you can use a search-and-replace technique to change PRINT statements to LPRINT statements. As a result, the program will direct output to both the monitor and the printer. Proceed as follows:

1. With the original version of the HEART program on screen, place the cursor on the first character of the first PRINT statement on line 4.

2. Hold down the Shift key and press ↓ until all of the PRINT statements that form the heart have been highlighted.

3. Press Ctrl + Ins to copy the selected material to the clipboard.

4. Press ◄── to create a blank line. (When you do this the highlighting will disappear.)

5. Press Shift + Ins to paste the material in the clipboard to the new location. You should now have two duplicate sets of PRINT statements.

6. Save this version of the program as HEART2.BAS.

If you run the HEART2 program as it now stands, it will display two hearts on screen. Leave this version of the program in the Work screen; you will modify it in the next section to print one of these hearts on paper.

WORKING WITH THE SEARCH MENU

The QuickBASIC Search menu includes a Find option that you can use to locate any word, phrase, or mathematical expression used in your program. A second option, the Change command, is available when you want to make changes to a word or phrase in all or part of your program. You will use this second feature to change PRINT to LPRINT in the HEART2 program.

USING THE FIND COMMAND

To find a word or phrase in your program, select the Find command in the Search menu to open the Find dialog box. The cursor will be in a input box labeled

Find What

This box automatically contains whatever word was at the cursor position when you invoked the Find command. You can search for this word without making any changes to the dialog box, or you can type in any other word or phrase you want to search for. There are two default search conditions: The search will locate all matches regardless of case and will locate the word you are searching for whether it stands alone or is part of some larger word. You can change either or both of these conditions before initiating the search. To conduct a search that is case-sensitive, press Alt +M to select *Match Upper/Lower Case*. To find whole word matches, press Alt +W to select the *Whole Word* option. When you want to repeat a search for the same word, using the same search conditions, you can use the F3 shortcut key.

If you mark a block of text before initiating the Find command, the selected block will automatically be entered in the *Find What* box when you start a search. This is a fast way to initiate a search for longer expressions.

Practice the Find command with the HEART2 program by following these steps:

1. Position the cursor on any occurence of the word PRINT.

2. Press Alt, then S, then F to initiate the search.

3. Press ◄┘ to accept the default search conditions. As a result, the next instance of the word PRINT is highlighted.

4. Press F3 to repeat the search automatically. Each time you repeat the search, the cursor will move to the next occurence of the word PRINT. After the last PRINT statement has been reached, the search will continue with the first line of the program.

5. Press any cursor-control key to remove the highlighting.

The Find command is a fast way to locate variables and expressions in longer programs.

USING THE CHANGE COMMAND

Remember to use Tab to move from *Find What* to *Change To*. If you press ◄┘ before you have entered the modified expression, your search-and-replace operation will begin without the correct information.

The QuickBASIC Change command allows you to modify a variable or command statement in all or part of your program. To use it, select the Change command from the Search menu. When the Change dialog box opens, enter a word or phrase into the *Find What* input area as you did with the Find command. Then press Tab to move to the *Change To* input area and type the word or phrase you want to replace your former entry with. You can then select between a *Find and Verify* option and a *Change All* option. If you select *Find and Verify*, QuickBASIC will stop each time it finds what you are looking for, allowing you to choose between making the change or skipping over it. If you choose *Change All*, changes will be made automatically throughout the program. *Find and Verify* is the default option and almost always the wiser choice. Using *Change All* is likely to result in some modifications you hadn't anticipated.

The next exercise uses the Change command to change PRINT to LPRINT in the second part of the HEART2 program.

1. Position the cursor on the blank line between the two sets of identical PRINT statements in the HEART2 program.

2. Press Alt, then S, then C to initiate the search-and-replace action. The most recent search expression—PRINT—is automatically placed in the *Find What* box. (If you have searched for other words, you will need to type PRINT into the *Find What* box.)

3. Press Tab to move to the *Change To* box and type LPRINT.

4. Press ← to proceed using the *Find and Verify* option. The next instance of the word PRINT will be highlighted, and you will be asked if you want to make the change to this word.

5. Press ← to change PRINT to LPRINT.

6. Continue to press ← each time you are asked to confirm a change until you reach the last line of your program. This is the last line you want to change.

7. Press Tab twice to select Cancel and then press ← to cancel the command without making any more changes. (Pressing the Esc key has the same effect.)

8. Your program should now match Figure 4.1. Save this version of the program again as HEART2.

Before you run the program, check to be sure your printer is ready. The output should include a heart on the monitor and a second heart printed out by your printer.

```
'HEART2.BAS
'Heart shape
CLS
PRINT " ***    ***"
PRINT "***** *****"
PRINT "***********"
PRINT " ******* "
PRINT "   ***  "
PRINT "    *   "

LPRINT " ***    ***"
LPRINT "***** *****"
LPRINT "***********"
LPRINT " ******* "
LPRINT "   ***  "
LPRINT "    *   "
```

Figure 4.1: HEART2.BAS—Printing a valentine

You have now seen a variety of input and output commands and some new editing commands. The last section of this chapter will show you how to apply these tools to a programming application.

DEVELOPING THE INVOICE PROGRAM

The INVOICE program creates a bill of charges tailor-made for a company that rents out self-storage units. The program requests information about the customer and the unit being rented. In a more realistic application, this information would be saved to a disk file, but we'll get to that in a later chapter. Once the data has been entered, an invoice is created that includes the company letterhead, customer information, the current date, and columns summarizing charges, amount received, and amount due.

The date is printed using the DATE$ function, which you haven't seen yet. This function returns the date that was provided to the machine when you first booted it up. Dates are displayed in the form mm-dd-yyyy.

The invoice is displayed first on screen and then sent to the printer. The completed program is shown in Figure 4.2. You will develop it in two steps, producing on-screen output first and then adding a section that creates the printed invoice.

```
REM INVOICE.BAS
'Creates an invoice for rental of storage units

'Define variables for print statements
longline$ = STRING$(80, "=")
Shortline$ = STRING$(9, "-")
DecimalFormat$ = "######.##"
CurrencyFormat$ = "$$####.##"

'Get Customer information
CLS
LINE INPUT "First Name     :", FirstName$
LINE INPUT "Last Name      :", LastName$
LINE INPUT "Street Address :", Address$
INPUT "City           :", City$
INPUT "State          :", State$
INPUT "Zip Code       :", Zip$
PRINT

'Get Information to Calculate Amount due
INPUT "Unit Number    :", Unit$
INPUT "Rent           :", Rent
Deposit = 15
Charge = Rent + Deposit
PRINT
PRINT USING "Deposit is      $$####.## "; Deposit
PRINT USING "Total charge is $$####.##"; Charge
PRINT
INPUT "Amt Received    :", AmtRcd
AmtDue = Charge - AmtRcd

'Print Invoice
LOCATE 24, 1
INPUT "Press Enter to continue", Response$
CLS

'Print company letterhead
PRINT longline$
PRINT TAB(32); "ZZZ Rent-Z-Space"
PRINT TAB(31); "10 Cubby Hole Road"
PRINT TAB(27); "Alameda, California 94777"
PRINT longline$
PRINT

'Print Name and Date on one line
PRINT FirstName$; SPC(1); LastName$;   'semi-colon at end of this line
PRINT TAB(55); "Date: "; DATE$         'means this output goes on same line

'Print street address
PRINT Address$

'Print City, State, and Unit ID on one line
PRINT City$; ", "; State$; SPC(1); Zip$;
PRINT TAB(55); "Unit: "; Unit$
PRINT
PRINT longline$

'Print charges
PRINT
PRINT TAB(27); "Current Charges and Payment"
PRINT TAB(14); "Deposit";
PRINT USING DecimalFormat$; TAB(55); Deposit
PRINT TAB(14); "Rent";
PRINT USING DecimalFormat$; TAB(55); Rent
PRINT TAB(55); Shortline$
PRINT TAB(14); "TOTAL";
PRINT USING CurrencyFormat$; TAB(55); Charge
PRINT TAB(14); "Received";
```

Figure 4.2: The INVOICE program

```
PRINT USING DecimalFormat$; TAB(55); AmtRcd
PRINT TAB(55); Shortline$
PRINT TAB(14); "AMOUNT DUE";
PRINT USING CurrencyFormat$; TAB(55); AmtDue
PRINT
PRINT longline$

'Prepare printer to print invoice
LOCATE 24, 1
INPUT "Ready the printer and press Enter to continue", Response$

'Print company letterhead
LPRINT longline$
LPRINT TAB(32); "ZZZ Rent-Z-Space"
LPRINT TAB(31); "10 Cubby Hole Road"
LPRINT TAB(27); "Alameda, California 94777"
LPRINT longline$
LPRINT

'Print Name and Date on one line
LPRINT FirstName$; SPC(1); LastName$;   'semi-colon at end of this line
LPRINT TAB(55); "Date: "; DATE$          'means this output goes on same line

'Print street address
LPRINT Address$

'Print City, State, and Unit ID on one line
LPRINT City$; ", "; State$; SPC(1); Zip$;
LPRINT TAB(55); "Unit: "; Unit$
LPRINT
LPRINT longline$

'Print charges
LPRINT
LPRINT TAB(27); "Current Charges and Payment"
LPRINT TAB(14); "Deposit";
LPRINT USING DecimalFormat$; TAB(55); Deposit
LPRINT TAB(14); "Rent";
LPRINT USING DecimalFormat$; TAB(55); Rent
LPRINT TAB(55); Shortline$
LPRINT TAB(14); "TOTAL";
LPRINT USING CurrencyFormat$; TAB(55); Charge
LPRINT TAB(14); "Received";
LPRINT USING DecimalFormat$; TAB(55); AmtRcd
LPRINT TAB(55); Shortline$
LPRINT TAB(14); "AMOUNT DUE";
LPRINT USING CurrencyFormat$; TAB(55); AmtDue
LPRINT
LPRINT longline$

'Advance paper to top of next page
LPRINT CHR$(12)
```

Figure 4.2: The INVOICE program (continued)

To determine the proper position for centered text like the letterhead in this program, subtract the length of your output string from 80 and then divide by 2.

Clear the View window and enter the program, stopping after you have typed the remark statement that reads:

'Prepare printer to print Invoice

(This statement is at about line 76).

Run the program, supplying sample data in response to each input prompt. When you have answered the last input question, the Output screen should resemble Figure 4.3. Press ⏎ to display the invoice shown in Figure 4.4. Save the program as INVOICE. Save the file frequently as you make changes to it, so that you always have a recently updated file on disk to retrieve if you run into difficulties later on.

```
First Name     :Joe
Last Name      :Blow
Street Address :13 Elm St.
City           :Berkeley
State          :CA
Zip Code       :96705
Unit Number    :72
Rent           :55

Deposit is         $15.00
Total charge is    $70.00

Amt Received   :70




Press Enter to continue
```

Figure 4.3: The INVOICE program—Data entry

To complete the program, first type the following two lines under the *Prepare printer to print invoice* remark statement.

```
LOCATE 24, 1
INPUT "Ready the printer and press ⏎ to continue", Response$
```

You are now ready to make a copy of the section of program shown in bold face in Figure 4.2 and move it to the end of your program using the Copy command. Once you have done this, change the PRINT statements to LPRINT statements throughout the duplicate section of the program, using the Change command. When you do this, choose the *Find and Verify* option so that you can cancel the

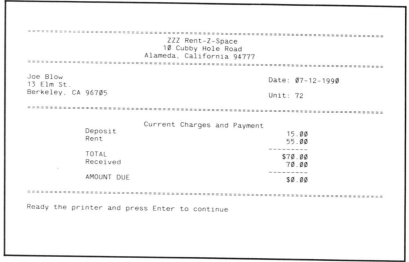

Figure 4.4: The INVOICE program—The finished invoice

command immediately after you have changed the *PRINT longline$* statement at the end of the program. Select the *Match Upper/Lowercase* option so that QuickBASIC will skip the word *Print* in the remark statement where it appears with lowercase letters; here print is used as an English word, not a BASIC command, and should not be changed to LPRINT.

At the end of the program add these two lines. The final line uses the ASCII code for form feed to advance the paper to the top of the next page. You will learn more about the CHR$ function in Chapter 8.

```
'Advance paper to top of next page
LPRINT CHR$(12)
```

Your program is now complete and should match the INVOICE program as it appears in Figure 4.2. This time when you run it, the prompt

Ready the printer and press ← to continue

appears on screen after the invoice has been displayed. When you press ← you should get a printed duplicate of the on-screen invoice.

SUMMARY

Carefully designed screens for input and output are an essential part of a good computer program. Although many advanced programming techniques have been developed in these areas, you can do a lot using only the commands covered in this chapter by paying careful attention to the layout and wording of input prompts and output screens.

Output is directed to the monitor using PRINT and to the printer using LPRINT. Syntax for PRINT and LPRINT statements is the same. Commas in these statements separate material at 14-space intervals, while semicolons place each item immediately after the previous one. Both can be placed at the end of a line when you want output to continue on the same line. You can also control the position of output to both the screen and the printer using SPC and TAB functions. The LOCATE statement affects the position of output on the monitor only by designating the row and column position to be used in the next PRINT statement.

The PRINT USING statement can be used to control the appearance of numeric output. PRINT USING statements include format strings consisting of special symbols that instruct the computer how numbers should be displayed. These symbols are summarized in Table 4.1.

Both INPUT and LINE INPUT statements can be used to receive input from the keyboard. An INPUT statement can be used to input both numeric and string variables. You can input several items with a single INPUT statement by using commas to separate the items. A LINE INPUT statement is used only for input of string values. In these statements the entire line is read into a variable; if commas are present, they are read in like any other character.

In addition to discussing input and output techniques, this chapter described the commands in the QuickBASIC Edit and Search menus. The Edit menu includes Cut, Copy, and Paste commands that allow you to manipulate blocks of material. The Search menu includes a Find command that allows you to locate words, phrases, or mathematical expressions in your program and a Change command that allows you to perform search-and-replace operations.

The INVOICE program incorporates the input and output commands you learned into a practical application. Creating this program also demonstrates how you can use the Edit and Search commands to speed the process of developing programs.

Every program you have created so far can be described as *linear*: Instructions are executed one after the other until the end of the program. To repeat a process you must run the program again from the beginning. Chapter 5 will introduce you to program *loops*. Loops in your program allow you to repeat commands without restarting the program. Because computers are so good at repetitive tasks, loops are an integral part of almost all computer programs.

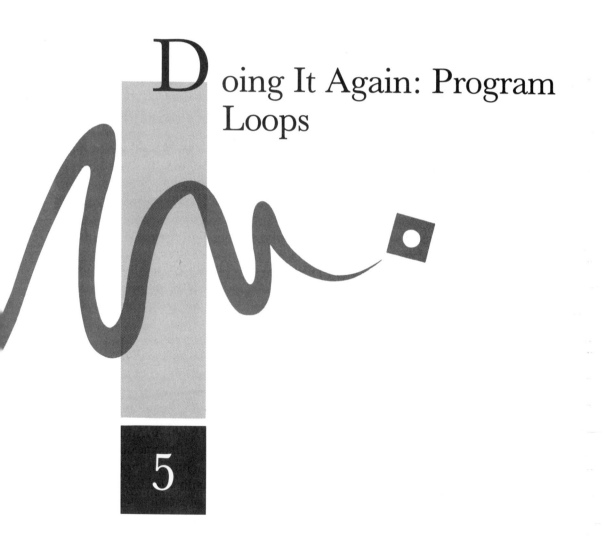

Doing It Again: Program Loops

5

CHAPTER *5* _____

WITH THIS CHAPTER YOU WILL BEGIN TO EXPLORE
program *control structures*. Control structures in your programs determine which tasks are accomplished, how often, and in what order. By
using these powerful programming tools, you can create programs
that allow the user to control the sequence of events. Program control
structures fall into two groups: *loops*, which are used to control repetitive processes; and *branches*, which allow choices to be made throughout program execution.

This chapter concentrates on program loops. We've all had the
experience of having to perform some task so often that it becomes
boring and tedious. You may have had this feeling while working
with practice problems earlier in this book, having to restart a program each time you wanted to try it out with different values. Computers work fast and are incapable of boredom—so when you find
yourself at a computer keyboard repeating the same command
sequences over and over again, you should always ask yourself how
you can get the computer to do this work for you. One way to get the
computer to take over this kind of task is to create programs that take
advantage of control loops.

Loops are created when a pair of keywords is placed at the beginning and end of a sequence of commands. The enclosed sequence of
commands is performed repeatedly until some condition has been
met. The term *iteration* is used to describe each occurrence of the
sequence of commands within a program loop. The paired keyword
combinations you will learn in this chapter are FOR...NEXT and
DO...LOOP.

CREATING FOR...NEXT LOOPS

In its simplest form, a FOR...NEXT loop uses a counter to keep
track of how many times an action has occurred. The action is

repeated until the counter reaches a specified limit. The program below uses a FOR...NEXT loop to print the message "I will not talk in class" 25 times. The counter in this example is the integer variable, **count %**, which is initially set equal to one and is automatically increased by one each time the program runs through the loop until it reaches its limit of 25. This limit could easily be raised to handle assignments given by even the sternest of first-grade teachers, although in extreme cases you might need to redefine count % as a long integer. Type in this program and check to be sure your printer is ready before running the program.

```
'Using FOR...NEXT to handle a repetitive task
FOR count% = 1 TO 25
    LPRINT "I will not talk in class"
NEXT count%
```

Notice that the command enclosed between the keywords FOR and NEXT has been indented. This standard way of setting off the command sequence within a program loop will make your programs much easier to read.

In the loop you just created, the counter has only one role: It keeps track of the number of times the action within the loop has occurred. Counter variables can also be incorporated into the program statements within the loop, as demonstrated in the next program, which prints a table of numbers and their squares. The variable **N %** is used to control the number of iterations of the loop and is also used as a changing data value within the loop. Type in and run the program.

```
'Using the counter in your program statements
CLS
PRINT "Number", "Square"
PRINT
FOR N% = 1 TO 10
    PRINT N%, N% ^ 2
NEXT N%
```

Your output should look like this:

Number	Square
1	1
2	4
3	9
4	16
5	25
6	36
7	49
8	64
9	81
10	100

In this program as in the previous example, the value of the counter increased automatically by one each time through the loop. The syntax of a FOR statement allows you to change this increment so that counters can either increase or decrease by any value you choose, as the programs in the next section demonstrate.

THE SYNTAX OF FOR...NEXT STATEMENTS

The syntax of a FOR...NEXT loop is summarized below. Information in italics is supplied by the programmer. Brackets are used to indicate optional expressions. Every FOR statement must be paired with a NEXT statement. If you try to run a program with a missing FOR or NEXT statement, an error message will be displayed on screen. This kind of error is picked up as part of the compiling process that occurs before program execution begins. The variable in a NEXT statement can be omitted, but including it generally makes a program easier to read.

FOR *counter* = *start* TO *stop* [STEP *increment*]

   '*Instructions within the loop*

NEXT [*counter*]

You can add the optional keyword STEP to a FOR statement when you want to control the size and direction of changes in the counter variable. Both counter variables and increment values can include any floating-point or integer value. When negative values are used for the increment, the counter variable decreases with each iteration of the loop, as the following program demonstrates:

```
'Using STEP to change the increment in a FOR...NEXT loop
CLS
FOR count% = 10 TO 1 STEP – 1
  PRINT count%
NEXT count%
PRINT
PRINT "BLAST OFF!"
```

The PRINT statement within the FOR...NEXT loop displays the decreasing value of the count% variable. Once count% reaches the stop value (= 1 here), the program exits the FOR...NEXT loop and continues on to execute the last two PRINT statements. Run the program. The output is shown here:

```
10
9
8
7
6
5
4
3
2
1

BLAST OFF!
```

USING VARIABLES AS ARGUMENTS IN FOR...NEXT LOOPS

Numeric arguments in any BASIC statement can be supplied as fixed values, variables, or expressions. (For example, a TAB statement might be given as TAB(3), TAB(N), or TAB(3 * N))

The syntax of a FOR statement includes four arguments: the name of the counter variable, and numeric arguments that provide starting, stopping, and increment values. So far you've only seen examples where these arguments are specified as fixed values, like those in this FOR statement:

```
FOR X = 5 TO 100 STEP 5
```

FOR...NEXT loops can be made more flexible, however, by using variables or expressions as arguments, in place of fixed values. In the FOR statement below, the details of execution depend on values for the variables A, B, and C:

FOR X = A TO B STEP C * −1

The temperature conversion program you will create next demonstrates the use of variable arguments in a FOR statement. The program listing is shown in Figure 5.1. Type in and save the program. It is explained in the text that follows.

```
REM TEMPCONV.BAS
'This program converts Fahrenheit to Celsius
'Variables are used as arguments in the FOR/NEXT loop
CLS
'Get values for start,stop and increment size
PRINT "This program converts Fahrenheit to Celsius"
PRINT
PRINT "Enter the range you would like to see."
INPUT "Low value  :", Low
INPUT "High value :", High
PRINT
INPUT "Enter an increment value :", Increment

'Print table in two columns
CLS
PRINT "Fahrenheit"; TAB(20); "Celsius"  'Heading
PRINT STRING$(30, "_")                    'Dividing Line
PRINT
FOR F = Low TO High STEP Increment
  C = 5 / 9 * (F - 32)
  PRINT USING "###.##"; TAB(2); F;      'Print Fahrenheit in column 1
  PRINT USING "###.##"; TAB(20); C      'Print Celsius in column 2
NEXT F
```

Figure 5.1: TEMPCONV.BAS: A temperature conversion program

The TEMPCONV program creates a table of equivalent Fahrenheit and Celsius temperatures. The user can control both the range of temperature values to be displayed and the size of the increment separating one value from the next. INPUT statements are used to receive and store starting, stopping, and increment values. The input questions, and sample user responses are shown here:

```
Enter the range you would like to see.
Low value  :97
High value :100
Enter an increment value :0.2
```

These values are stored in variables that are used in the FOR statement shown below. By using floating-point variables, the program allows the user to select fractional as well as whole number values for any or all of the arguments.

FOR F = Low TO High STEP Increment

Try running the program several times, entering different values at each of the input prompts. Figure 5.2 shows the output produced using the sample values above.

```
Fahrenheit          Celsius
_____

 97.00              36.11
 97.20              36.22
 97.40              36.33
 97.60              36.44
 97.80              36.56
 98.00              36.67
 98.20              36.78
 98.40              36.89
 98.60              37.00
 98.80              37.11
 99.00              37.22
 99.20              37.33
 99.40              37.44
 99.60              37.56
 99.80              37.67
100.00              37.78




Press any key to continue
```

Figure 5.2: Sample output from the TEMPCONV program

USING FLOWCHARTS TO VISUALIZE A SEQUENCE OF EVENTS

Many programmers find it useful to visualize the sequence of events in their programs by using diagrams known as flowcharts. A flowchart is a series of boxes connected by arrows. The boxes describe actions taken by the program, and the arrows indicate the path of program control. Symbols used in flowcharts have a standard meaning. Some common flowchart symbols are summarized in Table 5.1.

Table 5.1: Symbols Used in Flowcharts

SYMBOL	DESCRIPTION
⬭	**Terminal**. Marks the beginning or end of a program.
▭	**Process.** Contains a brief description of a numeric or text process.
▱	**Input/Output.** Describes an input or output procedure—any procedure that involves transfer of information from one part of a computer system to another.
◇	**Decision.** Indicates a point in the program where a decision between two possible actions takes place.
⬚	**Routine.** Describes a routine, or section of program code which incorporates several actions.
○	**Connector.** Contains an identifying symbol to connect one part of a program to another with the same symbol. This is used where using a continuous line is awkward or impossible.

Figure 5.3 uses a flowchart to describe the general actions performed by a FOR...NEXT loop.

Figure 5.4 is a flowchart describing the actions of the temperature conversion program. (See Figure 5.1 for the program listing.)

Flowcharts can be useful when you are designing a program and want to work out the overall logic before you become enmeshed in the details of statement syntax. They are also helpful as a method of sharing ideas with others.

USING DO...LOOP STATEMENTS

Another kind of program loop can be made by pairing DO and LOOP statements. DO...LOOPs control repetitive processes by performing a task until some condition has been met. This condition

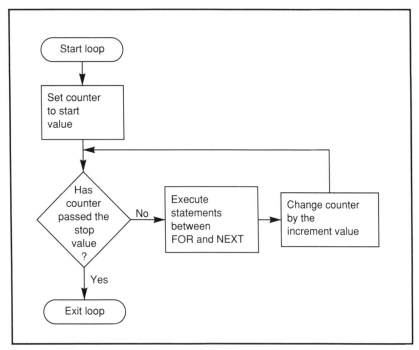

Figure 5.3: A flowchart showing the logic of a FOR...NEXT loop

may be supplied in any of three locations in the loop:

- As part of the DO statement, conditions may be set using either DO WHILE... or DO UNTIL... expressions.
- As part of the LOOP statement, conditions may be set using either LOOP WHILE... or LOOP UNTIL... expressions.
- Within the body of the loop, conditions may be set using branching program structures.

In the sections that follow you will first look at an endless DO...LOOP and learn how to interrupt program execution when you create an endless loop. Next you will learn how to add expressions to DO and LOOP statements that create conditions for ending the loop. The use of branching structures for exiting loops will be explained in Chapter 6.

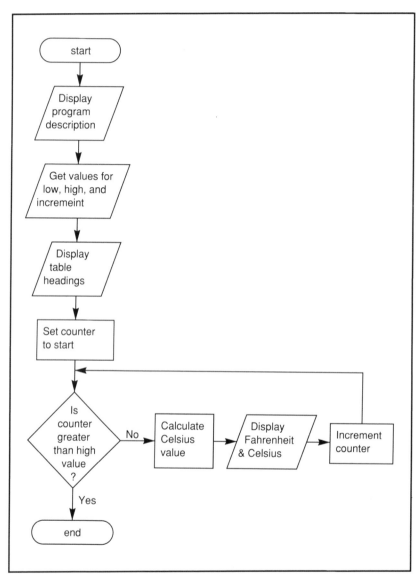

Figure 5.4: A flowchart of the TEMPCONV program

CREATING AND INTERRUPTING AN ENDLESS LOOP

When no condition is set for ending a loop, the computer will continue to perform its task endlessly until a machine limit is reached,

One common vari-
ety of program bug
is the unintentional per-
petual loop. The result is
either an endless parade
of values on screen or a
program that is hung up,
refusing to do anything.
Use Ctrl+Break to inter-
rupt program execution
when this happens.

power is cut off, or execution is interrupted by a keyboard command. The keyboard command that interrupts execution of a QuickBASIC program is Ctrl+Break. The following program is an example of an endless loop. Each time through the loop, the program increments the variable N by two and displays the results. Left unchecked, this program will count by twos until the value reached exceeds the range of the variable N, which is, by default, a single-precision variable. Type in the program as shown here.

```
'Demonstrates an endless loop
'Use Ctrl+Break to interrupt the program
CLS
N = 0
DO
   PRINT N
   N = N + 2
LOOP
```

Start the program and interrupt it using Ctrl+Break. You can interrupt execution of any program, at any time, with Ctrl+Break. When you do, you will be returned to the Work screen, and the program line that was about to be executed will be shown in high-intensity display.

The next sections of this chapter show you how to use WHILE... and UNTIL... expressions within a DO LOOP in order to describe conditions for ending the loop.

ADDING CONDITIONAL EXPRESSIONS USING DO/WHILE AND DO/UNTIL

When you create loops using paired DO...LOOP statements, you will want to tell the computer when it should stop repeating the process in the loop and continue on to subsequent program actions. There are two different approaches you can take. When you want a loop to continue to execute as long as some condition *remains* true, you can add a WHILE expression to your loop. When you want a loop to stop after some condition *becomes* true, you can use an UNTIL expression in your loop. These approaches are best understood by looking at examples.

USING WHILE IN A LOOP The endless loop you created in the last section counted by twos without limit. The following examples demonstrate different ways of stopping the loop after it has reached 10. One way is to tell the computer to continue counting as long as the numbers remain smaller than 12. To do this, you can add the phrase "WHILE N < 12", which tells the computer to continue as long as the expression N < 12 remains true. This expression can be added to the DO statement as shown here:

```
'Demonstrates DO/WHILE
CLS
DO WHILE N < 12
  PRINT N
  N = N + 2
LOOP
```

The same effect can be achieved by retyping the program and modifying the LOOP statement as shown here:

```
'Demonstrates LOOP/WHILE
CLS
DO
  PRINT N
  N = N + 2
LOOP WHILE N < 12
```

Try running both versions of the program. Although the two programs produce identical results, there is a difference between loops that have the conditional statement placed at the beginning and those that don't check conditions until the end of the loop. To see the difference, add a new line with the statement

```
N = 12
```

at the beginning of each of the two previous programs. When you run these modified programs, the condition of the expression N < 12 is false. The first program reaches the conditional statement before it performs the loop even once, with the result that *no* action takes place within the loop—the output is simply a clear screen. In the second program the first iteration of the loop occurs *before* the computer encounters the conditional statement, and the result is that the first value for N—in this case, 12—is displayed as output.

USING UNTIL IN A LOOP A second way to control a DO loop is to instruct the computer to continue repeating the action or set of actions until the conditional expression becomes true. In this case the conditional expression is preceded by the word UNTIL. Continuing with the same example, there are several new ways to have the computer stop counting at ten. In this first example, the expression N > 10 tells the computer to exit the loop as soon as any value for N is larger than 10. Run the program as shown here:

```
'Demonstrates DO/UNTIL using >
CLS
DO UNTIL N > 10
    PRINT N
    N = N + 2
LOOP
```

[handwritten marginal note: print across the screen ; or] [handwritten: N = 1   N = N + 2]

A conditional expression that checks to see if N = 12 has the same effect. Try the program again after making the modification shown below.

```
'Demonstrates DO/UNTIL using =
CLS
DO UNTIL N = 12
    PRINT N
    N = N + 2
LOOP
```

[handwritten marginal note: Do until N = (else)   N =]

If you change line 3 of the program above to read

```
DO UNTIL N = 11
```

the program continues to execute the loop indefinitely, because N = 11 is never true in this program. If you try this, use Ctrl+Break to interrupt program execution.

Expressions using UNTIL can also be placed at the end of the loop. You can use this technique to create still more programs that count by twos to ten. Try this out with the modification shown here:

```
'Demonstrates LOOP/UNTIL
CLS
DO
  PRINT N
  N = N + 2
LOOP UNTIL N > 10
```

The flexibility that DO/WHILE and DO/UNTIL loops offer makes them a powerful addition to your programming vocabulary. You will see them used throughout this book to perform a wide variety of tasks.

In the previous examples, conditions for exiting the loop were the result of internal program calculations. Conditional statements also frequently employ input from the user, as you will see in the next programming example, which is a modification of a program you created in Chapter 3. The modifications you make will also introduce you to a few new editing techniques.

EDITING TIPS FOR WORKING WITH INDENTED MATERIAL

Because material within a loop is generally indented in order to identify it and set it apart, QuickBASIC includes several features that make it easier to work with indented material. One of the first you're likely to notice is that pressing ⏎ returns you to the indentation level of the previous line, rather than to the far left of your screen. This feature is handy when you are writing a loop containing several statements that should all be indented to the same level. If the cursor is positioned on an indented line, pressing Home will move it to the first character of the line. The keystroke combination Ctrl +Q +S returns the cursor to the leftmost edge of your screen, but unless you are already familiar with this command from prior experience with WordStar, you may find it easier to press the Backspace key once or use the ← key to move the cursor from the current indentation level to the left edge of the screen.

CHANGING THE TAB SETTING

When you start to type a set of indented lines, you can set the indentation levels by using either the spacebar or the Tab key. The tab key is set to a default indentation of eight spaces. You can change this default by using the Display command in the Options menu. Follow these steps to change the tab setting to three spaces:

1. Open the Options Menu and select the *Display* command.
2. Press Alt + T to move the cursor to the *Tab Stops* option.
3. Type 3 to change tab stops to every third position.
4. Press ← to complete the command.

MODIFYING THE FORMAT PROGRAM

You may find it convenient at times to indent an entire block of material. In the following editing exercise, you will modify the FORMAT program you created in Chapter 3. This program allows you to experiment with ways to output numbers. In its original form, you must restart the program each time you want to try out new ideas. The modified version of the program includes a DO/WHILE loop that allows you to try as many different values as you like before exiting the program. As part of the editing process, you will indent a group of instructions that have been enclosed by the new DO and LOOP statements. The original program is shown here:

```
'FORMAT.BAS
'Demonstrates PRINT USING statement
CLS
LINE INPUT "Type in a sample format string:  "; format$
INPUT "What number would you like to see"; value#
PRINT
PRINT "The resulting value is:";
PRINT USING format$; TAB(36); value#
```

In the modified version shown below, an INPUT statement has been added displaying the following prompt:

```
Do another (Y/N)?
```

Your response to this question is stored in the string variable called Response$. This variable is subsequently used in the conditional expression of the LOOP statement, which reads as follows:

```
LOOP WHILE Response$ = "Y" OR Response$ = "y"
```

If your response was either an uppercase or lowercase Y, then the condition in this statement is true, and the program will repeat the commands within the loop. If you responded with an N, or in fact any other keyboard character, the conditional expression is no longer true and program execution will continue to the statement that displays the message "End of Program."

The modified version of the program is shown here, with additions to the original program shown in boldface. The following exercise explains the steps you can take to make these modifications.

```
'FORMAT2.BAS
'Demonstrates DO/LOOP and PRINT USING
CLS
DO
    LINE INPUT "Type in a sample format string:  "; format$
    INPUT "What number would you like to see"; value#
    PRINT
    PRINT "The resulting value is:";
    PRINT USING format$; TAB(36); value#
    PRINT
    INPUT "Do another (Y,N)"; Response$
    PRINT
LOOP WHILE Response$ = "Y" OR Response$ = "y"
```

To create the modified FORMAT2.BAS program, follow these instructions:

1. Retrieve or type in the original program.

2. Update the two introductory remark statements as shown and add the five new lines of code, which are shown in boldface. Don't bother to indent any of the new lines at this stage.

3. To indent the material within the loop, begin by placing the cursor on the first character of the LINE INPUT statement.

Select the next eight lines of text by pressing ↓ while you hold down the Shift key.

4. Press the Tab key to indent this entire eight-line block of text.

5. Use any of the cursor-control keys to unselect the block or click the left mouse button anywhere on the page.

Once you've completed the changes, try out your edited program. Many programs use a structure like this to allow the user to control how many times an activity is performed.

AN INTRODUCTION TO QUICKBASIC DEBUGGING TOOLS

Debugging tools are designed to help you catch errors in your programs, but they have an additional very useful function. Because debugging tools work by showing you exactly what is happening at any point in program execution, they provide beginners with a wonderful way to learn more about what happens when a program is running. Once you become familiar with QuickBASIC's debugging tools, you can use them to help you explore the sample programs in this book and to study working programs such as those provided with the QuickBASIC distribution diskettes. The tools that you learn now to help you understand how a program works will help you later when you want to understand why a program doesn't work. The next sections of this chapter will show you how to step gradually through a program, watching the values of variables change as each instruction in the program is executed. You will also learn how to make a running program pause at any point in its execution, giving you a chance to study and even alter variable values before continuing program execution.

STEPPING THROUGH A PROGRAM ONE LINE AT A TIME

One of the best ways to understand exactly what happens during program execution is to step through a program one line at a time. When you do this, you can follow the order of command execution and see the effect of each separate statement in the program. This is accomplished by pressing the F8 key. Each time you press this key the program performs exactly one statement. Your program listing remains on screen, and the line that is about to be executed is highlighted. This line is referred to as the *current* line. You can continue to execute the program line by line, or at any point in the process you can choose to have the computer continue execution at a normal pace from the current line. This is done with the *Continue* command in the Run menu, or by using the F5 shortcut key. The *Restart* command in the Run menu will reset your program, moving the current line back to the first executable line in your program. Unlike the *Start* command, the *Restart* command will not initiate program execution.

As you step through the program, you can see what is happening on the Output screen by pressing the F4 key. This toggle key moves display back and forth between the Work screen and the Output screen.

The next exercise demonstrates the use of these commands. Begin by opening the TEMPCONV program (Figure 5.1) that you created earlier.

1. With the TEMPCONV program on screen, press F8. The program ignores the initial remark statements and highlights the CLS statement, indicating that it is the current statement.

2. Press F8 again. The CLS statement will be executed, but you will not see the results because you are returned to the program statements in the Work screen rather than to the Output screen. The highlighting should indicate that the first PRINT statement is now the current line.

3. Continue to press F8 until the first INPUT statement is the current line. As you execute the PRINT commands, you can use the F4 key to switch to and from the Output screen to see the changes that are occurring there.

4. Press F8 to execute the INPUT statement. When an INPUT statement such as this is executed, you will have to provide input before continuing to move step by step through the program. Type in a value in response to the prompt and press ◄─┘.

5. You can continue to step through the program, or at any point you can press F5 to have the program return to normal execution, starting from whatever statement is current at the time.

ADDING BREAKPOINTS TO INTERRUPT PROGRAM EXECUTION

Placing a breakpoint in your program allows you to interrupt it at any point during program execution. To place a breakpoint, move the cursor to any line in your program and select *Toggle Breakpoint* from the Debug menu or use the F9 shortcut key. When you run the program, it will execute up to, but not including, this line and then show you your program listing with this line highlighted as the current line. To remove an individual breakpoint, move the cursor to the breakpoint line and repeat the Toggle Breakpoint command. You can set as many breakpoints as you like in a program. To clear all breakpoints with a single command, select *Clear all breakpoints* from the Debug menu.

The following exercise uses the TEMPCONV program to demonstrate these steps:

1. Move the cursor to the line that reads

   `'Print table in two columns`

2. Press F9 to set a breakpoint on this line. Depending on your monitor, the line will either change color or appear in reverse video.

3. Start the program and enter values at the input prompts. When you press ← after entering the last value, program execution will continue up to the breakpoint and then stop and return you to the Work screen. The breakpoint line will be highlighted as the current line.

4. You can continue from this point either by using F8 to move step by step through the program or by pressing F5 to continue normal program execution.

5. Clear the breakpoint by moving the cursor to the breakpoint line and pressing F9.

Leave the TEMPCONV program on screen. You will use it in the next section to learn how to watch the values of variables in your programs as they change during program execution.

WATCHING VARIABLE VALUES DURING PROGRAM EXECUTION

QuickBASIC includes debugging tools that allow you to watch the changes that occur to the value of any variable or expression in your program. This is an extremely useful technique for studying and understanding program performance. The Debug menu includes an *Add Watch* command that you can use to place the variable or expression you want to watch in a special *Watch window* that can be opened at the top of your Work screen. This window will show you the value of one or more watch items when you are returned to the Work screen at any point during program execution. If you run a program through to the end, the values displayed in the watch window will be the final values for the watched items. If you have set a breakpoint, you can see the values of the items at that point in program execution. If you step through the program line by line with the F8 key, you can watch exactly what happens to each watched item after each program statement has been executed.

The Debug menu also includes an *Instant Watch* command. To use this feature, place your cursor on a variable in your program and then activate the command. The dialog box that opens shows you the current value of that variable and also includes an option that lets you add the variable to the Watch window. The shortcut key combination Shift + F9 is the equivalent of selecting the *Instant Watch* command from the menus.

Use the TEMPCONV program to practice these commands in the following exercise. If you have set any breakpoints in the program, be sure they have been cleared before continuing.

1. Select *Add Watch* from the Debug menu. A dialog box opens that tells you to *Enter expression to be added*.

2. Type in the variable name **Low** and press ← to watch the value of this variable. The variable name will now appear in a Watch window that has been opened immediately below the Menu bar.

3. Use F9 to place a breakpoint at the line that reads

   FOR F = Low to High STEP Increment

4. Start your program. (Use Shift + F5 or select *Start* from the Run menu to be sure you are starting from the beginning of the program.)

5. Enter values for Low, High, and Increment as you are prompted to do so. After you enter the last value, program execution will continue to the breakpoint and you will be returned to the Work screen.

6. When execution stops, you will see the value of the watched variable, Low, in the Watch window. This will match the value you just supplied.

7. Move the cursor to the counter variable **F** in the breakpoint line. Press Shift + F9 to see an Instant Watch box that displays the value of this variable. Because the current statement has not yet executed, F is set to the default of zero at this point. Press ◄—¹ to close the box and add F to the Watch window. Your screen should now resemble Figure 5.5.

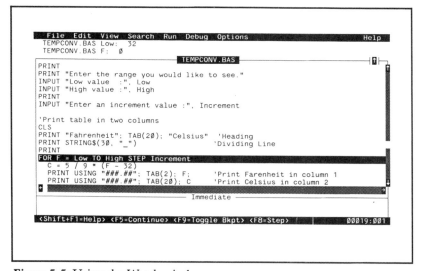

Figure 5.5: Using the Watch window

8. Press F8 to execute the current statement. Notice that the value of F in the Watch window changes. The FOR statement sets it equal to the value of Low as the first step in executing the FOR...NEXT loop.

9. Continue using the F8 key to step through the program until you have watched a few iterations of the FOR...NEXT loop. The value of F will change each time the NEXT statement is executed by the amount you entered for the increment value. Use F4 to toggle back and forth between the Work screen and the developing Output screen.

At this stage, you have probably realized that you don't want to step through an entire FOR...NEXT loop. You can use the following trick to take a shortcut out of a loop when you are stepping through a program.

10. Press F6 to move the cursor to the Immediate window.

11. Change the value of F to the high value you selected when you ran the program. For example, if you selected a high value of 100, you would type **F = 100** and then press ◄┘. (If you have forgotten the high value you set, you can use the Instant Watch command to see what it was set to.)

12. Press F8 to continue stepping through the program. Because you have changed the value of F, you will exit the loop as soon as you reach the FOR statement.

Using the QuickBASIC debugging tools as you work through the programs in this book will help you develop a solid understanding of how computer programs operate. Try them out on the short programming application that completes this chapter. This program uses both a FOR..NEXT loop and a DO/WHILE loop to control program execution.

THE GRADES PROGRAM

The GRADES program you will create next is designed for use by a teacher calculating student grade averages. A DO/WHILE loop allows the user to repeat the program for as many students as desired. The program also lets the user indicate how many test scores are available for each student. You have seen most of the techniques used in this program in the short samples you worked with earlier in this chapter, but you should take a closer look at the lines of the program that calculate the test average for each student. These are shown here:

```
'Calculate the sum of n% items
  FOR i% = 1 TO n%
    PRINT "Test Grade"; i%;
    INPUT " = = > ", Grade
    Sum = Sum + Grade
  NEXT i%

'Calculate average and initialize Sum for next student
Average = Sum / n%
```

The variable n% represents the number of grades to be averaged. Its value is provided by the user earlier in the program. During each iteration of the FOR...NEXT loop, the user enters a new test grade that is stored in the variable called Grade. This value is added to a variable called Sum. With each trip through the loop, the value of Grade is replaced by a new value, and the value of Sum is increased by that amount. After the final iteration of the loop, Sum will contain the sum of all of the entered test scores. A line of the program that follows the FOR...NEXT loop calculates the average by dividing this value by the number of test scores.

Because the program can be repeated for an indeterminate number of students, the value of Sum must be reset to zero each time. This process of setting a variable to the correct initial value is known as *initializing* the variable.

The complete program is shown in Figure 5.6. Enter the program and practice with it until you are familiar with its output. When you are comfortable with it, try experimenting with the debugging commands in the Run and Debug menus that allow you to study program execution in greater detail.

```
REM GRADES.BAS
'This program calculates student grade averages
'A DO...LOOP allows calculation of as many averages as desired.
'A FOR...NEXT loop allows calculation of variable numbers of test scores.

'Initialize Sum to zero
Sum = 0

DO
  CLS
  'Use an integer variable to store the number of grades
  INPUT "How many grades for this student"; n%
  PRINT

  'Calculate the sum of n% items
  FOR i% = 1 TO n%
    PRINT "Test Grade"; i%;
    INPUT "==> ", Grade
    Sum = Sum + Grade
  NEXT i%

  'Calculate average and initialize Sum for next student
  Average = Sum / n%
  Sum = 0

  'Display results to nearest tenth
  PRINT
  PRINT USING "The Average for this student is ===> ###.#"; Average

  'Place input prompt at bottom of screen
  LOCATE 24, 1
  INPUT "Calculate another grade average? (Y/N) ", Response$
LOOP WHILE Response$ = "Y" OR Response$ = "y"

CLS
PRINT "End of program"
```

Figure 5.6: The GRADES.BAS program listing

SUMMARY

One method of controlling the flow of events in a program is through the use of loop structures for managing repetitive operations. FOR...NEXT loops use a counter variable to determine how many times the sequence of commands within the loop should be executed. When a simple FOR statement is used, this counter is incremented by one with each iteration of the loop until the specified limit is reached. The STEP keyword can be added to a FOR statement in order to increase or decrease the value of the counter variable by values other than one. DO...LOOPS are used to execute repetitive tasks that are performed until some condition is met. This condition can be specified in either a WHILE or an UNTIL expression, placed at either the beginning or end of the loop.

This chapter also introduced a selection of debugging tools in the Run and Debug menus that enable you to watch the values of variables and control the rate at which statements in your program are executed. To control program execution, you can use F9 to interrupt the program at a specified point, F8 to step through the program one line at a time, and F5 to continue program execution from the current statement. Variables can be watched by using either the Add Watch or the Instant Watch (Shift+F9) commands in the Debug menu. These commands are used to display the values of variables in the Watch window of the Work screen.

The next chapter continues your introduction to program control structures by showing you how to use branching control structures in your program. These powerful structures are an integral part of program decision-making processes.

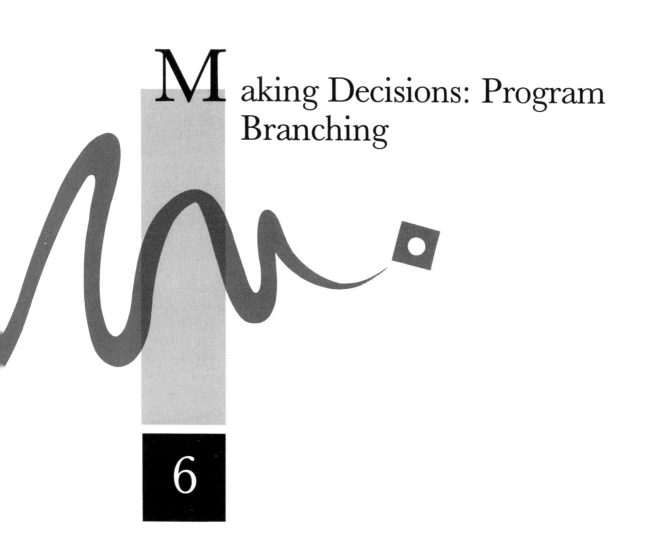

Making Decisions: Program Branching

CHAPTER *6* _____

THIS CHAPTER WILL CONCENTRATE ON BRANCHING
program structures. These structures enable your program to
respond in a predetermined way to the varying circumstances it
encounters. It is these structures that allow you to write effective,
interactive programs that can respond to input from the individual at
the keyboard.

Decisions using branching structures are a familiar part of daily
life. For example, the expression "If the shoe fits, wear it" sets up a
particular kind of decision structure: The first part of the expression
describes a condition that can be either true or false, followed by a
statement of action whose outcome depends on the truth or falsity of
the initial condition. In the world of computer programming, assertions that are either true or false are known as *Boolean expressions*—a
phrase that may appear a bit intimidating at first glance, but is not
really difficult to grasp. One of the aims of this chapter is to give you a
comfortable sense of how to work with Boolean expressions.

Program samples in this chapter will cover QuickBASIC's two
kinds of branching structures: IF...THEN and SELECT CASE.
First we will look at single-line IF...THEN and IF...THEN...ELSE
statements, which have been a traditional part of BASIC programming. Next we will take a look at the newer, block form of the
IF...THEN...ELSE statement, which simplifies complicated decision structures and makes for much more readable program code.
Finally, we will look at SELECT CASE statements, the newest of
QuickBASIC's decision structures.

_____ *USING IF...THEN STATEMENTS* _____

In its simplest form, an IF...THEN statement evaluates an expression and, if the expression is true, performs some activity. The action
is dependent on the truth of the statement. In the sample below, the
user supplies a value for the variable N. An IF...THEN statement is

then used to determine if the variable is greater than 0. The word *Positive* is displayed only when this condition is true. Execution then continues to the line that displays *Good-bye*.

```
CLS
INPUT "Enter a Number: ", N
IF N > 0 THEN PRINT "Positive"
PRINT "Good-bye"
```

If you enter a positive number, the Output screen shows three lines as seen here:

```
Enter a Number: 8
Positive
Good-bye
```

A negative number results in only two lines of output:

```
Enter a Number: −3
Good-bye
```

The logic of this simple IF...THEN statement is shown in Figure 6.1.

In the preceding example, the dependent action (printing *Positive*) takes place only when the expression being evaluated is true. When you want your program to take one action if the condition is true and a second action if it is false, you can add an ELSE clause to the IF...THEN statement, as shown in the example below.

```
CLS
INPUT "Enter a Number: ", N
IF N > 0 THEN PRINT "Positive" ELSE PRINT "Zero or Negative"
PRINT "Good-bye"
```

Adding an ELSE clause to an IF...THEN statement means that it will always result in some action, in this case a choice between identifying the number as *Positive* or *Zero or Negative*. A negative value now gives the following output.

```
Enter a Number: −3
Zero or Negative
Good-bye
```

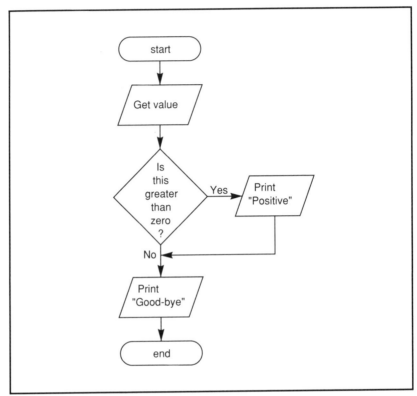

Figure 6.1: The logic of a sample IF...THEN statement

Figure 6.2 shows the logic of this IF...THEN...ELSE statement.

In these two examples, the actions being controlled by the IF...THEN statement are simple output statements. A more powerful application of branching statements is to control the flow of events within a program. To accomplish this, the THEN clause is followed by a statement that directs program control to some new part of the program. In the next section of this chapter, you will learn how to use branching structures as a new way to exit from program loops. In Chapter 7, you will learn how to control program flow by using branching structures in conjunction with separate sections of program code known as procedures.

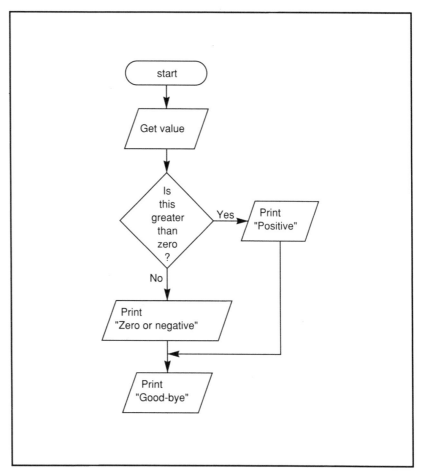

Figure 6.2: The logic of a sample IF...THEN...ELSE statement

A NEW WAY TO EXIT FROM LOOP STRUCTURES

IF...THEN statements can be used within both FOR...NEXT and DO...LOOP structures to set conditions for exiting from within a loop. Here is the general syntax for using IF...THEN EXIT statements to leave a DO..LOOP structure.

```
IF expression THEN EXIT DO
```

EXIT statements such as this can be used instead of WHILE or UNTIL expressions, as shown in the example below.

```
CLS
DO
  PRINT X
  X = X + 1
  IF X = 4 THEN EXIT DO
LOOP
```

The output of this program is:

```
0
1
2
3
```

EXIT statements can be placed anywhere within a loop. As soon as the condition within the statement is found to be true, program execution leaves the loop and continues at the first program line following the LOOP statement. This provides some additional flexibility over WHILE and UNTIL expressions, which can only be used to control iteration of the entire sequence of statements within the loop. One or more EXIT statements can also be used in addition to a WHILE or UNTIL expression in order to provide alternative conditions for exiting a loop.

You can also place conditional exit statements within a FOR...NEXT loop. In this case the syntax is:

IF *expression* THEN EXIT FOR

The output of this sample program is identical to that of the previous program. The EXIT statement intercedes before the counter variable in the FOR statement reaches its original limit.

```
CLS
FOR X = 0 TO 10
  IF X = 4 THEN EXIT FOR
  PRINT X
NEXT X
```

Conditional EXIT statements placed within a FOR...NEXT loop can be useful when you want your program to respond efficiently to unpredictable conditions. For instance, in a routine that is searching a list of items for one particular item, you can use an EXIT statement to be sure that iterations of the loop stop as soon as the item has been found. This approach is applied in the PRIME.BAS program that you will create later in this chapter. But before doing anything further with decision structures, we should take a closer look at the conditional statements that govern their actions.

SORTING OUT RELATIONAL AND LOGICAL OPERATIONS

The three innocent-looking little dots between IF and THEN in the phrase IF...THEN...ELSE are stand-ins for an assertion that might be either simple or quite complex. In this section, we will take a closer look at the structure of these assertions.

Study the three assertions in the sample below. The program is designed to tell the user whether her porridge is too hot (more than 180° F), too cold (less than 140° F), or just right (anywhere between these two temperatures).

```
CLS
INPUT "What is the temperature of the porridge"; T
IF T > 180 THEN PRINT "This porridge is too hot."
IF T < 140 THEN PRINT "This porridge is too cold."
IF T > = 140 AND T < = 180 THEN PRINT "This is just right!"
```

Two possible Output screens are shown here.

```
What is the temperature of the porridge? 212
This porridge is too hot.
```

```
What is the temperature of the porridge? 150
This is just right!
```

In the first IF...THEN statement, the assertion $T > 180$, which is read "T is greater than 180," is known as a *relational operation*. A relational operation compares two items and establishes that the comparison is either true or false. The symbol used between the items being compared is called a *relational operator*. Six relational operators are available in BASIC. Some of these symbols are identical to mathematical symbols you may already be familiar with, but in other cases a combination of keyboard characters is used to represent a single mathematical symbol. Table 6.1 summarizes BASIC relational operators, including their mathematical equivalents and their written meanings.

Table 6.1: Relational Operators Used in BASIC

OPERATOR	MATH	MEANING
=	=	Equal to
< >	≠	Not equal to
<	<	Less than
< =	≤	Less than or equal to
>	>	Greater than
> =	≥	Greater than or equal to

The assertion in the last line of the porridge program reads as follows.

    T > = 140 AND T < = 180

This is an example of a compound expression. The word *AND* connects two separate relational operations. In this context **AND** is known as a *logical operator*. Its effect here is to make this expression true only if *both* of the two relational operations are true. Only when both these conditions are met is the porridge just right. Note that the variable name must be repeated in each expression. This expression is equivalent to the mathematical expression:

    140 ≤ T ≥ 180

You saw a second example of a logical operator in the GRADES program in Chapter 5 in the following line.

    LOOP WHILE Response$ = "Y" OR Response$ = "y"

The relational operations here are connected by the logical operator **OR**. When OR is used in this way, the entire expression is true if *either* of the two expressions is true.

The logical operators AND and OR are always placed between two expressions. A third logical operator, **NOT**, is used in front of a single expression. Its effect is to reverse the logical value of the expression. In the example below, the expression NOT X = 0 is used to avoid division by zero in the THEN clause. The expression NOT X = 0 is true when X = 0 is false.

```
IF NOT X = 0 THEN A = B / X
```

It is easy to get lost in the logic of expressions using NOT, and fortunately it is often possible to achieve the same effect in a simpler way. The two statements below are equivalent, but the second statement is far easier to read and understand.

```
IF NOT X < = 0 THEN PRINT "X is positive"
IF X > 0 THEN PRINT "X is positive"
```

When an expression requires more than one operation, the operations are performed in a predetermined order of precedence. NOT operations precede AND operations which precede OR operations. Relational operations are always performed before logical operations, and arithmetic operations precede them both. Parentheses can be used to change the order of operations, or simply to make a complex expression easier to read. The following two statements are equivalent. Both are true when the variable Balance *is not* equal to zero and the variable City *is* equal to "Albany".

```
IF NOT Balance = 0 AND City = "Albany"
IF NOT (Balance = 0) AND (City = "Albany")
```

In this next statement, however, the condition is true when Balance *is not* equal to zero and City *is not* equal to "Albany".

```
IF NOT (Balance = 0 AND City = "Albany")
```

An online summary of all six logical operators can be found under the heading *logical operators truth table* in the Index from the Help menu.

Three additional logical operators are also available: **XOR**, **EQV**, and **IMP**. The role of each of the six logical operators is summarized in Table 6.2. Of the six operators, AND and OR are by far the most useful and commonly used.

Table 6.2: Logical Operators Listed in Order of Precedence

SAMPLE USAGE	EFFECT
NOT *expression1*	True when *expression1* is false.
expression1 **AND** *expression2*	True when *expression1* and *expression2* are both true.
expression1 **OR** *expression2*	True when either or both of the two expressions are true.
expression1 **XOR** *expression2*	True when either one of the two expressions is true and the other is false.
expression1 **EQV** *expression2*	True when *expression1* and *expression2* are equivalent—either both are true or both are false.
expression1 **IMP** *expression2*	False when *expression1* is true and *expression2* is false. All other combinations are true. (*Expression1* implies *expression2*.)

RELATIONAL OPERATIONS USING STRING VALUES

An online ASCII code summary can be found under the heading *ASCII Character Codes* in the Table of Contents from the Help menu.

In addition to using relational operations to compare numeric values, you can also use these operations to compare string values. When two string values are compared, the ASCII code values of corresponding characters within the two strings are compared, and at the first difference, the string whose character has a greater ASCII code is determined to be "greater." (A list of ASCII codes is given in Appendix C.) A few aspects of the ASCII code are worth noting here. Uppercase letters are coded in alphabetical order, and these codes are all smaller than those for lowercase letters. In other words, string values of the same case are correctly compared in alphabetical order, but not string values using different cases. Later you will learn how to modify string values to ensure matching case. The digits 0-9 have code values smaller than any letters of the alphabet. All of the following assertions are true:

```
CAIN > ABEL
CAIN < abel
1B < A
"2" < "ONE"
AAAA < B
"1111" < "2"
```

When numerals are compared as string values rather than as numeric values, a different set of rules applies—although the number 10 is greater than the number 2, the string value "10" is less than the string value "2".

Relational operations using string values are useful in placing, for example, lists of names in alphabetical order, but care must be taken—particularly in comparisons that employ string representations of numeric values—to ensure that you get the results you expect.

TAKING ADVANTAGE OF BLOCK IF...END IF STATEMENTS

In the decision structures we have looked at so far, only two alternative actions have been possible. It is frequently useful, however, to allow more that two possible reponses to a conditional statement. Block IF...END IF statements provide a straightforward way to control program execution where several avenues of action are possible. The general syntax of an IF...END IF structure is shown here.

```
IF condition1 THEN
    'statements executed if condition1 is true
[ELSEIF condition2 THEN]
    'statements executed if conditon2 is true
[ELSEIF condition3 THEN]
    'statements executed if condition3 is true
        .
        .
        .
[ELSE]
    'statements executed if no prior condition
    'is true
END IF
```

During execution of this block of statements, the condition in the initial IF...THEN statement is evaluated first. If this condition is found to be true, the program statement or statements immediately below it are executed, and the remaining sections of the block are skipped over entirely, so that program execution continues with the line following the END IF statement. However, if the first condition is found to be false, program execution continues with the first in the series of ELSEIF statements that follow. As soon as a true condition is found, the statement block beneath that condition is executed, and no further conditions are evaluated. If no conditions are found to be true, the statement block beneath the ELSE clause is executed.

A block IF...END IF structure can include as many ELSEIF statements as you choose. Both the ELSEIF and ELSE clauses are optional.

The porridge program that you created in the previous section can be rewritten using a block IF...END IF structure as follows.

```
CLS
INPUT "What is the temperature of the porridge"; Temp
IF Temp > 180 THEN
    PRINT "This porridge is too hot."
ELSEIF Temp < 140 THEN
    PRINT "This porridge is too cold."
ELSE
    PRINT "This porridge is just right!"
END IF
```

Block IF...END IF structures are often easier to write and maintain than single-line statements. In the modified version of the porridge program above, the use of a block structure means that the compound expression (T > = 140 AND T < = 180) used in the first version of the program is unnecessary.

Even in its simplest form, with no ELSEIF or ELSE statements, an IF...END IF structure is useful because it allows you to include a long list of actions to be performed when a single condition is met, as shown here.

```
IF expression THEN
    'action1
```

```
'action2
   .
   .
   .
END IF
```

NESTED IF...THEN STRUCTURES

The next program introduces the idea of *nested* structures: When one program structure is contained within another, it is referred to as a nested structure. The next sample program shows how one block IF...END IF can be nested within another. This strategy is useful when the answer to one question leads to another question.

When you run this program, you are asked to enter an integer value. The program then identifies this number as odd or even and further identifies those even values that are divisible by six. The first IF...THEN statement uses a MOD operation to decide if the number is even by testing to see if the remainder is zero when the number is divided by two. When this condition is true, the output message *Even* is printed, and a nested IF...THEN statement checks to see whether the number is also divisible by three. When this is also true, you can conclude that the number is also divisible by six, and this conclusion is also displayed. On the other hand, when the first IF...THEN condition is found to be false, program execution moves directly to the ELSE statement and the output message *Odd* is printed.

Enter the program as it appears below, and try it with a range of values until you have seen each of the possible outcomes.

```
CLS
INPUT "Enter an integer value: ", n%
IF n% MOD 2 = 0 THEN
   PRINT "This is an even number."
   IF n% MOD 3 = 0 THEN
      PRINT "It is also divisible by 6."
   END IF
ELSE
   PRINT "This is an odd number"
END IF
```

Three possible Output screens are shown here.

```
Enter an integer value: 12
This is an even number.
It is also divisible by 6.

Enter an integer value: 8
This is an even number.

Enter an integer value: 9
This is an odd number
```

Notice that the nested structure that tests for divisibility by three is executed only when it has already been determined that the number is even.

USING SELECT CASE STATEMENTS

QuickBASIC offers an additional structure for controlling decisions, the SELECT CASE structure. This alternative enables you to handle multiple-choice decisions with uncluttered, easy-to-read program code.

The next sample program will give you a general sense of the structure of a SELECT CASE statement before you look at its syntax in detail. The program asks for a letter from a to c and stores your response with a variable called Letter$. This variable is used in a SELECT CASE structure that results in one of four possible actions, based on the value of Letter$. The letters a, b, and c produce brief educational messages; any other value (including uppercase A,B, or C) will result in an EXIT statement that terminates execution of the DO loop.

```
CLS
PRINT "Any key other than a,b or c exits this program"
DO
   INPUT "Enter a letter from a-c: ", Letter$
   SELECT CASE Letter$
      CASE "a"
         PRINT "a is for AND"
```

```
              CASE "b"
                 PRINT "b is for Boolean"
              CASE "c"
                 PRINT "c is for computer"
              CASE ELSE
                 PRINT "Good-bye"
                 EXIT DO
           END SELECT
           PRINT
        LOOP
```

Run the program, testing it with the letters a,b,c, and d. The Output screen will look like this:

```
        Any key other than a,b, or c exits this program
        Enter a letter from a-c: a
        a is for AND

        Enter a letter from a-c: b
        b is for Boolean

        Enter a letter from a-c: c
        c is for computer

        Enter a letter from a-c: d
        Good-bye
```

In this example the SELECT statement made choices based on the value of a string variable, and each value of that variable produced a different response. The variations that can be made on this basic theme are described in the next section.

Block IF...THEN...ELSE statements can always be constructed that are equivalent to SELECT CASE statements. Use of SELECT CASE is a matter of programmer preference.

EXPANDING YOUR UNDERSTANDING OF SELECT CASE

To take full advantage of the SELECT CASE structure, you will want to become familiar with the various ways this structure can be used. The general syntax of a SELECT CASE statement is summarized below. The computer searches the CASE statement expression lists for a value that matches the test expression in the SELECT

CASE statement. If a match is found, the block of statements beneath that CASE statement is executed, and no more CASE statements are examined. If no match is found, the statements under the CASE ELSE statement are executed. There must be at least one CASE clause within the block; and you can add as many additional CASE clauses as you choose. The CASE ELSE clause is optional.

```
SELECT CASE TestExpression
  CASE ExpressionList1
    'Statements executed if TestExpression is
    'found in ExpressionList1
  [CASE ExpressionList2]
    'Statements executed if TestExpression is
    'found in ExpressionList2
    .
    .
    .
  [CASE ELSE]
    'Statements executed if the TestExpression
    'is not found in any ExpressionList.
END SELECT
```

The test expression used in the SELECT CASE statement can be a string variable, a numeric variable, or any valid QuickBASIC expression. This expression is matched against the expression lists that follow each CASE clause.

An expression list can be a single numeric or string value, a variable, an expression, a list of values, a range of values, or any combination of these. You can define a range of values using relational operators by adding the keyword IS to the CASE clause. These are all valid CASE statements:

```
CASE 2
CASE 3,4
CASE UpperValue/2
CASE IS > 10
CASE -1,-4, IS < -5
CASE IS > "M"
```

Ranges of values can also be defined by using the TO keyword in a CASE statement. When TO is used to define a range, the smaller value must be the first one given. These two CASE statements both use TO as a way of defining a range:

```
CASE "A" TO "M"
CASE IS < 0, 10 TO 20, IS > 30
```

These variations make SELECT CASE a very flexible programming tool. In the next section, you will see how to use this tool to create a simple on-screen menu.

MENUDEMO.BAS: A MENU DEMONSTRATION PROGRAM

Many programming applications use on-screen menus that allow the user a choice of possible activities. SELECT CASE statements are an ideal way of creating this kind of multiple-choice decision structure. A relatively easy menu to create is one that presents the user with a list of items, any one of which can be selected with an appropriate letter or number choice.

MENUDEMO is a short program that shows you how to set up this kind of simple menu. The program listing is shown in Figure 6.3. The first section of the program results in an on-screen display of the following menu:

```
MENU DEMONSTRATION PROGRAM
1. First Menu Choice
2. Second Menu Choice
3. Peace on Earth
4. Quit

What will it be? ----> 
```

Notice that a new punctuation mark, the colon (:), is used in the program lines that create this menu. A colon allows you to place two separate BASIC instructions on a single line. For example, the single line

```
LOCATE 6, 20: PRINT "1. First Menu Choice"
```

is exactly equivalent to these two lines of code.

```
'REM MENUDEMO.BAS
'Demonstrates the use of SELECT CASE in an idealized menu
'In an idealized menu.
CLS

DO

'Display menu choices on screen
LOCATE 3, 20: PRINT "MENU DEMONSTRATION PROGRAM"
LOCATE 6, 20: PRINT "1. First Menu Choice"
LOCATE 7, 20: PRINT "2. Second Menu Choice"
LOCATE 8, 20: PRINT "3. Peace on Earth"
LOCATE 9, 20: PRINT "4. Quit"

'Get choice from user
LOCATE 11, 20: INPUT "What will it be? ---->", Choice


'Position cursor and respond to menu choices
LOCATE 15, 5
SELECT CASE Choice
   CASE 1
     PRINT "The first menu choice is unavailable at this time."
   CASE 2
     PRINT "Choice two is coming soon to this computer!     "
   CASE 3
     PRINT "What can one small computer do?                 "
   CASE 4
     EXIT DO
   CASE ELSE
     BEEP
     LOCATE 12, 20
     PRINT "Enter 1, 2, 3, or 4"
END SELECT

LOOP
```

Figure 6.3: MENUDEMO.BAS

LOCATE 6,20
PRINT "1. First Menu Choice"

Colons are often used to combine two short lines of related code—in this case the LOCATE statement is combined with the message to be printed at the given location. Use colons where they will make your programs easier to read.

The MENUDEMO program is designed to respond to both valid and invalid menu choices. This is handled with the SELECT CASE structure. Choices 1, 2, and 3 result in a short message displayed on screen beneath the menu choices. Notice that trailing spaces have been included in the PRINT statements that generate these messages. Because these messages are all displayed in the same position on screen, blank spaces in the shorter messages have been added so that each message will completely replace any prior message that has already been displayed.

The instructions that create the menu display are contained within a DO...LOOP structure, so the program continues to display the menu and respond to choices until choice 4 is entered. When 4 is the choice, the statement block beneath CASE 4 is executed, and the EXIT DO statement terminates the loop.

When any value other than 1, 2, 3, or 4 is entered, the CASE ELSE statement block is executed. This block begins with a BEEP statement, which produces the nasty note familiar to computer users telling them that something is amiss. The beep is followed by this short explanatory message:

Enter 1, 2, 3, or 4

After this message is displayed, program execution loops back to the INPUT statement, which allows the user to try another choice.

Type in the program and try running it with every conceivable sort of menu choice. For example, try pressing ↵ without first selecting a choice, or use F1 rather than 1, or Q rather than 4. Always test any program with a complete spectrum of appropriate and inappropriate responses in order to find out how it responds to them. Confused computer users are a frantic lot who are apt to press almost anything in an attempt to get the response they are hoping for, and a well-written, "user-friendly" program should anticipate a broad range of input errors.

This particular program has *not* anticipated certain problems. For example, it does nothing to help the user who presses a number from 1 to 4, but fails to press ↵. It also results in a confusing "Redo from start" message if the user accidently enters a letter rather than a number. As you work your way through this book, you will be learning tools that can help you anticipate and minimize potential sources of confusion such as these.

UNDERSTANDING LOGICAL VALUES

The defining characteristic of a Boolean expression is that it is either *true* or *false*. True and false are known as *logical values*, and some understanding of how these values are handled by the computer is useful. Each Boolean expression that is encountered is evaluated and assigned an integer value as follows:

- A **false** condition is assigned the value 0.

- A **true** condition is assigned the value −1.

To understand this concept, look at the output of these two statements.

```
PRINT 5 > 2
PRINT 2 > 5
```

The output is

```
−1
 0
```

This output results from the fact that 5 > 2 is a true expression, and is therefore set equal to negative one. On the other hand, 2 > 5 is false, so it is evaluated as zero.

It is the integer value of a Boolean expression that determines the outcome of a decision statement. These two statements produce identical results:

```
IF 2 + 2 = 4 THEN PRINT "True"
IF −1 THEN PRINT "True"
```

The results are identical because the true assertion *2 + 2 = 4* is evaluated as -1, and this value controls the action in the THEN clause.

QuickBASIC uses only two values (− 1 and 0) when it evaluates a logical expression, but any integer can take the place of a logical expression in a decision statement—only zero is read as false; *any* other integer is read as true. In other words, you can replace the − 1 in the second statement above with any integer other than zero without changing its effect.

In the next sections you'll take a closer look at logical values and learn how to apply your knowledge to program development.

WATCHING THE VALUES OF BOOLEAN EXPRESSIONS

One way to understand how the computer treats Boolean expressions is to use QuickBASIC's debugging tools. In the next exercise, you will create a short program and use QuickBASIC's debugging tools in order to see how the computer handles the logical values assigned to a sample Boolean expression. The program you will use has been called WATCH.BAS and is shown here:

```
REM WATCH.BAS
'Watch the values of X, XSquared, and XSquared = X
' to understand the way logical values work.
CLS
FOR X = -2 TO 2
  XSquared = X ^ 2
  IF XSquared = X THEN PRINT X
NEXT X
```

This program tests the integer values from -2 to 2 and lists those values for which X is equal to X^2. Enter the program into the Work screen and then do the following.

1. Position the cursor on the variable **X** and press Shift +F9 and then ⬅ to place this variable in the Watch window.

2. Move the cursor to **XSquared** and add this variable to the Watch window in the same way.

3. To select the expresssion *XSquared = X*, move to the first letter of this expression, hold down the Shift key, and press the → key until the entire expression is highlighted.

4. Press Shift +F9 and then ⬅ to add this expression to the Watch window.

5. Step through the program using the F8 key until *NEXT X* is the current statement, noting the changes that occur in the Watch window as each program statement is executed. Figure 6.4 shows what the work screen will look like at this point in program execution. Because X = -2 and XSquared = -4, the expression XSquared = X is false, and the logical value *0* is displayed as the value of this expression.

```
┌─────────────────────────────────────────────────────────────────────────┐
│  File  Edit  View  Search  Run  Debug  Options                     Help   │
│ WATCH.BAS X: -2                                                           │
│ WATCH.BAS XSquared:  4                                                    │
│ WATCH.BAS XSquared = X:  Ø                                                │
│ ─────────────────────────────────── WATCH.BAS ──────────────────────[■]┐ │
│ REM WATCH.REM                                                         [↑]│
│ 'Lists values of X between -2 and 2 where X = X^2                         │
│ 'Watch the values of X, XSquared, and XSquared = X                        │
│ '   to understand the way logical values work.                           │
│ CLS                                                                       │
│ FOR X = -2 TO 2                                                           │
│   XSquared = X ^ 2                                                        │
│   IF XSquared = X THEN PRINT X                                            │
│ NEXT X                                                                    │
│                                                                           │
│                                                                           │
│                                                                           │
│ [←]                                                                    [→]│
│ ──────────────────────────── Immediate ──────────────────────────────    │
│                                                                           │
│ <Shift+F1=Help> <F5=Continue> <F9=Toggle Bkpt> <F8=Step>        ØØØØ9:ØØ1 │
└─────────────────────────────────────────────────────────────────────────┘
```

Figure 6.4: Watching the value of a logical expression

6. Continue to press F8 until X has been set equal to zero and *NEXT X* is again the current statement. The values of the watched items will now be

   X: 0
   XSquared: 0
   X = XSquared: − 1

   Because the values of X and XSquared are now equal, the expression *X = XSquared* is true, and its new logical value, − 1, is displayed in the Watch window.

7. Press F4 to see that *0*—the current value of X—has been displayed on the Output screen. Press F4 again to return to the Work screen.

8. Continue to use F8 to step through the program or use F5 to complete program execution at normal speed.

You have seen that to the computer 0 is the same as false and − 1 is the same as true. To human programmers, however, these values have little intrinsic meaning. One programming technique that facilitates work with logical values is the use of Boolean constants and variables. This is the subject of the next section.

WORKING WITH BOOLEAN CONSTANTS AND VARIABLES

Boolean constants and variables are used to control some decision-making problems in a way that helps make programs easier to write and to read. As an example, suppose you are writing a program that includes a search routine within a DO loop. You would like program execution to exit from the loop as soon as the item being searched for is found. The following two lines could both have this effect:

```
IF – 1 THEN EXIT DO
IF Found THEN EXIT DO
```

When Found is equal to – 1, these lines are exactly equivalent to the computer, but the second is likely to be more meaningful to a person looking at the program. The variable **Found** is acting as a logical value. As soon as the item being searched for has been located, the value of **Found** should be set equal to – 1. This can be done in a way that makes the program easier to read by defining two *Boolean constants* in a CONST statement such as this:

```
CONST FALSE = 0, TRUE = NOT FALSE
```

Then, when the item being searched for has been found, you can include a statement that reads

```
Found = TRUE
```

TRUE is used in this statement in place of the value – 1. By using names like Found and TRUE, which are part of our vocabulary, we can communicate with a computer in a language that makes sense to us as well as to the computer. The program in the next section includes a sample application of Boolean constants and variables.

FINDING PRIME NUMBERS WITH PRIME.BAS

The program shown in Figure 6.5 can be used to identify prime numbers. A prime number is an integer whose only factors are one and the number itself. The program tests as many numbers as you

```
REM PRIME.BAS
'Tests to see if a given number is prime
'Demonstrates Boolean variables and EXIT

'Setup
DEFINT A-Z                              'Variables are integers
CONST FALSE = 0, TRUE = NOT FALSE       'Define boolean constants
CLS

PRINT "This program tests for prime numbers."
DO
   Prime = TRUE                         'Set Boolean variable to true.
   INPUT "What number would you like to test (0 or Enter to quit)";
Value
   IF Value = 0 THEN EXIT DO
   FOR Test = 2 TO Value \ 2
      IF Value MOD Test = 0 THEN        'If Test is a factor of Value,
then
         Prime = FALSE                  'change value of Boolean
variable
         EXIT FOR                       'and exit the FOR...NEXT loop
      END IF
   NEXT Test
   IF Prime THEN PRINT "Prime" ELSE PRINT "Not prime"
   PRINT
LOOP
```

Figure 6.5: PRIME.BAS

choose, identifying each number as *Prime* or *Not Prime*. To exit the program, you enter a zero or simply press ⏎. A sample Output screen might look like this:

> This program tests for prime numbers.
> What number would you like to test (0 or Enter to quit)? 71
> Prime
>
> What number would you like to test (0 or Enter to quit)? 15
> Not Prime
>
> What number would you like to test (0 or Enter to quit)? 0

In this example 71, which has no factors other than one and 71, is identified as a prime number, while 15, which is divisible by three and five, is identified as *Not Prime*. When zero is entered, there is no response because this value is used to exit the program.

In order to test for factors, the program uses the MOD operation. A FOR...NEXT loop is set up that divides the number being tested by a series of test values, starting with 2, to see if any of these values are factors. If the expression *Value MOD Test* = *0* is true, then a factor has been found. When this happens, the Boolean variable **Prime** is defined as FALSE and an EXIT statement is used to terminate the FOR...NEXT loop. If no factor is found, the FOR...NEXT loop continues until every possible test value has been tried. It is impossible for a factor to be greater than half the value of the number being tested, so the upper limit for test values is set at Value \ 2.

After the test for factors is complete, the value of the Boolean variable **Prime** is used to determine which of the two output messages—*Prime* or *Not Prime*—will be printed. At the beginning of each iteration of the DO loop, Prime is redefined as TRUE.

This program takes a long time to identify large prime values because of the large number of MOD operations that must take place. (The largest legal prime value within the range of the integer variables used in this program is 32749. Enter this value to see how long the response time is on your system.) It is possible to write a program that could speed up the search for large prime values, but such a program would be somewhat longer and more complicated than the one shown here. This points to a common programming trade-off: So-called brute force programs that are relatively easy to write may be slower to operate. On the other hand, more elegant programs that run more quickly may take considerably longer to develop. One approach is not better than the other—the choice you make between these two styles will depend on the application involved.

SUMMARY

Decision structures in a program allow it to evaluate an expression and respond by branching to one of several options, based on the conditions stated in the expression. QuickBASIC provides two kinds of decision structures: IF...THEN and SELECT CASE statements. Single-line IF...THEN and IF...THEN...ELSE statements can be used to control simple decisions. When more complex decisions are involved, the block IF...END IF structure is easier to work with. This structure can be used to control multiple-choice decisions. The actions described in a block IF...END IF structure may consist of as many lines of program code as you choose. IF...THEN structures can be nested in order to handle situations where the results of one choice lead to some new decision.

SELECT CASE structures offer an alternative way of handling multiple-choice decisions. The MENUDEMO program in this chapter demonstrates how to use SELECT CASE to create a simple on-screen menu.

The final section of this chapter explained how BASIC handles logical values. By using QuickBASIC debugging tools, it is possible to watch the integer values assigned to logical expressions during program execution. Logical expressions that are false are evaluated as zero, while true expressions are evaluated as −1. The PRIME program in this chapter demonstrates the use of Boolean constants and variables as a way of working with these logical values.

Branching structures are useful as a means of managing the variety of tasks performed during execution of a typical program. Because programs often involve many discrete tasks, it is helpful to take an approach to writing programs that allows you to concentrate on one task at a time. This strategy of program development is the subject of the next chapter.

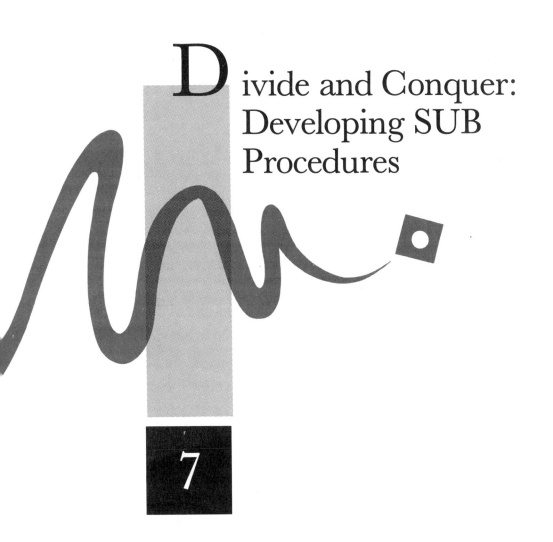

Divide and Conquer: Developing SUB Procedures

7

CHAPTER 7 _____

IMAGINE TRYING TO READ A BOOK THAT HAD BEEN
written without a table of contents, chapters, or even paragraphs.
Even if all the information you needed were in such a book, you
would probably give up in frustrated confusion long before you had
found it. Computer programs, like books, need to be organized in
order to make them easier to work with. In fact, writing computer
programs can be a great way to develop your organizational skills.

The large number of tasks in a typical computer program must
each be coded with great attention to detail. The most effective way
of handling this complexity is to divide the program into small
tasks of manageable size. To make this process easier, QuickBASIC
enables you to create discrete sections of program code called *proce-*
dures. These procedures make it possible to isolate individual tasks
within separate, self-contained units of code. By using procedures,
and keeping each procedure short and straightforward, you can
divide even the longest of programs into small, manageable units.
Each procedure can be called on to perform its task as frequently as
necessary. You may also find that procedures you develop for one
program can be used as building blocks in the development of subsequent programs. QuickBASIC offers several methods of helping you
incorporate established procedures into new programs.

■ QuickBASIC
can handle GO-
SUB...RETURN rou-
tines from earlier versions
of BASIC, but SUB proce-
dures offer greater flexibility and ease of use.

This chapter includes many short sample programs that demonstrate key concepts you will want to understand to make effective use
of QuickBASIC SUB procedures. Once you understand these concepts, you can study the LOAN and MORTGAGE programs to see
how SUB procedures have been applied in these somewhat longer
programs.

_____ *WORKING WITH SUB PROCEDURES* ___

A SUB procedure is a set of commands defined by the programmer in a SUB...END SUB structure. Each SUB procedure is given a

unique name. This name can be up to 40 characters long and must be unique: It cannot appear as a variable or procedure name in any other part of your program. In its simplest form, a SUB procedure has the following syntax:

```
SUB ProcedureName
  'Statements that make up the procedure
END SUB
```

Once you have defined a procedure in a program, you can call on it to perform its task from anywhere in the program in either of two ways. You can use the keyword CALL followed by the procedure name, or you can use the procedure name alone. When the procedure is called, the statements that make up the procedure will be executed until the END SUB statement has been reached. Program execution will then return to the first executable program line *after* the one that called the procedure. You can also use EXIT SUB statements within a procedure as an alternative way of exiting the procedure before the END SUB statement is reached.

The SUBDEMO program shown below uses two short SUB procedures. The *Dashes* procedure displays a line of dashes on screen, and the *Stars* procedure displays a line of asterisks. Don't enter the program into the Work screen yet. The exercises will take you step by step through the creation of the SUBDEMO program as a means of demonstrating those features of the QuickBASIC environment that are provided to help you work with SUB procedures in your programs.

```
REM SUBDEMO.BAS
'Introduction to SUB procedures
CALL Dashes   'Calls the procedure with CALL
Stars         'Calls the procedure without CALL

SUB Dashes
  PRINT STRING$(80, " = ")
END SUB

SUB Stars
  PRINT STRING$ (80, "*")
END SUB
```

TYPING SUB TO CREATE A PROCEDURE

In the QuickBASIC environment, SUB procedures are displayed separately from the main body of the program. The Title bar of the View window identifies which part of the program you are working with at any given time. One way to create a SUB procedure is to type the keyword SUB followed by a procedure name. When you press ← after typing this line, the main body of your program will disappear from the View window and be replaced by the new procedure, with the END SUB statement automatically added. You can then proceed to type in the statements that make up the procedure definition.

Begin to create the SUBDEMO program as follows:

1. Type the first four lines of the SUBDEMO program. These lines make up the *module-level* code of the program. Module-level statements are those that are not part of a program procedure.

2. Save the partially completed program as SUBDEMO so that the Title bar in the View window reads *SUBDEMO.BAS*.

3. With the cursor on the blank line beneath the fourth line, type

   ```
   SUB Dashes
   ```

   and press ←.

4. The statements that make up the module-level code will disappear, and the View window will now display the following:

   ```
   SUB Dashes

   END SUB
   ```

   The Title bar will read *SUBDEMO.Dashes*, indicating that the Dashes procedure of the SUBDEMO program is now occupying the active window.

5. Type the following in the line between the SUB and END SUB statements to complete the definition of this procedure:

   ```
   PRINT STRING$(80, " = ")
   ```

Now that you've created a procedure, you need to learn how to return to the main body of your program. The next exercise shows you how.

DISPLAYING AND DELETING PROCEDURES

Procedures are always listed in alphabetical order. When you print a program, procedures will be arranged alphabetically following the module-level code.

You can move different sections of your program into the View window by using the SUBs command in the View menu. This command opens a dialog box that displays the name of your program and, beneath this, the name of each procedure you have created. The F2 shortcut key will also open this dialog box. You can then select the section of program you would like to work by highlighting it and pressing ◄─┘ to accept the default *Edit in Active* action. This action moves the highlighted procedure into the View window.

To return the main body of the SUBDEMO program to the View window, do the following:

1. Press F2 to open the SUBs dialog box. The dialog box will show the program structure as seen here.

   SUBDEMO.BAS
   Dashes

2. Check to be sure that *SUBDEMO.BAS* is selected and press ◄─┘. The main body of your program will return to the View window.

You can also move from one procedure to the next using the *Next SUB* command in the View menu, or use the shortcut key combination Shift +F2. This command moves you alphabetically forward through the procedures in your program. Pressing Ctrl +F2 moves you backward through the procedures.

The SUBs command, which can be used to select a procedure for display, can also be used to delete a procedure from your program. To delete a procedure, highlight the name of that procedure in the SUBs dialog box and then select the *Delete* action.

USING THE EDIT MENU TO CREATE A PROCEDURE

A second method of creating SUB procedures using the Quick-BASIC menus is also available, but this option is available only when you have selected to work with QuickBASIC's Full Menus option. If you have been working with Easy Menus up to this point, change to the full menus by selecting the *Full Menus* command from the Options window. Full menus will be used throughout the remainder of the examples in this book.

The New SUB command in the expanded Edit menu can be used to create new SUB procedures. When you select this command, a New SUB dialog box opens that contains an input area for the name of the new procedure. The content of this input area is determined by the location of your cursor when you invoke the New SUB command. If you position the cursor on a blank line, the box will be empty. If the cursor is on a word that is part of a program statement, the box will contain that word. You can use this feature to save yourself a bit of typing, as demonstrated in the next exercise, which also completes the creation of the SUBDEMO program.

1. Check to be sure that the main module of the SUBDEMO program is in the View window and position the cursor anywhere on the word *Stars* in line four.

2. Select the New SUB command from the full Edit menu. The New SUB dialog box will open with the procedure name *Stars* already entered in the input area.

3. Press ◄┘ to create the new procedure. The view screen will show the following:

   ```
   SUB Stars
   END SUB
   ```

4. Open a blank line beneath the SUB statement and type in the following line in order to complete the definition of this procedure:

   ```
   PRINT STRING$ (80, "*")
   ```

5. Return to the main module of the program using the F2 shortcut key.

Once you have completed creating the SUBDEMO program, save it again. When you are working with the expanded menus, you can use the *Save* command, which is one of the options in the expanded Files menu. This command automatically saves your program using the current program name and format. No dialog box opens when you use the Save command unless you are saving a new, untitled, program for the first time.

After you have saved the program, you will find that the following two program statements have been added automatically to the beginning of your program.

DECLARE statements are always generated at the top of a program. You can use Cut and Paste commands to move DECLARE statements to a position below the introductory remarks in your program.

```
DECLARE SUB Dashes ( )
DECLARE SUB Stars ( )
```

When you are working in the QuickBASIC environment, declaration statements such as these are generated automatically whenever you save a program that contains procedures and does not already include declaration statements for those procedures. DECLARE statements must be present in order to compile a program in which procedure calls precede procedure definitions.

Because SUB procedures are displayed as discrete units, separate from each other and from the main body of your program, it is possible and often useful to view two procedures, or a procedure and the main module of a program, on screen at the same time. The next section of this chapter shows you how.

DIVIDING THE VIEW WINDOW

QuickBASIC allows you to partition the View area into two separate windows enabling you to view and work with two sections of your program simultaneously. There are two ways to divide the View window:

- Open the SUBs dialog box using F2 or by selecting the SUBs command in the View menu. Highlight the procedure you want to work with and then select the *Edit in Split* action. The selected procedure will appear in the lower half of your screen, while the top half displays the contents of the original View window.

- Select the *Split* command from the View window. Two windows will open, each containing the same section of your program. Use F6 to control which window is active and then use the SUBs command to choose the procedure you want to see displayed in the active window.

After you have split the View window, you can use Ctrl +F10 to make the active window occupy the entire Work screen. Pressing Ctrl +F10 again returns you to the split display.

Use the SUBDEMO program to practice these techniques as described here.

1. Have the main module of the SUBDEMO program in the View window and press F2 to open the SUBs dialog box.

2. Highlight the procedure name, *Dashes*.

3. Select *Edit in Split* either by using the Tab key and pressing ⏎ or by pressing Alt +S. The split View window is shown in Figure 7.1.

4. Press Ctrl +F10 to make the active window occupy the full Work screen. Repeat the Ctrl +F10 command to return to the split screen.

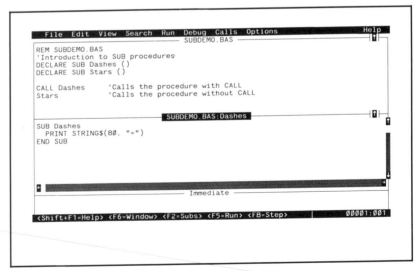

Figure 7.1: Splitting the View window

5. The window that contains the Dashes procedure is the active window. Press Shift + F6. This will activate the top window, and the SUBDEMO.BAS Title bar will be highlighted.

6. Use the *Split* command in the View window to return to a single View window. The main module of your program, which occupies the active window, remains on screen.

LOAN.BAS: *USING PROCEDURES IN* *A MENU-DRIVEN PROGRAM*

SUB procedures are ideally suited for the creation of menu-driven programs like LOAN.BAS, the program you will be exploring in this section. LOAN.BAS displays the following on-screen menu.

```
THIS IS THE LOAN ASSISTANT
Your choices are the following:

1. Calculate monthly payments on a loan
2. Calculate the cost of a loan
Q. Quit

Enter your choice here ---->
```

Choice 1 asks the user to input values for the principal (the amount of a loan), the yearly interest rate, and the term of a loan. The output supplies the monthly payments for the loan. The example shows the monthly payments for a five-year loan of $5,000 at 10.75% interest.

```
Principal..............................5000          Monthly Payment
Yearly Interest rate (%).........10.75                  $108.09
Term of the loan (months)......60
```

Choice 2 asks the user for the principal, monthly payments, and number of payments on a loan. The output supplies the total cost of the interest payments made on this loan. To determine the cost of the loan describe above, the following input values would be entered.

Principal...........................5000
Amount of each payment....108.09
Total number of payments...60

The output below shows that this loan costs $1,485.40 in interest payments.

Total Payments : $6,485.40
Cost of Loan   : $1,485.40

The LOAN program is shown in Figure 7.2. The main module of the program is very similar to the MENUDEMO program you developed in the last chapter. In this program, the first two CASE statements are used to call two different procedures, Payment and LoanCost, which correspond to the first two menu choices.

The Quit procedure in this program is changed a bit from the one used in MENUDEMO. When the user selects *Q* to quit, the program responds by asking for confirmation with this prompt message:

Exit the program now? (Y,N)

```
REM LOAN.BAS
'A menu driven program which uses subroutines to calculate
'loan information

DECLARE SUB LoanCost ()
DECLARE SUB Pause ()
DECLARE SUB Payment ()

'Setup
CLS
CONST FALSE = 0, TRUE = NOT FALSE
Done = FALSE

DO
   'Display menu
   LOCATE 3, 20: PRINT "THIS IS THE LOAN ASSISTANT"
   LOCATE 4, 20: PRINT "Your choices are the following:"
   LOCATE 7, 20: PRINT "1. Calculate monthly payments on a loan"
   LOCATE 8, 20: PRINT "2. Calculate the cost of a loan"
   LOCATE 9, 20: PRINT "Q. Quit"

   'Erase any previous choice and get a choice from user
   LOCATE 11, 48: PRINT "  "
   LOCATE 11, 20: INPUT "Enter your choice here ---->", Choice$
```

Figure 7.2: The LOAN program listing

```
      'Respond to choices
      SELECT CASE Choice$
         CASE "1"
            CALL Payment
         CASE "2"
            CALL LoanCost
         CASE "Q", "q"
            LOCATE 11, 20: INPUT "Exit the program now? (Y,N)  ", check$
            IF check$ = "Y" OR check$ = "y" THEN Done = TRUE
         CASE ELSE
            BEEP
      END SELECT

LOOP UNTIL Done

'-----------------------------------------------------------
'Calculate the total interest paid on a loan
'-----------------------------------------------------------
SUB LoanCost
   'Get values
   LOCATE 18, 1
   INPUT "Principal................ ", Principal
   INPUT "Amount of each payment.... ", Pmt
   INPUT "Total number of payments.. ", Term

   'Calculate total payments and cost of loan
   TotalPmt = Pmt * Term
   Cost = TotalPmt - Principal

   'Display results
   LOCATE 18, 40
   PRINT USING "Total Payments: $$######,.##"; TotalPmt
   LOCATE 19, 40
   PRINT USING "Cost of Loan  : $$######,.##"; Cost

   'Call subroutine that clears the screen
   Pause
END SUB

'-----------------------------------------------------------
'Pause program execution befor clearing the screen
'-----------------------------------------------------------
SUB Pause
   'Wait to clear the screen
   LOCATE 25, 1
   INPUT "Press Enter to continue", Response$
   CLS
END SUB

'-----------------------------------------------------------
'Calculate the monthly payments required to pay back a loan
'-----------------------------------------------------------
SUB Payment
   'Get values
   LOCATE 18, 1
   INPUT "Principal................ ", Principal
   INPUT "Yearly Interest rate (%)... ", Rate
   INPUT "Term of the loan (months).. ", Term

   'Calculate monthly payment
   Interest = Rate / 100      'Convert interest rate to decimal
   Interest = Interest / 12   'Calculate monthly interest rate
   'The following formula calculates payments per period
   Pmt = Principal * (Interest / (1 - (1 + Interest) ^ -Term))

   'Display results
   LOCATE 18, 45: PRINT "Monthly Payment"
   LOCATE 19, 45: PRINT USING "$$######,.##"; Pmt

   Pause    'Call subroutine that clears the screen
END SUB
```

Figure 7.2: The LOAN program listing (continued)

The user's response to this question is used to control the value of a Boolean variable called **Done**. A response of y or Y sets the value of this variable to TRUE. This in turn causes the program to exit from the menu display loop when execution reaches this statement:

LOOP UNTIL Done

Notice that the program includes a third procedure, Pause, which is called from within each of the other procedures. This procedure is used to pause program execution before the screen is cleared.

Each procedure is preceded by remark statements that set it apart visually and explain its function. To create these remark statements, first create the SUB procedure. With the procedure in the View window, move to the first character of the first line and press ◄─┘. A Dialog box with the following message will appear:

Blank lines not allowed before SUB/FUNCTION line.
Is remark OK?

Press ◄─┘ in response to this question to open up a new line above the SUB line. The QuickBASIC editor will automatically place an apostrophe at the beginning of the line.

The SUBDEMO and LOAN programs you have been studying use entirely self-contained procedures—in neither program are variable values exchanged between the SUB procedures and any other part of the program. To create more flexible and useful programs, however, you will need to know how to pass information from one part of a program to another. The remainder of this chapter explores some tools you can use to handle this exchange of information.

VARIABLES AND SUB PROCEDURES

QuickBASIC provides you with a variety of techniques for passing information back and forth between a procedure and other parts of a program. You'll find that this flexibility is useful for handling the broad range of tasks that procedures are used for. Some procedures may require data from the main body of your program, while others can act as entirely independent units. Depending on circumstances, it can be useful to pass the value of a variable to just one procedure, or to make it available to procedures throughout your program. You may or may not want the changes that affect a variable within a procedure to affect that variable's value when the program returns to the module-level code. Many programmers develop a library of standard procedures that can be plugged directly into any program, and these procedures must be able to exchange data accurately with the programs that include them. QuickBASIC can comfortably accommodate all of these considerations, and the sample programs that follow are designed to help you develop a clear understanding of what is involved.

GLOBAL AND LOCAL VARIABLES

A *global* variable is one that is available throughout a program. Each time the value of a global variable is changed, the change is reflected in all subsequent occurrences of that variable in any section of the same program. In contrast, the effect of a *local* variable is confined to a specific unit of code. Changing the value of a local variable in one part of a program will not affect an identically named variable in a different part of the same program. In earlier versions of BASIC, all variables were global, but difficulties often arose with long programs because of the danger of inadvertently using the same variable name for two different purposes. Such errors can create insidious, hard-to-find bugs in a program.

In QuickBASIC SUB procedures, all variables are local by default. A variable that is assigned a value in the main body of the program will not affect a variable of the same name within a SUB procedure. Conversely, a value given to a variable in a procedure will not affect a variable of the same name in the module-level code. This is demonstrated in the following program:

```
CLS
A = 1
PRINT "Before calling the procedure: A ="; A
CALL Demo
PRINT "After calling the procedure: A ="; A
```

```
SUB Demo
   A = 2 * A
   PRINT "Within the Demo procedure: A ="; A
END SUB
```

Because the value of a variable in the module-level code does not affect the value of a variable of the same name in a procedure, the variable called **A** in the Demo procedure is treated like any BASIC variable that has not been assigned a value. It is set equal to zero. This is the resulting output:

```
Before calling the procedure: A = 1
Within the Demo procedure: A = 0
After calling the procedure: A = 1
```

You can demonstrate the difference between the two variables called **A** by using the Watch window. If the main body of your program is on screen, when you add the variable A to the Watch window, it will be identified as shown here. (If you have saved the program, *Untitled* will be replaced with the program's file name.)

```
Untitled: A
```

This indicates that it is the *module-level* variable that is being watched. To watch the procedure-level value of A, you must first move the Demo procedure into the active View window. If you then repeat the same exact watch command, you will add a second variable to the Watch window that will be identified as follows:

```
Demo A:
```

The *procedure-level* variable is identified with both the procedure name and the variable name to distinguish it from variables elsewhere in your program with the same name. If you step through your program using F8, only one variable can be watched at a time. The variable that is in the section of code that is not being executed will be identified as <*Not watchable*> in the Watch window.

THE EFFECT OF A MODULE-LEVEL COMMON SHARED STATEMENT   Although it is often useful for procedure-level variables to be locally defined, there may also be some variable or variables that you would like to use globally throughout your program. You can select any variable you would like to use in this way by including a COMMON SHARED statement in the module-level code of your program. The syntax of this statement is shown here:

COMMON SHARED variable1, variable2, ...

Any variables in this list will be treated as global variables.

Insert a blank line above the *CLS* statement in the program shown above and add this statement to that line:

COMMON SHARED A

The output of the program now looks like this:

Before calling the procedure: A = 1
Within the Demo procedure: A = 2
After calling the procedure: A = 2

Because of the addition of the COMMON SHARED statement, the value of A that is set equal to 1 in the main module is now available to the Demo procedure. The statement "A = 2 * A" will now set A to equal 2. This value is shown in the second line of output. The new value of A is, in turn, available to the main module, and this is reflected in the final line of output.

THE EFFECT OF A SHARED STATEMENT   You may want some of your procedures to share variables with the main module of your code, while variables in other procedures remain local. If, for instance, you were to develop a long program using both common procedures that you have standardized for use in many programs and other procedures that are unique to that program only, you might want to use local variables in the standard procedures and global variables in the procedures unique to the program. By placing a SHARED statement within a procedure, you can designate a list of variables used in that procedure to be shared with the main body of your program. These variables will be shared with the module-level code, but *not* with variables of the same name in other procedures. This program demonstrates the use of the SHARED statement:

```
CLS
A = 1
PRINT "Before calling the procedures: A ="; A
CALL DemoShared
CALL DemoUnshared
PRINT "After calling the procedures: A ="; A

SUB DemoShared
   SHARED A
   A = 2 * A
   PRINT "In the DemoShared procedure: A ="; A
END SUB

SUB DemoUnshared
   A = A * 2
   PRINT "In the DemoUnshared procedure: A ="; A
END SUB
```

The output of this program looks like this:

```
Before calling the procedures: A = 1
In the DemoShared procedure: A = 2
In the DemoUnshared procedure: A = 0
After calling the procedures: A = 2
```

Notice that the SHARED statement in the DemoShared procedure affects the value of the shared variable called **A** in that procedure and also affects the value of A when execution returns to the module-level code. However, the value of A in DemoUnshared remains independent.

WORKING WITH ARGUMENTS AND PARAMETERS

A very powerful and flexible way of passing data from one part of your program to another is through the use of arguments and parameters. An *argument* is a constant, variable, or expression included as part of the statement that calls a procedure. Within the procedure definition, each argument is matched by a corresponding variable name known as a *parameter*. Parameters are listed in the SUB statement, and have a one-to-one correspondence with the arguments listed where the procedure is called. Figure 7.3 shows how arguments and parameters are used. An argument must always be paired with a parameter of the same data-type. When the procedure is executed, each parameter takes on the value of its corresponding argument.

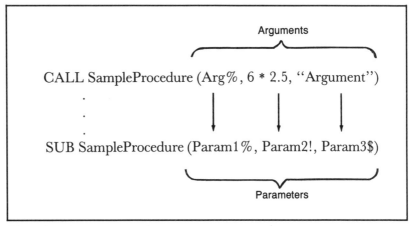

Figure 7.3: Arguments and parameters

PASSING VALUES TO A PROCEDURE The following program contains a SUB procedure called RootTable that creates a list of numbers and their square roots. The BASIC function SQR is introduced here. This function is always followed by an expression in parentheses, and can be used to find the square root of that value. Module-level INPUT statements ask the user to supply a starting value (Low) and a stopping value (High) for the numbers to be displayed in the table. In the CALL statement, Low and High are used as arguments to pass their values to the parameters **Begin** and **Finish** in the RootTable procedure. These two variables are used in the FOR...NEXT loop that creates the table.

```
CLS
INPUT "Display square roots starting with -->", Low
INPUT "                        and stopping with -->", High
PRINT
CALL RootTable(Low, High)
```

```
SUB RootTable (Begin, Finish)
  PRINT "Number", "Square Root"
  FOR N = Begin TO Finish
    PRINT N,
    PRINT USING "######.####"; SQR(N)
  NEXT N
END SUB
```

A sample run of the program is shown here:

```
Display square roots starting with --> 20
              and stopping with --> 24
    Number      Square Root
     20           4.4721
     21           4.5826
     22           4.6904
     23           4.7958
     24           4.8990
```

When you use a CALL statement to call a QuickBASIC procedure, the arguments must be listed within parentheses. However, if you call a procedure without using CALL, the arguments should be listed without parentheses. In the program above, you can change the line that now reads

```
CALL RootTable(Low, High)
```

to read

```
RootTable Low, High
```

These two statements are equivalent, and the change will not affect the program's performance.

COMMON SHARED and SHARED statements can only share information between variables with the same name in the different sections of your program. Arguments and parameters are more flexible because they allow you to pass the value of an expression or variable in one part of your program to a variable in another section that may or may not have the same name.

A variable used as an argument can have a different name from its corresponding parameter. It can also have the same name.

STRING VALUES AND CONSTANTS IN PROCEDURES The next sample program illustrates the kind of standard procedure that can be used as an extension of the BASIC language in order to handle a frequently encountered task. The program uses a string variable as a parameter in a procedure that prints text in a centered position on a page. This program also illustrates an important difference between the behavior of variables and constants in SUB procedures: Unlike variables, constants defined in the module-level code are treated as global values. The procedure uses constant values for the left and right margin positions. Because these are global values, they are automatically available during execution of the Center procedure.

The LEN function introduced here is always followed by a string expression contained within parentheses. The function counts the number of characters in that expression and returns this numeric value.

Here is the program listing. Be sure your printer is ready before running the program.

```
CONST LEFT = 10, RIGHT = 70
Sample$ = "Centering between margins of 10 and 70"
Center Sample$
LPRINT TAB(LEFT); STRING$(60, "–")
Center DATE$

SUB Center (Phrase$)
   LineLen = RIGHT – LEFT
   PhraseLen = LEN(Phrase$)
   Position = LEFT + (LineLen – PhraseLen) \ 2
   LPRINT TAB(Position); Phrase$
END SUB
```

Sample output from this program is shown here.

Centering between margins of 10 and 70

07-28-1990

USING STATIC IN PROCEDURE DEFINITIONS Ordinarily, variable values within a QuickBASIC SUB procedure are reset each time the procedure is called, in the same way that all variable values are reset each time you restart a program. If you want to preserve the value of all the variables in a procedure between procedure calls, you can do so by adding the STATIC attribute to the SUB statement in your procedure definition using this syntax:

SUB *Procedure* (*Parameterlist*) STATIC

To preserve the value of some—but not all—variables between procedure calls, include a STATIC statement within your procedure definition, using this syntax:

STATIC *variablelist*

The program sample that follows uses the STATIC attribute to preserve the value of the variable **X** between calls of the StaticDemo procedure. Each time the procedure is called from the module-level FOR...NEXT loop, X retains its previous value. The program produces an Output screen that contains a column of values for X, starting with zero and ending with nine.

```
CLS
FOR N = 1 TO 10
   CALL StaticDemo
NEXT N

'Using STATIC preserves the value of X between calls
SUB StaticDemo STATIC
   PRINT X
   X = X + 1
END SUB
```

To understand how STATIC functions, remove the word STATIC from the procedure definition and run the program again. When you run the modified program, the value for X is reset to 0 each time the procedure is called and, as a result, the printed value of X is always zero.

PASSING ARGUMENTS BY VALUE AND BY REFERENCE   The arguments you include in a procedure call may be variables, constants, or expressions. Variable arguments are handled in a way that has an important effect on how a program functions. When a variable is used in an argument list, it is passed to the procedure by *reference*. When data is passed by reference, the same memory location is used for both the argument and the parameter. Thus any change that occurs to the value of the parameter during execution of the procedure will also affect the subsequent value of the module-level variable that was passed to that procedure. In contrast, when a constant or an expression is used in an argument list, it is passed to the procedure by *value*. When data is passed by value, it is first copied to a temporary memory location, and the procedure has access only to this copy of the data. This means that variables included as part of an expression in an argument list are *not* affected by changes to the corresponding parameters.

The practical implications of these technical differences can be summarized as follows:

- When you *do* want a procedure to influence the value of a variable in the calling program, use the *variable* as an argument when you call the procedure. The result is a two-way communication between the calling program and the procedure regarding the value of this variable.

- When you *don't* want a procedure to influence the value of a variable in the calling program, use an *expression* to pass the variable to the procedure. Change a variable into an expression by enclosing it in parentheses. The result is that the procedure acts independently and leaves the original value of the variable unchanged.

The sample program used below requests an item price and a number of items from the user. It then calls a procedure that calculates a 10% discount based on the item price. A statement calculating the total value of the items is placed in both the procedure and in the calling program. These two calculations can be used to demonstrate the difference between passing a variable by reference and value. If you want the discounted price to be used in both the procedure-level calculation and the subsequent module-level calculation, you simply include the variable in the argument list that calls the Discount procedure, as shown here. Because the variable is passed by reference, the procedure-level calculation and the subsequent module-level calculation produce identical results.

```
CLS
INPUT " Enter the price of one item: ", ItemPrice
INPUT " Enter the number of items: ", N%
CALL Discount(ItemPrice, N%)
PRINT "Module-level value of the items: "; ItemPrice * N%

SUB Discount (Price, Count%)
   Price = .9 * Price
   PRINT "Procedure-level value of the items:"; Count% * Price
END SUB
```

A sample output screen would look like this:

```
Enter the price of one item: 5
Enter the number of items: 10
Procedure-level value of the items: 45
Module-level value of the items: 45
```

However, if you want the procedure to calculate the discount, but you want the calling program to preserve the original item price, you can place the Price variable in parentheses in the procedure call in order to pass it by value to the Discount procedure. The modified CALL statement looks like this:

```
CALL Discount((ItemPrice), N%)
```

Modified in this way, the program will use the original item price when it calculates the total value after performing the Discount procedure, rather than using the discounted price as it did when the variable was passed by reference. Using the same values for price and number of items, the output would now look like this:

```
Enter the price of one item: 5
Enter the number of items: 10
Procedure-level value of the items: 45
Module-level value of the items: 50
```

The module-level figure for the value of the items is now different from the procedure-level value. Because the item price was passed by value, the module-level calculation is performed using the original item price.

MORTGAGE.BAS: USING ARGUMENTS IN A LOAN APPLICATION

The MORTGAGE program is an application that uses arguments to pass values to parameters in the program's procedures. The program prints a table of monthly mortgage payments like the one shown in Figure 7.4. The low and high values for the Loan Amount, the term of the mortgage, and the lowest of the four Interest Rates in the table are all chosen by the user. The program then passes these values as arguments to a procedure that uses nested FOR...NEXT loops to create the table. The program also contains a procedure called DisplayHelp that displays an optional explanation of the input items.

```
MONTHLY PAYMENTS FOR A 30 YEAR MORTGAGE

Loan Amount                           Interest Rates
                     10.00%      10.50%      11.00%      11.50%
================================================================
      $50,000       438.79      457.37      476.16      495.15
      $51,000       447.56      466.52      485.68      505.05
      $52,000       456.34      475.66      495.21      514.95
      $53,000       465.11      484.81      504.73      524.85
      $54,000       473.89      493.96      514.25      534.76
      $55,000       482.66      503.11      523.78      544.66
```

Figure 7.4: Monthly payments calculated by the MORTGAGE program

Before you try the MORTGAGE program, you might want to experiment with the short sample program below, which demonstrates the way nested FOR..NEXT loops can be used to create a table.

```
CLS
FOR Row = 1 TO 3
  FOR Column = 1 TO 3
    PRINT "Row"; Row; "Col"; Column,
  NEXT Column
  PRINT
NEXT Row
```

This program generates the table shown here:

Row 1 Col 1	Row 1 Col 2	Row 1 Col 3
Row 2 Col 1	Row 2 Col 2	Row 2 Col 3
Row 3 Col 1	Row 3 Col 2	Row 3 Col 3

Each iteration of the outer FOR...NEXT loop produces one row in the table. The PRINT statement that precedes the *NEXT Row* statement serves the purpose of moving output to a new line once each row is complete. The inner FOR...NEXT loop generates the three items of output in each row. A good way to get a sense of how the program works is to add the variables **Row** and **Column** to the Watch window and step through the program one line at a time with the F8 key.

The MORTGAGE program uses a very similar structure in the *Table* procedure to create the table of monthly mortgage payments using the values passed to it from the main module. The complete program listing is shown in Figure 7.5.

The MORTGAGE program combines many of the programming techniques you have learned. Once you understand it as it appears here, try experimenting with changes to the program. A good way to start is to use the Search and Change commands to change LPRINT

```
REM MORTGAGE.BAS
'This program creates a table of mortgage payments
'The parameters of the Table procedure are used in
'nested FOR...NEXT loops to create this table.

DECLARE SUB DisplayHelp ()
DECLARE SUB Table (InitPrin!, FinalPrin!, InitRate!, Term!)

'Welcome message
CLS
PRINT "THIS IS THE MORTGAGE MAGICIAN"
DisplayHelp

'Get values
LOCATE 14, 1
PRINT "Don't use commas -- Press Enter after each value"
PRINT STRING$(48, "-")
PRINT "Low Value     High Value     Interest Rate     Term"
LOCATE 17, 1: INPUT Initial
LOCATE 17, 14: INPUT Final
LOCATE 17, 28: INPUT Rate
LOCATE 17, 45: INPUT Term
```

Figure 7.5: The MORTGAGE program listing

```
'Wait for response that indicates the printer is ready
LOCATE 25, 1: INPUT "Ready the printer and press Enter", Ready$

'Print the Table
CALL Table(Initial, Final, Rate, Term)


'------------------------------------------------------------
'Display an explanation of terms
'------------------------------------------------------------
SUB DisplayHelp
   PRINT
   PRINT "To prepare a table of monthly mortgage payments, you will"
   PRINT "need to enter the following values:"
   PRINT
   PRINT "Low Value:      The lowest loan amount you want in the table"
   PRINT "High Value:     The highest loan amount you want in the table"
   PRINT "Interest Rate: The lowest interest rate you want in the table"
   PRINT "               Use decimal form "
   PRINT "               For example 10.5% = .105"
   PRINT "Term of Loan:  The term of the loan measured in months"
   PRINT "               15 years = 180     30 years = 360   "
END SUB

'-------------------------------------------------------------
'Display a table of monthly payments for a range of loan amounts
'-------------------------------------------------------------
SUB Table (InitPrin, FinalPrin, InitRate, Term)
   'Define Format strings
   Val$ = "$$########,"
   Pmt$ = "######,.##"
   Pct$ = "######,.##%"

   'Print Headings - note the use of punctuation
   LPRINT "MONTHLY PAYMENTS FOR A"; Term / 12; "YEAR MORTGAGE"
   LPRINT
   LPRINT "Loan Amount"; TAB(40); "Interest Rates"
   'Print interest headings as percentages
   Rate = InitRate * 100
   FOR Position = 15 TO 60 STEP 15
      LPRINT USING Pct$; TAB(Position); Rate;
      Rate = Rate + .5
   NEXT Position
   LPRINT STRING$(80, "=")

   'Print Table using nested FOR...NEXT loops
   'Each iteration of the outer loop creates one row in the table
   'The nested loop calculates and displays values across the row
   FOR Prin = InitPrin TO FinalPrin STEP 1000
      'Reset annual interest to initial rate at start of each row
      AnnualInterest = InitRate
      LPRINT USING Val$; Prin;
      FOR Position = 15 TO 60 STEP 15
         'Calculate monthly interest for use in the formula
         Interest = AnnualInterest / 12
         Payment = Prin * (Interest / (1 - (1 + Interest) ^ -Term))
         LPRINT USING Pmt$; TAB(Position); Payment;
         'Increment annual interest by half a percent
         AnnualInterest = AnnualInterest + .005
      NEXT Position
      LPRINT      'This statement positions next output on a new row
   NEXT Prin
END SUB
```

Figure 7.5: The MORTGAGE program listing (continued)

to PRINT in order to produce on-screen display. This will help you save paper and time as you continue your experimenting. You might want to try changing the intervals used between interest rates or values for the loan principal, or see if you can create a table with five interest rates rather than four. Making changes to a program is a good way to make mistakes, and making mistakes is an excellent way to learn.

SUMMARY

SUB procedures are used as a way of dividing the job of writing a program into smaller tasks of manageable size. Each SUB procedure has a unique name and is defined in a **SUB...END SUB** structure. The procedure can be called by name from any point in the program with or without using the **CALL** keyword.

The QuickBASIC environment provides a variety of menu options for working with SUB procedures. These include commands for creating deleting procedures and for displaying procedures using a single View window or using a split screen.

Variables available throughout a program are known as **global**. In contrast, **local** variables are available only in a particular procedure. Variables used in QuickBASIC procedures are local by default. Constant values that are defined using a CONST statement in the main module of a program are always global. Variables can be made global by listing them in a **COMMON SHARED** statement. Variables within a particular procedure can be made available to the module-level code of a program by listing them in a **SHARED** statement within the procedure. Variables in a procedure are reset each time the procedure is called unless a **STATIC** statement is used. If the word STATIC is included in the SUB statement, then all variables used in that procedure retain their value between procedure calls. A STATIC statement can also be included within a procedure definition followed by a list of variables. In this case only those variables retain their value between procedure calls.

When a procedure is called, the values of specific variables can be passed to that procedure by listing them as **arguments** in the call statement. These arguments correspond to **parameters**, which are listed in the SUB statement of the procedure definition. When the arguments listed in a procedure call are variables, they are passed to the procedure by value, and any change to the corresponding parameters will also affect the value of the variable arguments. When the arguments listed in a procedure call are expressions, they are passed to the procedure by reference, and the values of variables used in the expressions will not be affected by events in the procedure.

The application programs in the following chapters will give you an opportunity to see the wide range of tasks that can be handled using program procedures.

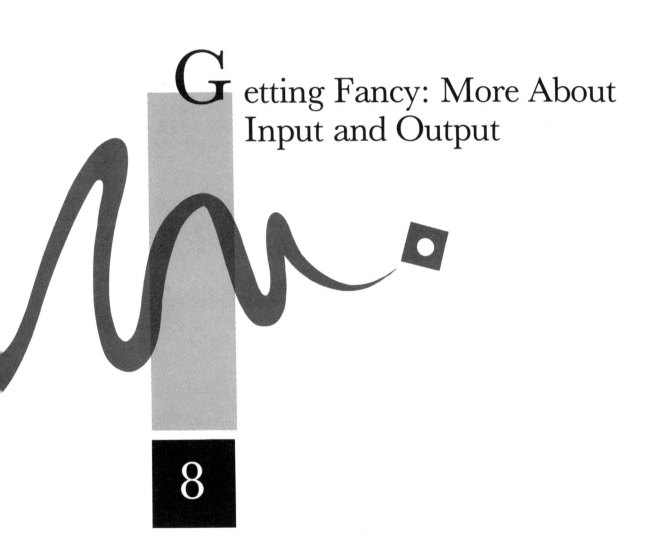

Getting Fancy: More About Input and Output

8

CHAPTER 8

THIS CHAPTER INTRODUCES PROGRAMMING techniques that will help you develop enjoyable, user-friendly programs. These are grouped here because they can help you obtain tighter control over your programs and because they can make programming more fun. If you are a first-time programmer, you might find more detail here than you need. If this is the case, study only the short, sample programs. These will give you enough background to proceed with the following chapters. You can return to explore the details later.

We'll start by looking at two new ways of getting input from the keyboard, the INPUT$ and INKEY$ functions. Understanding how to work with these functions will help you write more responsive programs. A discussion of the codes used to store keyboard characters in memory is included to help you work with keyboard input more effectively. The 256 codes used for this purpose are known as ASCII codes, an abbreviation for American Standard Code for Information Interchange.

Next we'll take a look at ways of enhancing program displays on the monitor. In this section you'll learn how to control the brightness and color of screen output using the COLOR statement. You'll also learn how to divide the Output screen into viewports with VIEW PRINT. This allows you much greater flexibility when you are designing output displays. Many of these techniques are incorporated into the ASCII.BAS program, which creates an on-screen display of ASCII character codes.

After studying visual output techniques, you'll learn how to use the SOUND and PLAY statements to create output you can hear. Your friends and associates will be especially pleased to be within hearing distance while you work on this section.

The final section of this chapter shows you a new way of storing data within a program using paired READ and DATA statements. This technique is applied in the MUSIC.BAS program that concludes the chapter.

MORE WAYS OF GETTING INPUT FROM THE KEYBOARD

The INPUT statement you have been using for keyboard input is a handy and flexible tool, but it has these two potential drawbacks:

- The user must remember to press ◄━┛ after typing in keyboard input.

- The INPUT statement cannot handle all the keys on a standard computer keyboard. To write programs that can respond to keys such as the cursor-control keys and the function keys, you will need to learn some additional programming methods.

In the sections that follow, you will learn how to handle these two programming concerns.

USING INPUT$

If you want your program to respond instantly to the touch of a key, you can use the INPUT$ function. When the computer encounters this function within a program statement, it waits for a specified number of characters from the keyboard, or reads a specified number of characters from a disk file, and then returns them as a character string to the program statement. In this chapter you'll learn how to use INPUT$ to get information from the keyboard. (You'll learn how to use INPUT$ with disk files in Chapter 11.) To use INPUT$ for keyboard input, you specify a number of keystrokes in parentheses. For example, this statement

```
UserInput$ = INPUT$(2)
```

causes the program to pause until two keys have been pressed and then assigns those two characters to the UserInput$ variable.

The sample program below prompts you to press a key and then waits for input. As soon as you touch a key, the program responds by assigning the returned value to the variable called **AnyKey$** and then printing that value.

```
CLS
PRINT "Press any key"
AnyKey$ = INPUT$(1)
PRINT "You pressed "; AnyKey$
```

When you run this program, notice that the key you press is not echoed to the screen automatically. It appears on screen here only because of the final PRINT statement. You may find it helpful to compare the program above to this similar one, which uses an INPUT statement:

```
CLS
INPUT "Press any key, then press Enter ", Anykey$
PRINT "You pressed "; Anykey$
```

Because an INPUT statement does echo the keyboard characters to the screen, the key you pressed will appear twice in the INPUT version of the program. When you want INPUT$ to echo characters to the screen, you can combine it with a PRINT statement as shown here:

```
X$ = INPUT$(1): PRINT X$
```

The INPUT$ function is a nice way of handling menu choices. It is used in this way in the MUSIC program at the end of this chapter.

USING INKEY$

An additional device for receiving input from the keyboard is the INKEY$ function. Unlike INPUT$, INKEY$ is used without an argument. INKEY$ reads a single value from the area of memory that stores values for the keystrokes that are pressed during program execution. If no character is waiting in this buffer, INKEY$ returns a null string to the program statement. INKEY$ is commonly used within a loop, which continues to operate until INKEY$ no longer returns the null string. This technique is demonstrated here.

```
CLS
PRINT "Press any key"
DO
   AnyKey$ = INKEY$
LOOP WHILE AnyKey$ = ""
PRINT "You pressed "; AnyKey$
```

Notice that no cursor appears on screen when INKEY$ is used to receive keyboard input.

WORKING WITH ASCII CODES

Many keys on a computer keyboard correspond directly with familiar letter, number, and character keys that are also part of a typewriter keyboard. But computer keyboards also include keys that are not represented by familiar characters. These include the Esc key, the function keys, and keystroke combinations using the Ctrl and Alt keys. In order to handle keyboard input that falls in this second category, you need to understand how to work with ASCII codes.

ASCII code tables are available in Appendix C of this book and also through Quick-BASIC's online table of contents.

Every character on a keyboard is stored in memory using a standard ASCII code value. ASCII codes are integer values between 0 and 255, which is the range of values that can be stored in a single byte of memory. Two functions, ASC and CHR$, enable you to work with ASCII code values for reading keyboard input and controlling screen output. The ASC function returns the ASCII code value of the first character of a string expression. For example, the following statement prints the number 90, which is the ASCII code value for an uppercase Z:

```
PRINT ASC("Z")
```

The inverse action is performed by the CHR$ function, which displays the character string that corresponds to a given ASCII code. This next statement uses the ASCII code value 90 to print an uppercase Z:

```
PRINT CHR$(90)
```

The 256 ASCII display characters include some that are not on your keyboard. You can use ASCII codes when you want to display these characters. For instance, the ASCII code for the Greek letter pi (π) is 227. The following statement displays this character on screen:

```
PRINT CHR$(227)
```

The ASCII.BAS program that you will create later in this chapter displays each of the available output characters.

When a key or keystroke is pressed, it is stored in memory with an ASCII code. The standard typewriter characters are all stored using a one-byte code. A second group of keystrokes is stored in memory using an extended, two-byte code. With this second group, the initial byte is always the null character (ASCII code 0), and the second byte contains an ASCII code number that identifies the character. Two-byte keys and key combinations include the cursor-control keys, the function keys, and keystroke combinations that use the Alt key.

The KEYCODE program shown in Figure 8.1 will help you understand how to use the INKEY\$ function to get a complete range of keyboard input, including keys that use two-byte identification codes. You can also use it as a reference tool to identify the codes that are used to identify various keystrokes. The program produces the following on-screen prompt:

Press any Key or Keystroke combination.

Following this prompt, INKEY\$ is used to receive keyboard input. The next statement reads as follows:

```
IF LEN(Choice$) = 1 THEN
```

The LEN function is used here to determine the length of the Choice\$ variable that has stored the keyboard input. This length will be either one or two bytes, depending on the keystroke or keystroke combination that was pressed. The block IF...END IF structure is used to give different output for one and two-byte codes.

```
REM KEYCODE.BAS
'Supplies ascii code for a key or keystroke combination
'INKEY$ is used to respond to keyboard input
'The LEN is used to identify (2-byte) codes
'The ASC function displays the ascii code for that key

CLS
PRINT "This program gives you information about the"
PRINT "ASCII codes used to store input from the keyboard."
PRINT
DO
  PRINT "Press any key or keystroke combination."
  DO
    Choice$ = INKEY$
  LOOP WHILE Choice$ = ""
  IF LEN(Choice$) = 1 THEN
      PRINT "Display character: "; Choice$
      PRINT "ASCII Code: "; ASC(Choice$)
  ELSEIF LEN(Choice$) = 2 THEN
      PRINT "This keystroke uses a two-byte code."
      PRINT "The first byte stores a null value."
      PRINT "ASCII code of second byte:  ";
      PRINT ASC(RIGHT$(Choice$, 1))
  END IF

  PRINT
  PRINT "Press any Key to Continue.  ESC to quit."
  PRINT
  Quit$ = INPUT$(1)
LOOP UNTIL ASC(Quit$) = 27
```

Figure 8.1: The KEYCODE program listing

If the keystroke uses a one-byte code, the program displays this code using this statement:

PRINT "ASCII Code: "; ASC(Choice$)

The ASC function used here returns the ASCII code for that key.

An example of a one-byte keystroke is an uppercase A. This gives the following output:

Display Character: A
ASCII Code: 65

Press the Esc key and you will see that it produces a special display character (a left-pointing arrow) and that its ASCII code value is 27. Output in this case looks like this:

Display Character: ←
ASCII Code: 27

If a keystroke using a two-byte code is used, the program prints the ASCII code of only the right-hand character of the two. This is accomplished in the following statement:

```
PRINT ASC(RIGHT$(Choice$,1))
```

You'll learn more about the RIGHT$ function in Chapter 10.

Try pressing the ↓ key in response to the prompt. This key uses a two-byte code and produces the following output:

```
This key uses a two-byte code.
The first byte stores a null value
The ASCII code of second byte:   80
```

Programs can use the differences between standard and extended code to respond differently to keystrokes that provide character information, such as letters and numbers, and those, such as the cursor-control keys, that allow the user to control input.

MORE WAYS OF CONTROLLING OUTPUT

The following sections show you some additional techniques you can use to control your program output. These include methods of controlling the color of text on the screen, the use of separate viewports to divide your screen into independent output areas, and ways of including sound in your program output. These techniques can help make your programs more useful as well as more fun.

THE COLOR STATEMENT

The COLOR statement is useful for both color and monochrome monitors. If you are working with a color monitor, you can use this statement to choose from a variety of different colors for the background color and text of your screen output. If you are working with a monochrome monitor, you can use this statement to highlight output by using reverse video or brighter text in some areas. The COLOR statement syntax is shown here.

```
COLOR ForegroundValue, BackGroundValue
```

 The online help screen for the COLOR statement includes a list of available colors and their number values.

The foreground value determines the color that will be used for text display, and the background value determines the background color of the screen. There are 8 possible background colors and 16 possible foreground colors. These are identified with numbers 0–7 for background and 0–15 for text. In addition, each of the text colors can appear in a blinking display. Blinking displays use numbers 16–31.

If you are working with a color monitor, you can use the following program to view all of the possible color combinations. The program uses nested FOR...NEXT loops to produce each of the possible pairs of values. Each pair of values is used in a COLOR statement to change the appearance of the screen. The background and foreground values are then displayed on screen using the color combination that results from this pair of values.

Using constants for color values (for example, CONST BLUE = 1, RED = 4) is a convenient way of working with colors.

```
REM COLOR.BAS
'Displays available on-screen color combinations
'Foreground (Fore) is text
'Background (Back) is screen color

CLS
PRINT "Color combinations available"
PRINT "Numbers are those used in the COLOR statement."
PRINT "COLOR (Foreground, Background)"
PRINT
FOR Fore = 0 TO 15
   FOR Back = 0 TO 7
      COLOR Fore, Back
      PRINT Fore; Back; TAB((Back + 1) * 10);
   NEXT Back
NEXT Fore
```

If you are working with a monochrome monitor, you can still use the COLOR statement to control the appearance of on-screen output. A monochrome monitor can produce ten different variations of text display. These are demonstrated in the next program, along with the pairs of values that produce each variation.

```
REM B&WCOLOR.BAS
'Video "color" displays
'for a monochrome monitor
```

```
CLS
COLOR 7, 0: PRINT "Normal = 7, 0"
COLOR 15, 0: PRINT "Bright = 15, 0"
COLOR 0, 7: PRINT "Reverse video = 0, 7"
COLOR 1, 0: PRINT "Underlined = 0, 1"
COLOR 9, 0: PRINT "Bright Underlined = 9, 0"
PRINT : PRINT : PRINT
COLOR 22, 0: PRINT "Blinking = 22, 0"
COLOR 16, 7: PRINT "Blinking Reverse Video = 16, 7"
COLOR 31, 0: PRINT "Blinking Bright = 31, 0"
COLOR 17, 0: PRINT "Blinking Underlined = 17, 0"
COLOR 25, 0: PRINT "Blinking Bright Underlined = 25, 0"
```

Effective color choices can make your programs easier to use by making the monitor screen easier to read.

THE VIEW PRINT STATEMENT

Another technique that can make a monitor screen easier to read is dividing it into separate regions or *viewports*. The VIEW PRINT statement is a convenient way of dividing the output screen into viewports. Using different viewports allows you to use different parts of your screen in different ways. For instance, you might want helpful instructions to remain constantly on display in one part of the screen, while a separate viewport is used to display changing program output. The VIEW PRINT statement syntax is shown here:

VIEW PRINT *TopValue* TO *BottomValue*

The two arguments define the top and bottom rows of a viewport. Once a VIEW PRINT statement has been executed, all subsequent program output is directed to the area within these two values, until the viewport is redefined with a new VIEW PRINT statement. Other parts of the screen remain unchanged. A CLS statement will clear only the output within the currently active viewport. Using the VIEW PRINT statement alone, with no arguments, resets the viewport to occupy the full screen.

The next program demonstrates the use of the VIEW PRINT statement. The first VIEW PRINT statement is used to define a viewport that occupies the first ten lines of the screen. A FOR..NEXT loop then displays numbers from 1 to 12. When all ten lines of the viewport have been filled, the number 1 scrolls out of view. In order to slow down the output so you can watch this process, the program uses a SLEEP statement. This statement causes program execution to pause for the number of seconds specified in the argument. After the 12 numbers have been displayed, a new viewport is defined, using the bottom of the screen. The PRINT statements that follow direct output to this new viewport without affecting the output that is already on screen.

```
CLS
VIEW PRINT 1 TO 10
FOR x = 1 TO 12
    PRINT x
    SLEEP 1
NEXT x

VIEW PRINT 15 TO 25
PRINT "VIEW PRINT sets boundaries for the viewport."
PRINT "The screen display outside these boundaries"
PRINT "remains unchanged."
```

THE ASCII.BAS PROGRAM

The ASCII.BAS program shown in Figure 8.2 combines several of the techniques you have learned so far. By using the statement PRINT CHR$(N), which sends the display character for the code value N to the screen, this program shows the character display for each of the 255 ASCII codes. A SELECT CASE structure is used to send special messages for some of the codes because using certain codes with PRINT CHR$ will change the position of output on screen, rather than simply displaying a character on screen. These special codes are useful within LPRINT statements, where they can be used to control the printer. For example, LPRINT CHR$(12) can be used to advance the printer to the top of a new page.

```
REM ASCII.BAS
'Displays the ASCII character codes

DECLARE SUB PrintReverse (Item$)

'Clear screen and display headings
CLS
LOCATE 1, 1: PRINT "ASCII code", "Character or other effect"

'Display instructions at bottom of screen, leaving heading on screen
VIEW PRINT 24 TO 25
PRINT "Press any key to continue. ";
PrintReverse "ESC"
PRINT " to stop."

'Set viewport so that instructions and headings remain on screen
VIEW PRINT 3 TO 23

'Display output for ASCII codes 1 - 255
FOR N = 1 TO 255
    'Display special messages for some codes
    SELECT CASE N
      CASE 7
         PRINT N, , "Bell sound"
         PRINT CHR$(N);
      CASE 10
         PRINT N, , "Line Forward"
      CASE 11
         PRINT N, , "Output to top of screen"
      CASE 12
         PRINT N, , "Advance to new page"
      CASE 13
         PRINT N, , "Carriage Return"
      'For all others, show onscreen character display using CHR$
      CASE ELSE
         PRINT N, CHR$(N)
    END SELECT

    'Pause output every twenty lines
    IF N MOD 20 = 0 THEN
        DO
           Anykey$ = INKEY$
        LOOP WHILE Anykey$ = ""
        'Exit if Esc key is pressed
        IF ASC(Anykey$) = 27 THEN EXIT FOR
    END IF
NEXT N

'Clear message at bottom of screen
VIEW PRINT 24 TO 25
CLS
'Display the item$ string using reverse video
SUB PrintReverse (Item$)
    COLOR 0, 7
    PRINT Item$;
    COLOR 7, 0
END SUB
```

Figure 8.2: The ASCII program listing

Viewports are used to create a heading at the top of the screen and instructions at the bottom of the screen that remain in place while different code values scroll through the center of the screen. The reverse video display, which provides accent in the instructions display, is accomplished with a COLOR statement in the PrintReverse procedure. This procedure displays a character string in reverse video and then resets the colors for normal display. The MOD statement in this program is used to produce a pause in the display after every 20 lines of output. At this point, the INKEY$ statement is used to receive keyboard input. Pressing the Esc key at this point will interrupt execution of the program. Pressing almost any other key continues the on-screen display; however, a few keystroke combinations override INKEY$. One of these exceptions is the PrtSc key; pressing this key will send the current screen display to the printer and will not cause program execution to resume.

HEARING THINGS

In addition to producing visual output, computers can also produce a range of sounds. You can use sounds to alert the person using a program to events as they occur during program execution, or simply to make a program more fun to use. Most computer games use sound, and the addition of sound can be a particularly nice touch if you are creating educational programs. The next two sections of this chapter will give you an introduction to two new statements, SOUND and PLAY, which can be used to produce a range of auditory results.

MAKING SOUNDS USING SOUND The SOUND statement produces sounds of a given pitch and duration. Pitch is determined by frequency, which is measured in cycles per second. Higher values for frequency produce higher pitches. QuickBASIC SOUND statements can accept integer frequencies between 37 and 32,767, but the actual range of pitches you can produce will be limited by your system's sound device. Duration is measured in "clock ticks." There are 18.2 clock ticks per second. The SOUND statement syntax is shown here.

SOUND *frequency,duration*

You can use the next sample program to get a feel for different frequencies and durations. The program prompts the user for values for frequency and duration and then generates a sound using those values.

```
CLS
PRINT "Use this program to explore the SOUND statement"

INPUT "Frequency (37–32767)"; Frequency
INPUT "Duration (0–65535)"; Duration
SOUND Frequency, Duration
```

By combining different SOUND statements in different ways, you can create a variety of different sounds, such as those created by this program.

```
'Rising tone
FOR n = 200 TO 2000 STEP 100
    SOUND n, 1
NEXT n

'Oscillating tones
FOR n = 1 TO 6
    SOUND 2000, 3
    SOUND 1500, 3
NEXT n

'Final note
SOUND 2000, 6
```

If you know the frequencies of musical notes (for example, A = 440), it is possible to use the SOUND statement to generate music. In the following section you will learn an additional music-making tool that is more closely tied to the way we think about music.

PLAYING MUSIC USING PLAY   The PLAY statement is used specifically for generating musical output. While the arguments in the SOUND statement are based on the physics of sound, the PLAY statement uses a notation that is based on music theory. Pitch is selected by using letter names (A-G) and octaves to chose notes. Duration of sound is measured using musical whole notes, half notes, quarter notes, etc.; and by using beats per minute to control the tempo of these notes.

Each PLAY statement is followed by a *command string* containing one or more codes used to set tone, duration, and tempo. A selection of these codes is summarized here.

A-G   These letters select notes in the current octave. Sharps and flats are indicated with + for sharp, and – for flat.

O*n*   Sets the current Octave. The range for *n* is 0–6. Octave one (O1) starts at middle C.

L*n*   Sets the length of a note. The range for *n* is 1–64. The longest note is a whole note, which is specified using L1. A half note (L2) is held for half as long. The shortest note (L64), is one sixty-fourth the length of a whole note.

T*n*   Sets tempo by indicating the number of quarter notes per minute. The range for *n* is 32–255, and the default is 120 quarter note beats per minute.

Any combination of the above symbols can be included in a PLAY statement command string. Settings for octave, note length, and tempo remain in place until changed. This example plays an ascending C major scale using half notes and the default tempo.

PLAY "O1 L2 CDEFGAB O2 C"

If this next example follows the previous one, it continues the ascending scale in octave two, but plays each note for only an eighth note duration.

PLAY "L8 CDEFGAB O3 C"

You can learn more about the PLAY command by using the online Help index to display the PLAY Help screen.

If you are musically inclined, with a little practice you can learn to convert written music to PLAY statement command strings as a way of including musical output in your programs.

STORING DATA VALUES WITHIN A PROGRAM LISTING

There may be occasions when you want your program to store lists of data values for reference purposes. These might be either string or numeric values. You can always use assignment statements to store such values, but a more convenient way is to include this information in list form in a special data section of the program.

USING READ AND DATA STATEMENTS

Two paired statements, READ and DATA, are useful when you want to store lists of data values for variables in your program. A DATA statement contains a list of one or more data values to be assigned to a variable or variables listed in a READ statement located elsewhere in the same program. Items in both READ and DATA statements are separated by commas. When the computer encounters a READ statement, it searches for a DATA statement and uses the values listed there to assign values to the variables listed in the READ statement. Each new variable in a READ statement list is assigned the next available value from the DATA list. If all the data in a DATA statement has been assigned to a variable, the program searches for additional DATA statements. DATA statements can be placed before or after the READ statement, but must be in the module-level code.

Use this program to see how READ and DATA statements work.

```
CLS
READ X, Y
READ Z
PRINT X, Y, Z

DATA 1
DATA 2,3
```

The output from this program shows the values that have been assigned to X, Y, and Z:

```
1          2          3
```

The first variable in the first READ statement, X, is set equal to 1, using the first value in the first DATA statement. Because this is the only value listed in the first DATA statement, the value for Y is read from the next DATA statement. When program execution continues to the second READ statement, the value of Z is set to 3, using the final available DATA value.

In this next program, the READ statement is placed within a program loop. Each time the READ statement is executed, it uses the next available DATA value. Notice that quotation marks are not necessary when string values are listed in a DATA statement.

```
CLS
PRINT "Number", "Name"
FOR M = 1 TO 12
   READ Month$
   PRINT M, Month$
NEXT M

DATA Jan, Feb, Mar, Apr, May, Jun
DATA Jul, Aug, Sep, Oct, Nov, Dec
```

The output of this program is a paired list of month numbers and names. The first few rows are shown here.

Number	Name
1	Jan
2	Feb
3	Mar
.	.
.	.
.	.

If a READ statement is encountered after all of the items in a program's DATA statements have already been used, program execution will be interrupted and an "Out of DATA" error message will be displayed. You can create this error by changing the FOR statement in the program above to read as follows:

```
FOR M = 1 TO 13
```

When the program tries to read in a thirteenth value for the variable named Month$, no new DATA values are available. The error message is displayed, and you are returned to the program code with the READ statement at which the error occurred highlighted. You can fix an error such as this by reducing the number of variables to be read, adding to the data available, or instructing the program to reread the DATA available starting again at the beginning of the list. The next section shows you how to accomplish this last option.

USING THE RESTORE STATEMENT

When you want your program to read data from the *beginning* of a list of values in a DATA statement regardless of any previous READ statements, you can use a RESTORE statement. When a READ statement is encountered after a RESTORE statement has been executed, assignment of values will return to the first value in the first DATA statement. Try this short program to see how RESTORE works.

```
CLS
READ J, K
RESTORE
READ L, M
PRINT J; K; L; M

DATA 1,2,3,4
```

The output is shown below. Because of the RESTORE statement, the value for L and M are read from the beginning of the DATA list.

```
1 2 1 2
```

Remove the RESTORE statement from the program, and the output will look like this.

```
1 2 3 4
```

The RESTORE statement can also be used when you have included more than one list of data in your program and you want to direct a READ statement to one particular list. You'll learn how to do this in the section that follows.

USING LINE IDENTIFIERS
WITH A RESTORE STATEMENT

If you want to include several different data lists in the same program, you need some way of controlling which list is used when a READ statement is encountered. It is possible to do this by identifying different data sections of your program using *line identifiers*. Any line in a BASIC statement can begin with a line identifier, which can be either a number or a character string. Character-string line identifiers must begin with a letter and end with a colon. You can label your data lists by using line identifiers. Each DATA statement can have its own identifier, or you can precede a group of DATA statements with a single line identifier. Once you have labeled DATA with a line identifier, you can direct a READ statement to the labeled data by including a line identifier as part of a RESTORE statement. When data is read into memory with a subsequent READ statement, the computer will begin its search for data at the line that was identified in the RESTORE statement. This technique is used in the next program to read even values into one list of variables and odd values into a second list.

```
CLS
RESTORE Odd
READ A, B
RESTORE Even
READ X, Y
PRINT A, B, X, Y

Even: DATA 2,4
Odd: DATA 1,3
```

The output of this program is shown here.

```
1              3              2              4
```

Because of the "RESTORE Odd" statement, the first READ statement uses the data that has been labeled with "Odd:", although this is not the first DATA statement. The second RESTORE directs the next READ statement to the data identified as "Even:". The MUSIC program that follows shows how this technique can be put to use in a programming application.

THE MUSIC PROGRAM

The MUSIC.BAS program is a short application that demonstrates many of the techniques introduced in this chapter. The module-level code for this program is shown in Figure 8.3 and the SUB procedures are shown in Figure 8.4. The program is menu driven, and offers the user the following four menu choices:

1. Amazing Grace
2. Where Oh Where (has my little dog gone?)
3. Use the keyboard to play a tune
4. Quit

```
REM MUSIC.BAS
'A menu generated, music-making program
DECLARE SUB Highlight (Item$)
DECLARE SUB Keyboard ()
DECLARE SUB ReadMusic ()

CLS
DO
    'Display Menu, using the Highlight procedure to highlight choices
    LOCATE 1, 1
    Highlight "THE MUSIC MAKER MENU"
    PRINT
    PRINT
    Highlight "1. ": PRINT "Amazing Grace"
    Highlight "2. ": PRINT "Where Oh Where (has my little dog gone)"
    Highlight "3. ": PRINT "Use the keyboard to play a tune"
    Highlight "4. ": PRINT "Quit"
    PRINT
    'Use INPUT$ to allow instant response to keyboard choice
    Choice$ = INPUT$(1)

    'Respond to choice
    SELECT CASE Choice$
      CASE "1"
          'Select data for using a line identifier
          RESTORE Grace:
          'Call the procedure which uses these data
          ReadMusic
      CASE "2"
          RESTORE DogGone:
          ReadMusic
      CASE "3"
          CLS
          Keyboard
    END SELECT
LOOP UNTIL Choice$ = "4"

'Data for PLAY statement command strings
Grace:
DATA "T90 O3 L4 D","L2 G L8 B G", "L2 B L4 A", "L2 G L4 E",
DATA "L2 D L4 D","L2 G L8 B G", "L2 B 14 A", "O4 L1 D", "stop"

DogGone:
DATA "T180 O3 L2 C O2 L4 A","L4 F E F", "G G E","L2 C O3 L4 C"
DATA "L2 D L4 C", "O2 B- A G", "O3 L1 C", "stop"
```

Figure 8.3: The MUSIC program module-level code

```
'--------------------- Highlight ------------------------
'Display an item using bright text
'-------------------------------------------------------
SUB Highlight (Item$)
    COLOR 15, 1
    PRINT Item$;
    COLOR 7, 1
END SUB


'---------------------- Keyboard ----------------------
'Play notes in response to keyboard choice
'-------------------------------------------------------
SUB Keyboard
    PRINT "Use the keys 1 - 8 to play a tune"
    PRINT "Press ";
    Highlight "Esc "
    PRINT "to return to the menu"
    DO
      'Get a keyboard choice
      DO
        NoteKey$ = INKEY$
      LOOP WHILE NoteKey$ = ""
      'Respond to choices by playing eighth note tones in Octave 2
      SELECT CASE NoteKey$
          CASE "1": PLAY "L8 O2 C"
          CASE "2": PLAY "L8 O2 D"
          CASE "3": PLAY "L8 O2 E"
          CASE "4": PLAY "L8 O2 F"
          CASE "5": PLAY "L8 O2 G"
          CASE "6": PLAY "L8 O2 A"
          CASE "7": PLAY "L8 O2 B "
          CASE "8": PLAY "L8 O3 C"
      END SELECT
      'Use Esc key to exit from loop
    LOOP UNTIL ASC(NoteKey$) = 27
    CLS
END SUB

'--------------------- ReadMusic -------------------------
'Use DATA values for PLAY command string to play a song
'-------------------------------------------------------
SUB ReadMusic
    DO
      READ Measure$
      IF Measure$ = "stop" THEN EXIT DO
      PLAY Measure$
    LOOP
END SUB
```

Figure 8.4: The MUSIC program SUB procedures

The first two choices play a few measures of the song whose title is shown. The ReadMusic procedure accomplishes this by reading command string values for a PLAY statement from one of two DATA lists. Each string value in the list corresponds to one measure of music. RESTORE statements placed within the SELECT CASE structure are used to select the correct data for each of the two songs.

The third option allows the user to play simple tunes using the first eight number keys on the keyboard. The Keyboard procedure that accomplishes this begins by displaying these instructions on screen:

Use the keys 1–8 to play a tune
Press **Esc** to return to the menu

The Keyboard procedure use the INKEY$ function to get keyboard input. The inner DO...LOOP contains this function, and causes program execution to pause until some key has been pressed. A SELECT CASE structure uses PLAY statements to produce different notes in the C scale to correspond to each of the 1–8 keys. All other keys, except the Esc key, produce no effect. When Esc is pressed, the conditions for exiting the outer DO...LOOP are met, and program execution continues on to the CLS statement, which is the last statement in this procedure.

The fourth menu choice is the quit option. The last statement in the loop that generates the menu reads as follows:

LOOP UNTIL Choice$ = "4"

As a result, choice 4 causes the program to exit from the loop. This is the last executable statement in the program.

The Highlight procedure defined in the program uses a COLOR statement to get brighter on-screen display of text. This procedure is used to highlight the numbers that correspond to the four menu choices in the program.

SUMMARY

A variety of tools for controlling program input and output were introduced in this chapter.

- **INPUT$**($n$) can be used to receive n characters from the keyboard. Using this function allows your program to respond instantly to keyboard input, without waiting for the ◄┘ key to be pressed.

- **INKEY$** is an additional way to receive keyboard input. This function can handle keys that use extended two-byte ASCII code values. Because this function can return a null value, it is commonly used within a loop that pauses during execution until some other value is entered.

- **COLOR**(*Foreground*, *Background*) can be used with both color and monochrome monitors to control the appearance of the monitor screen and the text display.

- **VIEW PRINT** *Top* **TO** *Bottom* limits the output to the monitor screen to those rows specified.

- **SOUND**(*Frequency*, *Duration*) produces sound of the specified frequency and duration.

- **PLAY** *commandstring* uses a command string containing special codes to produce musical output.

These commands can be used to make program output livelier and easier to understand.

READ and **DATA** statements were also introduced in this chapter. These paired statements can be used as a convenient way of incorporating lists of data into your program code. Where more than one list of data is included, you can use line identifiers in combination with **RESTORE** statements as a way of specifying which DATA statements should be used by a particular READ statement.

You have already been introduced to several examples of BASIC functions. Examples of functions used in this chapter include INPUT$, INKEY$, LEN, CHR$, and ASC. In Chapter 9 you will learn what makes functions different from other kinds of programming tools and learn more about using functions in your programs.

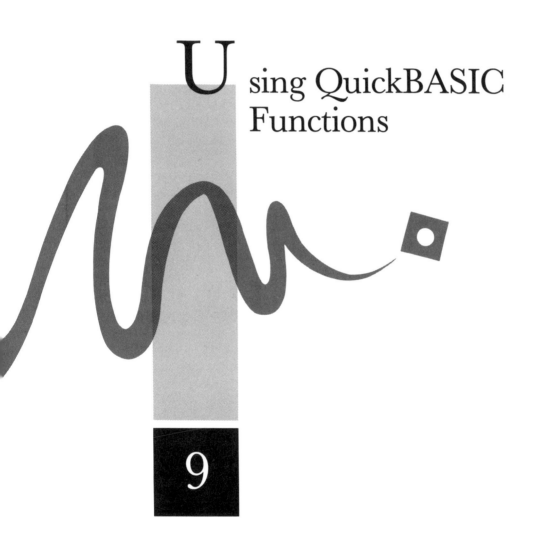

Using QuickBASIC Functions

9

CHAPTER 9

THE KEYWORDS THAT MAKE UP THE QUICKBASIC programming language can be divided into two categories, statements and functions. Statements perform some specific task, but functions perform a task and then *return a value* to the program. When a program line that contains a function is executed, the function expression is replaced by the returned value. In this chapter you will learn more about the functions that are a built-in part of the Quick-BASIC programming language, and you will also learn how to create your own, user-defined functions.

The first group of functions covered here are designed to help you work with string expressions. The short programming application FILTER.BAS demonstrates the use of several string-processing functions. Next, you will learn two ways of creating your own functions: DEF FN statements and FUNCTION procedures. The sample application FILTERFN incorporates user-defined functions in a modified version of the FILTER program. You can use these two programs to compare FUNCTION and SUB procedures.

The BASIC programming language also includes built-in numeric functions, many of which correspond directly to mathematical functions you may already be familiar with from algebra or trigonometry. These numeric functions are summarized briefly in the next section of this chapter.

In the last part of the chapter, you will learn how to introduce random values into a program using the RND function. The final program in this chapter, MULTIPLY.BAS, uses this function and several string-processing functions in a teaching application.

UNDERSTANDING THE FUNCTION OF A FUNCTION

You can picture functions as data processing "machines." Each machine is provided with a list of values, which are the raw materials the machine works with. These raw materials are processed according to the rules that define the function, and a single finished product emerges from the machine. In programming terms, the raw materials are the arguments of the function, and the finished product is the returned value. Figure 9.1 is a diagram of five different function "machines." Each diagram provides the name of a function and an example of what it does. Notice that function arguments can be either single numeric or string values, or can include any combination of one or more input values. Each set of arguments produces exactly one returned value, and this returned value can also be either a numeric or a string value. BASIC functions that return string values are identified with a dollar sign at the end of the function name. The first four functions shown in Figure 9.1 are part of the BASIC language. The last diagram suggests a possible user-defined function.

Every function expression must be incorporated into a program statement. During execution of that statement, the computer uses the returned value of the function expression as it would use any other value. The statement

    PRINT LEN("Gentlemen")

has the same effect as

    PRINT 9

because the number 9 is the value returned by the function expression LEN("Gentlemen").

QuickBASIC provides a large variety of functions. Although you are unlikely to use them all, it is useful to have an overall sense of what functions are available. The next sections of this chapter provide you with a brief introduction to many of the most commonly used functions.

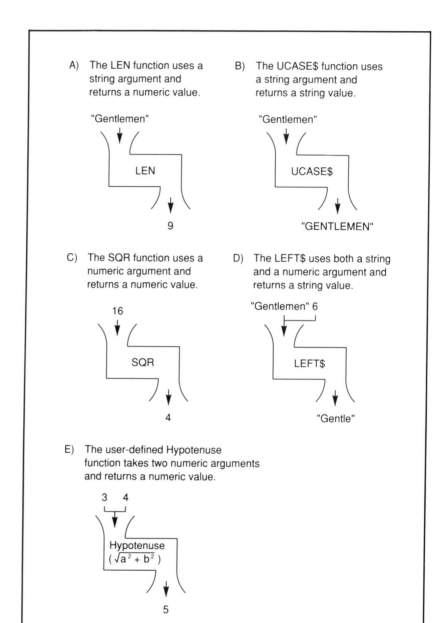

A) The LEN function uses a string argument and returns a numeric value.

"Gentlemen"

LEN

9

B) The UCASE$ function uses a string argument and returns a string value.

"Gentlemen"

UCASE$

"GENTLEMEN"

C) The SQR function uses a numeric argument and returns a numeric value.

16

SQR

4

D) The LEFT$ uses both a string and a numeric argument and returns a string value.

"Gentlemen" 6

LEFT$

"Gentle"

E) The user-defined Hypotenuse function takes two numeric arguments and returns a numeric value.

3   4

Hypotenuse
$(\sqrt{a^2 + b^2})$

5

Figure 9.1: Picturing the function of five functions

USING FUNCTIONS IN STRING PROCESSING

String-processing functions allow you to work with string values. As you study programming, you're likely to be surprised at the broad range of ways that you discover to apply these techniques. String-processing functions are introduced in the next sections of this chapter.

CONVERTING BETWEEN NUMBERS AND STRINGS

Two BASIC functions, VAL and STR$, allow you to convert numbers back and forth from numeric to string form. Before learning these functions, study the sample program shown below. In this program, the DATA values 3 and 4 are read first into the numeric variables A and B and then into the string variables A$ and B$. By adding the two values as numbers and then as string variables, the program illustrates an important difference between these two kinds of values.

```
CLS
READ A, B
RESTORE
READ A$, B$
PRINT A + B, A$ + B$
DATA 3, 4
```

The output of this program is shown here:

```
7               34
```

When two single-precision numbers, 3 and 4, are added, the result is another single-precision number, 7. However, adding the two one-byte string variables, ''3'' and ''4'', results in the two-byte string, ''34.'' Because string values and numeric values behave differently, it is important to be able to convert data back and forth between the two. The VAL and STR$ functions described here accomplish this conversion.

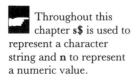 Throughout this chapter **s$** is used to represent a character string and **n** to represent a numeric value.

VAL(*s$*)   VAL takes a string argument and returns the numeric value represented by the string.

**STR$**(*n*)   STR$ takes a numeric argument and returns the string of characters used to represent that number.

Add the line

```
PRINT STR$(A) + STR$(B), VAL(A$) + VAL(B$)
```

to the sample program in order to demonstrate the effect of these two functions.

VAL is useful when you want to use INKEY$, INPUT$, or LINE INPUT to receive numeric input because each of these requires the use of string values. STR$ is useful when you want to do string processing with numeric values.

SEARCHING A STRING

The INSTR function is a string processing function that searches a string for specified characters. This function requires two string arguments—the string to be searched and the characters you are searching for. The value returned by the INSTR function is a numeric value that corresponds to the position of the first occurrence of the searched-for characters. An optional numeric argument allows you to specify the starting position for the search. Here is the INSTR function syntax.

    INSTR ([*StartSearch*,] *LookInString$*, *LookForString$*)

The sample program below suggests how INSTR can be used to determine if a valid menu option has been chosen. The program displays the abbreviated menu shown here.

    Press a highlighted character to select
    1. First Choice
    2. Second Choice

If you press a valid choice, the program immediately exits the menu display loop and displays the choice you made on screen. If you press any other character, the program responds with a BEEP and returns to the start of the loop to await a more suitable choice. The program tests for reasonable choices by defining a string that includes all the valid keystrokes and searching this string for the keyboard character you pressed, as shown here.

```
IF INSTR("1Ff2Ss", Choice$) = 0 THEN BEEP ELSE EXIT DO
```

Here is the complete program:

```
DO
    'Display Menu with highlighted letters and numbers
    CLS
    PRINT "Press a highlighted character."
    COLOR 15, 0: PRINT "1. F";
    COLOR 7, 0: PRINT "irst Choice"
    COLOR 15, 0: PRINT "2. S";
    COLOR 7, 0: PRINT "econd Choice"

    'Get a choice
    Choice$ = INPUT$(1)
    'Check to see if choice was valid
    IF INSTR("1Ff2Ss", Choice$) = 0 THEN BEEP ELSE EXIT
    DO LOOP

    PRINT
    PRINT "You selected "; Choice$
```

An additional application of the INSTR function is shown in the FILTER and FILTERFN programs later in this chapter.

SELECTING PORTIONS OF A STRING

Three BASIC string-processing functions—LEFT$, RIGHT$, and MID$—allow you to select particular portions of a string of characters. The action of these three functions is summarized below.

SYNTAX	*EFFECT*
LEFT$($s\$$, n)	Returns n characters from the leftmost portion of the $s\$$ string.

RIGHT$(*s$*, *n*)   Returns *n* characters from the
rightmost portion of the *s$* string.

MID$(*s$*, *n*, [*length*])   Starting at position *n*, returns the
number of characters specified by the
length. If no length is given, MID$
returns all the characters from *n* to the
end of the string.

Sample expressions using each of these functions are shown here
along with the string that is returned by each expression.

EXPRESSION	*RETURNED STRING*
LEFT$("Good Morning!", 4)	Good
RIGHT$("Good Morning!", 1)	!
MID$("Good Morning!", 6, 7)	Morning

The sample below calculates a person's age, based on year of
birth. The RIGHT$ function is used to trim the year from the cur-
rent date and the birth date. The current operating-system date is
supplied by using the DATE$ function, at which point the following
prompt appears on screen.

When were you born?

The user can supply a birth date in any form that ends with the year
of birth. All of these birth dates will give meaningful results:

March 1, 1947
'47
3/1/47

Once the year has been trimmed from each of the dates, the VAL
function is used to convert the years to numeric values so that they
can be used in calculation.

Here is the program listing:

```
'Get today's date and birth date
CLS
```

```
Today$ = DATE$
PRINT "When were you born? ";
LINE INPUT BirthDate$

'Trim off years
PresentYear$ = RIGHT$(Today$, 2)
BirthYear$ = RIGHT$(BirthDate$, 2)

'Calculate age and display results
Age = VAL(PresentYear$) – VAL(BirthYear$)
PRINT "After this year's birthday you are"; Age
```

ADDITIONAL STRING FUNCTIONS

It is possible to convert strings of characters to either uppercase or lowercase letters using the UCASE$ and LCASE$ functions. These functions act only on letters of the alphabet; numbers and other keyboard characters are not affected. The SPACE$ function returns a specified number of blank spaces. These functions are summarized here.

SYNTAX	*EFFECT*
UCASE$(s$)	Converts all of the letters in string s$ to uppercase letters.
LCASE$(s$)	Converts all of the letters in string s$ to lowercase letters.
SPACE$(n)	Returns n blank spaces.

Sample expressions using each of these functions are shown here along with the string that is returned by each expression.

EXPRESSION	*RETURNED STRING*
UCASE$("QuickBASIC 4.5")	QUICKBASIC 4.5
LCASE$("QuickBASIC 4.5")	quickbasic 4.5
"X" + SPACE$(2) + "X"	X X

In the sample shown below, UCASE$ and LCASE$ are used with LEFT$ and MID$ to produce a standardized display of an individual's first name in which only the first letter is uppercase.

```
CLS
INPUT "What is your first name"; F$
F$ = UCASE$(LEFT$(F$, 1)) + LCASE$(MID$(F$, 2))
PRINT "Your string-processed name is "; F$
```

A sample output screen produced by this program is shown here:

```
What is your first name? REBECCA
Your string-processed name is Rebecca
```

THE FILTER PROGRAM

String-processing functions can be important and useful tools when you are designing program input and output. You have seen in earlier programming examples that INPUT statements using numeric variables require the values to be entered without commas. This requirement can easily lead to confusion when a user is entering large values. The NumberFilter SUB procedure in the FILTER program demonstrates how string-processing functions can be used to allow a user to enter numbers with or without extra symbols such as commas and dollar signs. The FILTER program is shown in Figure 9.2.

The programs prompts the user as follows:

```
Type in two numbers (with or without commas)
```

LINE INPUT statements are used in order to allow for the possibility of commas in the input string. The two values are added together first as strings, and the result is displayed. Then the NumberFilter procedure is called in order to convert the strings to numeric form. These numeric values are then added, and the new result is also displayed.

A sample output screen is shown here:

```
Type in two numbers (with or without commas)
--> $11,111
--> $22,222
```

USING QUICKBASIC FUNCTIONS 213

```
REM FILTER.BAS
'Demonstrates string processing

DECLARE SUB NumberFilter (StringValue$, NumericValue!)
'Input two numbers as string values
CLS
PRINT "Type in two numbers (with or without commas)"
LINE INPUT "--> ", FirstValue$
LINE INPUT "--> ", SecondValue$

'Add the two string values
PRINT "Add the two strings --> ";
PRINT FirstValue$ + SecondValue$

'Filter out commas, etc. and convert to numeric values
CALL NumberFilter(FirstValue$, FirstValue)
CALL NumberFilter(SecondValue$, SecondValue)

'Add the two numeric values
PRINT "Add the two numbers -->";
PRINT FirstValue + SecondValue

'------------------- NumberFilter ---------------------
'Filters unwanted characters out of a number string and
'converts the 'cleaned up' string to a numeric value
'------------------------------------------------------
SUB NumberFilter (StringValue$, NumericValue)
  CleanString$ = ""
  StringLength = LEN(StringValue$)
  Valid$ = "0123456789.+-"

  'Check each character in the string to see if it is
  'a valid numeric character, and if it is, add it to
  'the CleanString$ variable.
  FOR N% = 1 TO StringLength
    Char$ = MID$(StringValue$, N%, 1)
    IF INSTR(Valid$, Char$) > 0 THEN
      CleanString$ = CleanString$ + Char$
    END IF
  NEXT N%

  'Convert the cleaned up string to a numeric value
  NumericValue = VAL(CleanString$)
END SUB
```

Figure 9.2: The FILTER program listing

Add the two strings --> $11,111$22,222
Add the two numbers --> 33333

The NumberFilter procedure defines a Valid$ string, which includes all valid numeric symbols. INSTR is used to test the characters in the input string one at a time and see if they are found in the Valid$ string. If a character is found to be a valid numeric symbol, it is added to the variable called CleanString$. Once each character has been tested, the CleanString$ variable is converted to a numeric value using the VAL function.

The numeric value created at the end of the NumberFilter function is passed back to module-level code by including it in the parameter list. This is one way to return a value to the main body of a program from a procedure. In the next sections of this chapter you will learn how to create your own functions that return values in the same manner as the built-in QuickBASIC functions. You will then learn how you can modify the FILTER program to return a numeric value in this new way.

USER-DEFINED FUNCTIONS

In addition to working with QuickBASIC's built-in functions, you have the option of creating your own, user-defined, functions. A user-defined function performs a set of tasks that you have defined somewhere in your program and then returns a value to the program. Each user-defined function is named using the same rules you use for naming variables. This includes the use of type-declaration characters ($, %, &, !, #) to determine the data-type of the returned value.

There are two ways of defining functions in a QuickBASIC program. One way is with DEF FN statements, which are incorporated directly into the main body of your program. A newer and more flexible addition to BASIC programming is the FUNCTION procedure, which is used to define functions in a manner similar to the definition of SUB procedures.

In the next sections of this chapter, you'll see several ways to define the same function. As an example, we will use the Hypotenuse function shown in Figure 9.1. This function uses the Pythagorean theorem familiar to most high-school algebra students to calculate the length of the hypotenuse of a right triangle, given the length of each of the other two sides.

The equation is shown below.

$$C = \sqrt{A^2 + B^2}$$

In our programming examples, A and B will be provided as arguments, and C will be the returned value.

USING DEF FN STATEMENTS

When you define a statement with DEF FN, you must be sure to define the function before you use it. DEF FN function definitions can be accomplished in a single-line or a block form. The syntax for a single-line DEF FN statement is shown here.

DEF FN*name* [(*Parameter1, Parameter2, ...*)] = *expression*

The FN of the DEF FN statement becomes part of the function name. Once a function has been defined in this way, you can use the function by including *FNname* in your program statements.

The sample below uses this syntax to define the FNHypotenuse function. The program uses this function to calculate and print the length of the hypotenuse of a right triangle when the other two sides are equal to 3 and 4.

```
'Define the function using A & B as parameters
DEF FNHypotenuse (A, B) = SQR(A ^ 2 + B ^ 2)
CLS
'Invoke the function using 3 & 4 as arguments
PRINT FNHypotenuse(3, 4)
```

A block form of the DEF FN statement is also available. The block syntax of a DEF FN statement is shown here:

DEF FN [(*Parameter1,Parameter2, ...*)]

```
'Program statements
.
FNname = expression
.
.
END DEF
```

Within the block of program statements that define the function, you must include a line that assigns a value to the function name. This is the value that will be returned by the function. Rewriting the Hypotenuse function in block form, the sample program above can be modified to read as follows: (The output of the two programs is identical.)

```
'Define the function using A & B as parameters
DEF FNHypotenuse (A, B)
   FNHypotenuse = SQR(A ^ 2 + B ^ 2)
```

```
END DEF
CLS
'Invoke the function using 3 & 4 as arguments
PRINT FNHypotenuse(3, 4)
```

Although block DEF FN structures can be used to define longer functions, the use of FUNCTION procedures, as described in the next section, is a more straightforward way to accomplish the same end.

DEFINING FUNCTION PROCEDURES

Displaying and altering FUNCTION procedures in the QuickBASIC environment is like working with SUB procedures. These techniques were covered in Chapter 7.

FUNCTION procedures allow you to define functions with a greater degree of flexibility and control than is afforded by DEF FN statements. A FUNCTION procedure is like a SUB procedure: You define it in a FUNCTION...END FUNCTION structure that is displayed independently on screen. FUNCTION procedures are arranged alphabetically along with SUB procedures at the end of your program. DECLARE FUNCTION statements are generated automatically when you save your program. Functions names defined in FUNCTION procedures do not include the FN prefix.

Like SUB procedures, FUNCTION procedures use local variables by default. Sharing values of variables between FUNCTION procedures and module-level code can be handled in the same way as with SUB procedures. These techniques were discussed in Chapter 7. Unlike SUB procedures, FUNCTION procedures return a value and are used within an expression in the same manner as built-in BASIC functions. The syntax of a FUNCTION definition is shown here. The value of the expression set equal to the *FunctionName* will be the value returned by the function when it is used in a program statement.

```
FUNCTION FunctionName [(Parameterlist)] [STATIC]
    .
    Program statements
    .
    FunctionName = expression
    .
    .
END FUNCTION
```

The sample program shown here uses a FUNCTION procedure to calculate the length of the hypotenuse of the same right triangle with legs equal to 3 and 4 that was used in the previous section.

```
CLS
PRINT Hypotenuse(3, 4)

'Calculate the Hypotenuse
'Parameters A & B are the lengths of the two legs
FUNCTION Hypotenuse (A, B)
   Hypotenuse = SQR(A ^ 2 + B ^ 2)
END FUNCTION
```

No data suffixes have been added in this example, so each of the values in this program is set as a single-precision value. If you save the program, the QuickBASIC editor will automatically generate the following declaration statement reflecting this fact:

```
DECLARE FUNCTION Hypotenuse! (A!, B!)
```

THE FILTERFN PROGRAM

In the FILTER program listed in Figure 9.2, a SUB procedure was used in order to remove extraneous characters from numeric input. The resulting numeric value was made available to the main body of that program by including it in the SUB procedure parameter list. By using a FUNCTION procedure to accomplish this same task, you can make the resulting value available to the program's main module more directly by defining this value as the function's returned value. The FILTERFN program shown in Figure 9.3 performs exactly the same tasks as the FILTER program, but uses a FUNCTION procedure rather than a SUB.

Study these two programs in order to understand how to work with QuickBASIC's two different kinds of procedures. As you can see from these examples, it is often possible to accomplish the same task in two different ways. Some procedures—those that accomplish a task with no exchange of data values—require the use of a SUB procedure. Other tasks, such as the number filtering procedure, lend themselves naturally to the use of a FUNCTION procedure.

```
REM FILTERFN.BAS
'Demonstrates string processing with a user-defined function

DECLARE FUNCTION NumberFilter (StringValue$)

'Input two numbers as string values
CLS
PRINT "Type in two numbers (with or without commas)"
LINE INPUT "--> ", FirstValue$
LINE INPUT "--> ", SecondValue$

'Add the two string values
PRINT "Add the two strings --> ";
PRINT FirstValue$ + SecondValue$

'Convert strings to numeric values and add the results
PRINT "Add the two numbers -->";
PRINT NumberFilter(FirstValue$) + NumberFilter(SecondValue$)

'-------------------- NumberFilter ---------------------
'Filters unwanted characters out of a number string and
'returns a numeric value
'-------------------------------------------------------
FUNCTION NumberFilter (StringValue$)
  CleanString$ = ""
  StringLength = LEN(StringValue$)
  Valid$ = "0123456789.+-"

  'Check each character in the string to see if it is
  'a valid numeric character, and if it is, add it to
  'the CleanString$ variable.
  FOR N% = 1 TO StringLength
    Char$ = MID$(StringValue$, N%, 1)
    IF INSTR(Valid$, Char$) > 0 THEN
      CleanString$ = CleanString$ + Char$
    END IF
  NEXT N%

  'Return the numeric value of the cleaned up string
  NumberFilter = VAL(CleanString$)
END FUNCTION
```

Figure 9.3: The FILTERFN program listing

USING MATHEMATICAL FUNCTIONS

In addition to the built-in string-processing functions you learned in the first sections of this chapter, QuickBASIC includes many mathematical functions. These are divided into four categories here: (1) Arithmetic functions include a mix of familiar algebraic functions; (2) integer functions provide three different ways of converting numeric values to integers; (3) trigonometric and (4) logarithmic functions correspond directly to the functions used in these two fields of mathematics. The usefulness of the logarithmic and trigonometric functions will depend entirely on your programming applications.

You may want to skip these sections unless you have a specific need for them. The arithmetic and integer functions, on the other hand, are generally useful, and a quick review of them will let you know what sorts of tasks they can accomplish.

ARITHMETIC FUNCTIONS

Each of the built-in numeric functions takes a single numeric expression as an argument and then returns a single numeric value. QuickBASIC's arithmetic functions are summarized here. They are demonstrated in the sample programs that follow.

SYNTAX	*EFFECT*
SQR(n)	Returns a value equal to the square root of n. The value of n cannot be a negative number.
ABS(n)	Returns a value equal to the absolute value of n. (If $n \geq 0$ then ABS(n) = n. If n < 0 then ABS(n) = $-n$.)
SGN(n)	Returns one of three values, depending on the sign of n. If n is positive, then SGN(n) = $+1$. If n is zero, then SGN = 0. If n is negative, then SGN(n) = -1.

The program below uses SGN to test for negative values before using an expression as an argument in the SQR function.

```
CLS
INPUT "Enter a number ", N
IF SGN(N) = - 1 THEN
   PRINT "That is a negative number."
   PRINT "No real square root value exists."
ELSE
   PRINT "The square root of that number is";
   PRINT SQR(N)
END IF
```

Two sample output screens are shown here:

Enter a number − 5
That is a negative number.
No real square root value exists.

Enter a number 25
The square root of that number is 5

The DISTANCE program uses both SQR and ABS in order to calculate the vertical, horizontal, and diagonal distances between two points on a coordinate plane. The two points are identified using standard (x,y) coordinates, where x represents the horizontal position of a point with respect to the origin (0, 0) and y represents the same point's vertical position. The program listing is given in Figure 9.4.

```
REM DISTANCE.BAS
'Calculates the distance between two points on a coordinate plane

'Get values for (x1,y1) and (x2,y2)
CLS
PRINT "Enter coordinates as x, y"
INPUT "First Point ", x1, y1
INPUT "Second Point ", x2, y2

'Use ABS to calculate vertical and horizontal distances
XDist = ABS(x1 - x2)
YDist = ABS(y1 - y2)

'Use SQR to calculate diagonal distance
DiagDist = SQR(XDist ^ 2 + YDist ^ 2)

'Display Results
PRINT "Horizontal Distance = "; XDist
PRINT "Vertical Distance = "; YDist
PRINT "Diagonal Distance = "; DiagDist
```

Figure 9.4: The DISTANCE program listing

A sample output screen produced by this program is shown here:

Enter coordinates as x, y
First Point − 2,3
Second Point 4, − 6
Horizontal Distance = 6
Vertical Distance = 9
Diagonal Distance = 10.81665

THE INTEGER FUNCTIONS

Each of the three QuickBASIC integer functions converts a numeric value to an integer in a different way. The actions of these three functions are summarized here.

SYNTAX	*EFFECT*
CINT(n)	Rounds n to the nearest integer value.
FIX(n)	Removes any fractional part of n.
INT(n)	Returns the largest integer less than or equal to n.

This program demonstrates the effect of these three functions.

```
CLS
PRINT "N", "CINT(N)", "FIX(N)", "INT(N)"
PRINT
FOR I% = 1 TO 6
   READ N
   PRINT N, CINT(N), FIX(N), INT(N)
NEXT I%

DATA – 1.6, – 1.3, – 0.6,0.6,1.3,1.6
```

The program gives the following output:

N	CINT(N)	FIX(N)	INT(N)
– 1.6	– 2	– 1	– 2
– 1.3	– 1	– 1	– 2
– .6	– 1	0	– 1
.6	1	0	0
1.3	1	1	1
1.6	2	1	1

TRIGONOMETRIC FUNCTIONS

BASIC provides four built-in trigonometric functions that calculate sine (SIN), cosine (COS), tangent (TAN), and arctangent (ATN). Each of these four functions uses radians for the measurement of an angle. Radians describe the size of an angle by using a measure equal to the length of the arc cut off by that angle in a circle whose radius is equal to one. An angle equal to $360°$ is equal to 2π radians. To convert an angle measured in degrees and minutes to its equivalent value in radians, use this formula:

```
Radians = (3.141593/180)*(Deg + Min/60)
```

The sample program shown here uses the trigonometric functions to create a table of trigonometric values for whole number degree measurements from 1 to 10.

```
CONST PI = 3.141593  'Define pi as a constant

CLS
PRINT "Degrees", "Sin", "Cos", "Tan": PRINT

FOR Degree = 1 TO 10
   Radian = PI / 180 * Degree
   PRINT Degree,
   PRINT USING "#.####"; SIN(Radian); SPC(8);
   PRINT USING "#.####"; COS(Radian); SPC(8);
   PRINT USING "#.####"; TAN(Radian)
NEXT Degree
```

The arctangent function(ATN) is the inverse of the TAN function. ATN returns the radian measure of the angle whose tangent is given in the argument. The relationship between ATN and TAN is shown by these two program lines,

```
PRINT TAN(1)
PRINT ATN(1.557408)
```

which produce the following output:

```
1.557408
1
```

In the first line, the angle whose measure is equal to one radian has a tangent value equal to 1.557408. The second line shows that the measure of the angle whose tangent is equal to 1.557408 is one radian.

LOGARITHMIC FUNCTIONS

QuickBASIC includes two logarithmic functions, the natural logarithm (LOG) and the exponential function (EXP). Logarithms are the inverse of exponential functions. The two expressions, $y = \log_a x$ and $x = a^y$ are equivalent. The value of a in the first equation is known as the base of the logarithmic function. The QuickBASIC LOG function calculates the natural logarithm, which uses the constant *e* (which is approximately equal to 2.718282) as its base. The EXP function raises this same constant to a given power. These two functions are summarized here.

SYNTAX   *EFFECT*

LOG(n)   Calculates $\log_e(n)$, also commonly written as $\ln(n)$.

EXP(n)   Calculates e^n.

QuickBASIC has no built-in function for calculating base-10 logarithms, also known as *common* logarithms. You can calculate common logarithms to single-precision accuracy with the following function:

```
FUNCTION Log10(x)
   Log10 = LOG(x) / LOG (10)
END FUNCTION
```

The sample program below demonstrates the relationship between logarithmic and exponential functions using both common and natural logarithms.

```
DECLARE FUNCTION Log10! (x!)
CONST e = 2.718282

CLS
PRINT "ln(e)", "e^(ln(e))", "Log(10)", "10^(Log(10))"
PRINT LOG(e),
PRINT EXP(LOG(e)),
PRINT Log10(10),
PRINT 10 ^ Log10(10)

FUNCTION Log10 (x)
   Log10 = LOG(x) / LOG(10)
END FUNCTION
```

The output of this program is shown here:

ln(e)	e^(ln(e))	Log(10)	10^(Log(10))
1	2.718282	1	10

GENERATING RANDOM NUMBERS

The RND function gives you the ability to generate numbers that are essentially random. This technique is an integral part of most game programs and can also be used to generate long lists of random data in order to test the speed and effectiveness of practical programs designed to handle large amounts of data. By generating random data, you can test these programs without having to provide hundreds or thousands of items of actual data. The RND function requires no argument. Each time it is called, it will return a different number between 0 and 1. It is used in this sample program, which generates a row of ten random numbers.

```
FOR n% = 1 TO 10
  PRINT USING "#.####"; RND; SPC(2);
NEXT n%
PRINT
```

If you run this program several times, you will see that the numbers generated each time are identical. To get numbers that are different each time you run a program, you must initialize (or *reseed*) the random number generator by using the RANDOMIZE statement. This statement uses a numeric argument to initialize the random number generator. The argument can be any integer value, and each different argument results in a different sequence of random numbers when the RND function is called. The TIMER function, which returns the number of seconds that have elapsed since midnight, is frequently used as a way of ensuring a different sequence of random numbers each time you run a program.

Modify the program above by inserting this statement at the beginning:

```
RANDOMIZE TIMER
```

With this change, the program will generate a new list of numbers each time it is run.

The RND function is often used to generate numbers that are not in the range of values between 0 and 1. By multiplying the randomly generated decimal fraction by 10 and then selecting only the integer part of the result, this expression generates numbers between 0 and 9:

```
INT(RND * 10)
```

To generate numbers from 1 to 10, you could modify the statement above as shown here:

```
INT(RND * 10) + 1
```

The easiest way to generate random integer values within a given range is to use the function definition shown below. The parameters *Low* and *High* correspond to the low and high values of your desired range.

```
FUNCTION RandomNumber (Low, High)
  RandomNumber = INT(RND * (High – Low + 1)) + Low
END FUNCTION
```

The MULTIPLY program in the next section employs a user-defined function like this one in order to generate numbers between 0 and 10. These values are used to create flashcard-like problems to assist a student with basic multiplication facts.

THE MULTIPLY PROGRAM

The MULTIPLY program is an example of computer-assisted instruction. It provides drill in multiplication using numbers between zero and ten. Although no computer can replace a caring teacher, computers have a degree of patience few human tutors can manage. Computers are suited for some educational tasks because no matter how many incorrect answers a student comes up with, a computer never displays one whit of exasperation. The module-level code of the program is shown in Figure 9.5.

```
REM MULTIPLY.BAS
'A multiplication flashcard program

DEFINT A-Z   'Select integers as default data type

'Procedure declarations
DECLARE SUB DisplayResults ()
DECLARE SUB Good ()
DECLARE FUNCTION RandNum% (Low%, High%)
DECLARE SUB Oops ()
DECLARE SUB Multiplication ()


'Declare and define gobal variables
COMMON SHARED Correct, Incorrect
COMMON SHARED Smile$, Esc$, SpaceBar$
Smile$ = CHR$(2): Esc$ = CHR$(27): SpaceBar$ = CHR$(32)

'Initialize random number generator and clear screen
RANDOMIZE TIMER
CLS

'Wait for instructions
DO
   VIEW PRINT 23 TO 25
   LOCATE 23, 1
   PRINT "Press the Spacebar to Start"
   PRINT "Press Esc to Stop"
   Choice$ = INPUT$(1)
   IF Choice$ = Esc$ THEN EXIT DO
   IF Choice$ = SpaceBar$ THEN Multiplication
LOOP
```

Figure 9.5: The MULTIPLY program module-level code

The core of the program is the Multiplication procedure. This procedure calls the user-defined RandNum function to generate two numbers from one to ten. These two procedures are shown in Figure 9.6. The user is asked for the product of these two numbers. String-processing functions are used in order to allow the user to input answers without pressing ◄┘ after each answer. (A disadvantage of the input procedure used here is that digits cannot be altered once a key has been pressed.) The student answer is compared against the correct answer.

If the answer is correct, the *Good* procedure is called. This procedure produces ascending tones that get higher with each correct answer. The global variable **Correct** is used to keep track of the number of correct answers. The *Good* procedure is shown in Figure 9.7. If the answer is incorrect, the correct answer is displayed on screen and the *Oops* procedure shown in Figure 9.8 is used to produce a descending tone.

DEFINT A-Z statements not shown in Figures 9.6 through 9.9 will be generated automatically as you add procedures to the MULTIPLY program.

```
'-----------------------Multiplication----------------------
'Display multiplication flashcards and respond to user input
'----------------------------------------------------------
SUB Multiplication
   VIEW PRINT: CLS                    'Clear the entire screen
   Correct = 0                        'Initialize variables
   Incorrect = 0

  FOR n = 1 TO 10
     'Create and display a multiplication problem
     X = RandNum(0, 10)    'Get random numbers
     Y = RandNum(0, 10)
     LOCATE 10, 32: PRINT SPACE$(15)       'Erase old answer
     LOCATE 10, 32: PRINT X; "x"; Y; "= ";

     'Calculate the correct answer and get user input
     Answer = X * Y
     'Determine the number of digits in the answer
     Digits = LEN(STR$(Answer)) - 1
     'Input that many digits and build StudentAns$
     FOR I = 1 TO Digits
        D$ = INPUT$(1): PRINT D$;
        StudentAns$ = StudentAns$ + D$
     NEXT I
     StudentAns = VAL(StudentAns$)   'Convert to numeric value
     StudentAns$ = ""                'Initialize the variable

     'Respond to correct and incorrect answers
     IF StudentAns = Answer THEN     'Correct answer
       CALL Good
     ELSE                            'Incorrect answer
       'Display all missed problems with the correct answer
       LOCATE 12 + Incorrect, 1
       PRINT X; "x"; Y; "="; Answer
       CALL Oops
     END IF
  NEXT n

  CALL DisplayResults                'Tally the results
END SUB


'-----------------------RandNum-----------------------------
'Generate random integers between Low and High values
'----------------------------------------------------------
FUNCTION RandNum (Low, High)
  RandNum = INT(RND * (High - Low + 1)) + Low
END FUNCTION
```

Figure 9.6: The Multiplication and RandNum procedures of the MULTIPLY program

After ten problems have been presented, the DisplayResults procedure shown in Figure 9.9 is called to display the total number of correct answers. Program control then returns to the main-module DO...LOOP, where the user can elect to continue with a new set of problems by pressing the spacebar, or leave the program by pressing Esc.

```
'--------------------------Good-------------------------------
'Respond to correct answers with ascending notes and a smile
'-------------------------------------------------------------
SUB Good STATIC
    VIEW PRINT 1 TO 2
    IF Correct = 0 THEN Pitch = 200
    FOR Freq = Pitch TO Pitch + 200 STEP 20
        SOUND Freq, 1
    NEXT Freq
    Pitch = Pitch + 30
    Correct = Correct + 1
    LOCATE 1, Correct * 2: PRINT Smile$
    VIEW PRINT
END SUB
```

Figure 9.7: The Good procedure of the MULTIPLY program

```
'--------------------------Oops-------------------------------
'Sound series of low notes and keep a tally of the number wrong
'-------------------------------------------------------------
SUB Oops STATIC
    FOR Freq = 200 TO 50 STEP -10
        SOUND Freq, 1
    NEXT Freq
    SOUND 100, 3
    Incorrect = Incorrect + 1
END SUB
```

Figure 9.8: The Oops procedure of the MULTIPLY program

```
'----------------------DisplayResults----------------------
'Display the number right and provide an appropriate message
'-----------------------------------------------------------
SUB DisplayResults
    LOCATE 3, 1      'Position the cursor

    SELECT CASE Correct
        'Play a tune if all are right
        CASE 10
            PRINT "You got them all right!"
            PLAY "T80 O4 L16 EEE L8 E O3 L4 G"
            PLAY "L16 AB O4 C L4 E L16 EFE L8 EDED O4 L2 C"
            PRINT "Excellent!"

        'or else display the score and a short message
        CASE ELSE
            PRINT "You got"; Correct; "right"
            IF Correct > 7 THEN PRINT "Good Work! ";
            PRINT "Keep Practicing "; Smile$
    END SELECT
END SUB
```

Figure 9.9: The DisplayResults procedure of the MULTIPLY program

For more practice, try modifying the program. Some easy alterations you might make include selecting a different number of problems for each sample-problem set, or changing the range of numbers
used in the sample problems. A more interesting modification might
allow the user to select these values. A still more challenging task is to
add procedures for addition, subtraction, and division, and create a
menu-driven program that allows the user to select any of these to
work on.

SUMMARY

A function takes input that is provided in the form of arguments
and processes that input according to the function definition. The
result is a value that is returned to the program at the point where a
function expression is used. QuickBASIC includes both built-in
string-processing and numeric functions.

In addition to these built-in functions, you can create user-defined
functions to meet your own needs. User-defined functions can be
incorporated into the module-level code with single-line or block-
form DEF FN statements. A more flexible way to define functions is
with a FUNCTION procedure. FUNCTION procedures are created and handled in much the same way as SUB procedures, but
unlike SUB procedures, FUNCTION procedures return a value.
This means that SUB procedures are always invoked with a procedure call, while FUNCTION procedures are invoked by incorporating the function name and arguments directly into a program
statement.

The last sections of this chapter introduced the use of the RND
function, which generates random values for use in your programs.
The MULTIPLY program demonstrated the use of RND in an educational application.

Chapter 10 introduces programming techniques that can be used
to handle long lists of data. You will see the RND function used in
this context in order to create large lists of randomly arranged data.

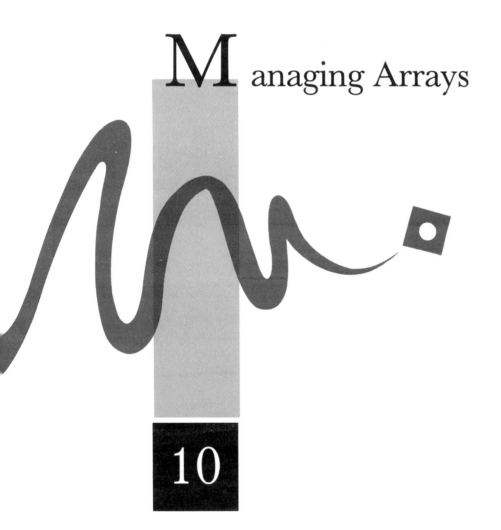

Managing Arrays

10

C H A P T E R **10**

BECAUSE COMPUTERS ARE IDEALLY SUITED FOR managing large amounts of information, data handling is at the heart of many computer programs. The next three chapters will concentrate on programming techniques that are essential to writing programs that can store, retrieve, and organize large quantities of data.

Data presented visually in list or table form is generally handled in a computer program by using an *array*. An array is a group of variables sharing the same name and filling the same purpose. In this chapter you will learn how to define and work with arrays and then apply these techniques in the MEAN&DEV program, which calculates two simple statistical values—mean and standard deviation.

The final sections of the chapter demonstrate how arrays can perform sort and search operations, two techniques common to many data-handling programs.

DEFINING AN ARRAY

An array is a data structure that uses a single variable name for an entire list or table of items. Each item in the array is identified by the use of a *subscript*, which is placed in parentheses following the variable name. For example, the subscripted variable

    Month$(3)

identifies the third item in an array of string variables called Month$.

In this sample program, a variable array is created in order to store and print four column headings.

```
ColumnHead$(1) = "Quarter 1"
ColumnHead$(2) = "Quarter 2"
ColumnHead$(3) = "Quarter 3"
ColumnHead$(4) = "Quarter 4"
```

```
CLS
FOR Column% = 1 TO 4
  PRINT ColumnHead$(Column%),
NEXT Column%
```

The output is shown here:

Quarter 1   Quarter 2   Quarter 3   Quarter 4

In order to work with an array, you must first reserve sufficient space in the computer's memory and then assign values to each element in the array. You can then work with arrays in a structured program in much the same way as you work with simple variables—that is, you can define arrays as either local or global, and pass arrays as arguments to FUNCTION and SUB procedures in your programs.

DESCRIBING AN ARRAY WITH THE DIM STATEMENT

The DIM statement is used to define the characteristics of the arrays you use in a program. These characteristics include the following:

- Whether the array is to be shared throughout the procedures in your program.

- The dimensions of the array, determined by the number of subscripts you plan to use with each variable name, and the range of values for each subscript.

- The data-type of the array values. As with simple variables, single-precision is the default data-type.

A DIM statement also initializes all the elements in an array, setting numeric values to zero and strings to the null value. A sample DIM statement is shown here.

DIM SHARED SampleArray(100) AS INTEGER

This statement defines SampleArray as a set of shared, integer variables. The subscript in the DIM statement means that sufficient memory is allocated to use subscripts that range from 0 to 100 in the array. Each element in the numeric SampleArray is also initialized to zero by this statement.

The general syntax of a DIM statement is

DIM [SHARED] *ArrayName* [(subscripts)] [AS *Datatype*]

If you include the keyword SHARED in your DIM statement, then your array will be defined as global and will be available to all procedures in your program. The AS clause in a dimension statement is used to declare the data-type of the variables in the array. When no AS clause is present, the array is assigned the default data-type.

The subscript value (or values) is used to describe the size of the array. Arrays with only one subscript are called *one-dimensional* arrays. You can also define multidimensional arrays with more that one subscript. The subscripts you include in your DIM statement determine the maximum size of each dimension in your array. The overall size of the array is determined by the number of dimensions and the size of each dimension. If you do not describe the size of an array in a DIM statement, the maximum value for each subscript is 10. If you use a subscript value that is beyond the range described in the DIM statement, you will get an error message that reads "Subscript out of range."

Subscripts in DIM statements can be a single numeric value or can use the TO keyword to describe the range of values to be used with the array. The following two statements are equivalent.

DIM Item(8)
DIM Item(0 TO 8)

Using TO allows you to use negative subscripts, as shown below. This statement reserves sufficient space for a total of 18 items in the Sample array, including negative, positive, and zero subscripts.

DIM Sample(– 12 TO 5)

In addition to being used to describe arrays, DIM statements can also describe simple variables when no subscript is used. The statement

DIM Maximum AS INTEGER

allows you to work with the integer variable called **Maximum** without using the % suffix. To make this variable global, you can declare it as follows.

DIM SHARED Maximum AS INTEGER

ASSIGNING DATA TO AN ARRAY

Array variables can be assigned values as you would any other variable. Most frequently this assignment is done within a program loop, in which each iteration of the loop assigns a new value to the array. The sample programs in this chapter demonstrate how you can use DATA statements and keyboard input in order to assign values to the variables in an array. Arrays can also be assigned values from disk files, using techniques you will learn in Chapters 11 and 12.

The MONTH program shown in Figure 10.1 uses an array variable to store month names in memory. DIM statements are used both to dimension the array and to declare the variable N as an integer. A FOR...NEXT loop is used to read these values in from a DATA statement. The program then uses the array as part of a process that converts dates from numeric to written form.

```
REM MONTH.BAS
'Working with an array

'Dimension statements
DIM Month$(1 TO 12)     'Allocate memory for the array
DIM N AS INTEGER        'Use DIM to select data type

'Assign values to the array
FOR N = 1 TO 12
   READ Month$(N)
NEXT N
DATA January, February, March, April, May, June, July
DATA August, September, October, November, December

'Use the array
CLS
DO
   INPUT "Type a date as MM/DD/YY (Enter to Stop) ", mmddyy$
   IF mmddyy$ = "" THEN EXIT DO
   N = VAL(LEFT$(mmddyy$, 2))
   PRINT "That date is in "; Month$(N); " 19"; RIGHT$(mmddyy$, 2)
LOOP
```

Figure 10.1: The MONTH program listing

Sample output from the MONTH program is shown below.

```
Type a date as MM/DD/YY (Enter to Stop) 12/25/90
That date is in December 1990
Type a date as MM/DD/YY (Enter to Stop) 1/1/91
That date is in January 1991
```

WORKING WITH ARRAYS

Because they can be used to handle quantities of data, arrays are an extremely flexible and useful programming tool. The next sections of this chapter describe a variety of techniques you can use to work effectively with array variables in your programs.

DEFINING STATIC AND DYNAMIC ARRAYS

QuickBASIC allows you to define two kinds of arrays, *static* and *dynamic*. Static arrays have a predetermined size that becomes a built-in part of a program when the program is compiled. If you use numeric expressions or constants as subscripts in a DIM statement, then the array is static. The MONTH program uses a static array.

A dynamic array is not allocated until a program runs—that is, the user can enter information that is used to determine an array size each time the program is run. Arrays dimensioned with variable subscripts are dynamic. The program lines shown here define a dynamic array:

```
INPUT "How many items in the list";HowMany
DIM Items$(HowMany)
```

Use a static array when you know in advance how many elements are in an array. Use a dynamic array when you cannot predict in advance how many elements the array will contain. Dynamic arrays are also useful if you are writing programs that use a great deal of memory because these arrays can be removed from memory, while memory allocated to a static array cannot be reallocated after the DIM statement has been executed.

MANAGING MEMORY

Because arrays can contain large amounts of information, you may find it necessary to work carefully within the memory limitations of your system. Under normal circumstances, QuickBASIC reserves 64K (64,284) bytes of random access memory (RAM) for each array. The amount of memory used by a numeric array will depend on the data-type as well as the size of the subscripts and the dimensions of the array. If you exceed the 64K limit, you will get a "Subscript out of range" error message when you try to run your program.

The array dimensioned below contains 10,000 single-precision elements. Because each single-precision element occupies 4 bytes of memory, it does not exceed the allotted space.

```
N!(100,100)
```

Because double-precision values occupy 8 bytes of memory, the change shown here makes the array exceed the 64K limit.

```
N#(100,100)
```

If your program includes several arrays, it is possible to use up all of the available memory. If you try to run a program that exceeds the available memory, you will get an "Out of memory" error message. To explore the amount of memory you have available with your system, experiment with a program similar to the one shown here. Keep adding additional arrays until you exceed the capacity of your system and get an "Out of memory error message" when you run the program.

```
n = 16000
DIM A(n)
DIM B(n)
DIM C(n)
DIM D(n)
DIM E(n)
  .
  .
  .
```

When you want to use several arrays at different points in a program, it is possible, using the ERASE statement, to increase the amount of available memory by removing one or more dynamic arrays from memory before allocating space for any additional arrays. You can demonstrate the effect of ERASE on the program you just created by deleting some of the dimensioned arrays to free up enough memory to be able to create additional arrays, as shown here.

```
.
.
.
DIM E(n)
ERASE A, B, C  'Remove these arrays from memory
DIM F(n)       'freeing up space for more arrays.
.
.
.
```

The ERASE command will only deallocate dynamic arrays. If you use ERASE with a static array, all of the elements of that array will be reinitialized, but the dimensions assigned in the DIM statement will remain the same.

PASSING AN ARRAY TO A PROCEDURE

When you want to work with arrays in a structured program, you can either define arrays as shared, or you can pass all of the elements in an array to procedures by using array names as arguments and parameters. As with simple variables, sharing an array means you refer to it by the same name throughout your program. When you pass an array as an argument, you can use different names in different parts of your program to refer to the same data items.

To pass all the elements of an array to a procedure, put the name of the array followed by an empty set of parentheses in the argument and parameter lists. The sample program shown next defines an array that contains the first 20 multiples of 10. All the elements of this array are passed to the PrintArray procedure, which displays these numbers on screen. Tens( ) is an argument that passes all the elements of this array to the Array( ) parameter.

```
DECLARE SUB PrintArray (Array!( ), Limit!)
DIM Tens(1 TO 20)
```

```
'Define array
FOR N = 1 TO 20
  Tens(N) = N * 10
NEXT N

'Call SUB procedure to print the array
CLS
PrintArray Tens( ), 20

SUB PrintArray (Array( ), Limit)
  FOR I = 1 TO Limit
    PRINT Array(I)
  NEXT I
END SUB
```

You can also pass individual elements of an array to a procedure by including the specific subscript values in parentheses after the array name. Each element can then be treated as if it were a simple variable. The modified program below prints out only the third element of the Tens( ) array.

```
DECLARE SUB PrintArray (Item!)
DIM Tens(1 TO 20)

'Define array
FOR n = 1 TO 20
  Tens(n) = n * 10
NEXT n

'Call SUB procedure to print an item in the array
CLS
PrintArray Tens(3)

SUB PrintArray (Item)
  PRINT Item
END SUB
```

THE MEAN&DEV PROGRAM

The MEAN&DEV program shown in Figure 10.2 is an application that uses an array to calculate two frequently used statistical values, mean and standard deviation. The mean is the arithmetic average of the items. Mean is calculated by adding a list of numeric values and dividing by the number of items on the list. The standard deviation is a measure of dispersion of values around the arithmetic mean. The standard deviation is small when the list of items includes items close in value and large when the values are widely dispersed. The standard deviation is calculated by summing the squares of the differences between the mean value and each value on the list and then dividing this sum by the number of items. The formulas for mean and standard deviation are shown here. V_n represents the array of data values, and N is the number of items.

$$ \text{Avg} = \frac{\sum V_n}{N} \qquad\qquad \text{Std} = \sqrt{\frac{\sum (V_n - \text{Avg})^2}{N}} $$

```
REM MEAN&DEV.BAS
'Calculate mean and standard deviation

'Procedure declarations
DECLARE FUNCTION Std! (Value!(), N%, Average!)
DECLARE FUNCTION Avg! (Value!(), N%)

DEFINT I-N              'Define integer variables
DIM DataVal(100)        'Dimension the array

'Display instructions
CLS
PRINT "Enter one value per line, then press Enter."
VIEW PRINT 3 TO 25     'so instructions remain on screen

DO
  'Initialize variables
  N = 0: Average = 0: StandardDev = 0

  'Create the array.
  DO
    INPUT Value$
    N = N + 1
    DataVal(N) = VAL(Value$)
    'Exit if a null value was entered
  LOOP UNTIL LEN(Value$) = 0
  N = N - 1                       'Remove the null value from the list

  'Perform calculations and display the results
  Average = Avg(DataVal(), N)
  StandardDev = Std(DataVal(), N, Average)
  PRINT "Average is"; Average;
  PRINT TAB(30); "Standard Deviation is"; StandardDev

  'Determine if there are more values
  PRINT : PRINT "Continue? (Y/N) ";
  More$ = UCASE$(INPUT$(1)): PRINT More$
LOOP WHILE More$ = "Y"
```

Figure 10.2: The MEAN&DEV program listing

```
'--------------------------Avg--------------------------
'Calculates the average of the items in the Value() array
'------------------------------------------------------
FUNCTION Avg (Value(), N)
  IF N = 0 THEN EXIT FUNCTION      'to avoid division by zero
  FOR I = 1 TO N
    Sum = Sum + Value(I)
  NEXT I
  Avg = Sum / N
END FUNCTION

'--------------------------Std--------------------------------
'Calculates the Standard Deviation of items in the Value() array
'------------------------------------------------------------
FUNCTION Std (Value(), N, Average)
  IF N = 0 THEN EXIT FUNCTION
  FOR J = 1 TO N
    DSquared = (Value(J) - Average) ^ 2
    SumDSquared = SumDSquared + DSquared
  NEXT J
  Std = SQR(SumDSquared / N)
END FUNCTION
```

Figure 10.2: The MEAN&DEV program listing (continued)

The user of this program can input up to 100 data items, a limit set by the DIM statement. Although this could be made larger, or defined with a dynamic array that prompts the user for the length of the list, a program such as this that does not allow the user to correct items that have already been entered would be very unwieldy for long lists of items. The data values are input as string variables and then converted to numeric values. This allows the program to exit the loop when ⏎ is pressed because pressing ⏎ inputs the null string, which is the only data value that has a length of zero.

As the values are entered, they are stored in the DataVal array. The elements in this array are passed as arguments to the FUNCTION procedures, which calculate average and standard deviation. These values are printed out, and the user is given the option of continuing with another list or exiting the program. Figure 10.3 shows a sample output screen.

PERFORMING SORT OPERATIONS

Data is generally encountered in a random fashion. In order to make randomly organized data useful, we sort it—usually in numeric or

```
    Enter one value per line, then press Enter.

    ? 12
    ? 13
    ? 12
    ? 13
    ?
    Average is 12.5              Standard Deviation is .5

    Continue? (Y/N) Y
    ? 12.5
    ? 12.5
    ? 12.5
    ?
    Average is 12.5              Standard Deviation is Ø

    Continue? (Y/N) N




    Press any key to continue
```

Figure 10.3: Sample output from the MEAN&DEV program

alphabetical order. This is a boring and tedious task to perform manually, and so computers are frequently called for when information needs to be sorted. When you encounter a standard programming task such as sorting, you don't actually need to think the problem through to its very roots. Programmers before you have encountered this same problem, and as a result you can avail yourself of many standard approaches when you need to sort data. A specific approach to solving a particular problem is known as an *algorithm*. The two following sections demonstrate two commonly encountered sorting algorithms, the bubble sort and the Shell sort. Spend as much or as little time with these algorithms as interests you. It is perfectly possible to incorporate a sorting routine into a program without having a thorough understanding of how it works.

THE BUBBLE SORT

The bubble sort is a good sort to begin with because it is simpler than most other sorting algorithms. The BUBBLE program shown in Figure 10.4 uses a bubble sort to sort out a short list of scrambled letters that have been read into an array using READ and DATA statements.

```
REM BUBBLE.BAS
'Reads an array and sorts the array with a bubble sort
'The array is printed after each pass through the sorting loop

DECLARE SUB BubbleSort (Item$())
DECLARE SUB PrintArray (Array$())

'Setup
DEFINT A-Z
CONST FALSE = 0, TRUE = NOT FALSE
DIM letter$(6)
DIM SHARED Count
Count = 6        'Number of items in list to be sorted
CLS

'Read scrambled letters into the array
FOR N = 1 TO Count
  READ letter$(N)
NEXT N
DATA C,B,F,A,D,E

'Sort the array showing the results after each swap
CALL BubbleSort(letter$())

'------------------------BubbleSort-----------------------
'Performs a bubble sort displaying changes on screen
'---------------------------------------------------------
SUB BubbleSort (Item$())
  'Display Headings
  PRINT "I", "Swapmade", "Limit", "Array"

  'Set number of items to be sorted
  Limit = Count

  DO
     Swapmade = FALSE
     PRINT

     FOR I = 1 TO Limit - 1
        'Display what's happening on screen
        PRINT I, Swapmade, Limit, : PrintArray Item$()

        'Switch any two items that are out of order
        IF Item$(I) > Item$(I + 1) THEN
           SWAP Item$(I), Item$(I + 1)
           Swapmade = I
        END IF

        'Change Limit for next pass to the last swapped item
        Limit = Swapmade
     NEXT I
     'Display results of final pass
     PRINT I, Swapmade, Limit, : PrintArray Item$()

  'Continue to sort while SwapMade has a non-zero (TRUE) value
  LOOP WHILE Swapmade

END SUB

'------------------------PrintArray-----------------------
'Prints all of the items in an array
'---------------------------------------------------------
SUB PrintArray (Array$())
  FOR I = 1 TO Count
    PRINT Array$(I);
  NEXT I
  PRINT
END SUB
```

Figure 10.4: The BUBBLE program listing

During a bubble sort, each item in a list is compared with the next item in the list. If the first item is larger than the second, the two items are exchanged. This exchange is done in BASIC using the SWAP statement. The second item in the list is then compared with the third, and so on through the list until the second-to-last item is compared with the last. The process is then repeated so that larger items gradually "bubble" their way to the end of the list, while smaller items work their way to the beginning. When a pass through the sorting loop includes no exchanges, the sort is complete.

In the bubble sort used here, the **Swapmade** variable acts as a *flag*. This variable is reset to zero at the beginning of each pass through the sorting loop. When a swap is made, **Swapmade** is set to mark the position at which the swap occurred. This serves two purposes: First, it is used to adjust the upper limit of the FOR...NEXT loop because it is unnecessary to sort beyond the point where the last swap occurred; second, it determines when the entire sort is complete because at this point its value remains zero.

The output of the BUBBLE program shows you what happens to the array and the variables used in the sorting routine after each comparison of values is made. This output is shown in Figure 10.5. To get a feel for the way the sort works, you might try working it through manually with

```
I          Swapmade    Limit      Array

1              Ø           6       CBFADE
2              1           1       BCFADE
3              1           1       BCFADE
4              3           3       BCAFDE
5              4           4       BCADFE
6              5           5       BCADEF

1              Ø           5       BCADEF
2              Ø           Ø       BCADEF
3              2           2       BACDEF
4              2           2       BACDEF
5              2           2       BACDEF

1              Ø           2       BACDEF
2              1           1       ABCDEF

1              Ø           1       ABCDEF



Press any key to continue
```

Figure 10.5: The BUBBLE program output

pencil and paper, or using the QuickBASIC debugging tools to move through the program step by step, watching the value of the program's variables in the Watch window. On the other hand, you might be perfectly satisfied to look at the bottom line and see that the array has in fact been sorted and move on to the Shell sort.

THE SHELL SORT

The bubble sort that was presented in the previous section is not fast enough to deal with large lists very efficiently. The faster Shell sort you will look at next (which gets its name from its developer, Donald Shell) also uses an exchange of elements, but begins by comparing elements that are separated by an interval that is equal to half the length of the list. Once this exchange is complete, the initial interval is cut in half. The routine then works its way through the list, comparing pairs of values separated by this smaller interval and exchanging those pairs that are out of order until no new exchanges are made. With each pass through the sort, the interval is narrowed, until finally adjacent elements are compared and the sort is completed. The final sort, when the interval of comparison is equal to one, is identical to a bubble sort. But because no element in the array is far from its correct position when the final sort occurs, it will not require the many passes that are necessary when comparisons *begin* with adjacent elements.

The SHELLSRT program shown in Figure 10.6 begins by creating a random list of four-letter "names." Although these mixed up combinations of letters are meaningless, they are an excellent way to test a routine without having to type in a large number of names. You can choose the size of list you want. The list of names is then generated by the MakeList SUB procedure and stored in the dynamic NameList$ array. This array is sorted with a Shell sort using the ShellSort procedure. The TIMER function is used in order to measure the time required to perform the sort procedure.

The program prints the array both before and after the sort by calling the PrintArray procedure. Use small arrays until you have satisfied yourself that the names are being correctly sorted. When you want to try out larger arrays, you can inactivate the two program lines that call the PrintArray procedure by inserting apostrophes at the beginning of these lines. Once this is done, try increasing the size

```
REM SHELLSORT.BAS
'Using a Shell sort on a randomly created list of 'names.'

DECLARE SUB ShellSort ()
DECLARE SUB PrintArray ()
DECLARE SUB MakeList ()

DEFINT A-Z
DIM SHARED ListSize
CONST FALSE = 0, TRUE = NOT FALSE

'Get a number for the size of the list
CLS
INPUT "How many names would you like to sort"; ListSize
DIM SHARED NameList$(ListSize)

'Generate a random list of 'names'
PRINT
PRINT "***Creating Random List***":
MakeList
PrintArray                'Print the array before the sort

'Sort the names with a Shell sort
PRINT "***Performing Shell Sort***"
Start! = TIMER            'Set the start time
ShellSort                 'Perform the sort
Finish! = TIMER           'Set the finish time
PrintArray                'Print the array after the sort

'Display the time required for the sort
PRINT "Shell sort time: "; Finish! - Start!; "seconds"

'---------------------MakeList---------------------------
'Generate a random list of 4-letter 'names'
'--------------------------------------------------------
SUB MakeList
   RANDOMIZE TIMER

   FOR I = 1 TO ListSize
     NameToSort$ = ""       'Start with null string
     'Build a scrambled name
     FOR N = 1 TO 4
        RandomAsciiCode = INT(RND(1) * 26 + 65)
        RandomLetter$ = CHR$(RandomAsciiCode)
        NameToSort$ = NameToSort$ + RandomLetter$
     NEXT N
     'Add the name to the array
     NameList$(I) = NameToSort$
   NEXT I

END SUB

'---------------------PrintArray-------------------------
'Display all the element of an array
'--------------------------------------------------------
SUB PrintArray
   FOR N = 1 TO ListSize
      PRINT NameList$(N),
   NEXT N
   PRINT
END SUB
```

Figure 10.6: The SHELLSRT program listing

```
'-----------------------ShellSort--------------------
'Use a Shell sort to sort the items in an array
'----------------------------------------------------
SUB ShellSort
    Interval = ListSize \ 2
    DO WHILE Interval > 0
        Limit = ListSize - Interval
        DO
            Swapmade = FALSE
            FOR N = 1 TO Limit
                IF NameList$(N) > NameList$(N + Interval) THEN
                    SWAP NameList$(N), NameList$(N + Interval)
                    Swapmade = N
                END IF
            NEXT N
            Limit = Swapmade - Interval
        LOOP WHILE Swapmade
        Interval = Interval \ 2
    LOOP
END SUB
```

Figure 10.6: The SHELLSRT program listing (continued)

of the array and watching how this affects the time required to perform the Shell sort.

An excellent programming exercise to test your understanding of these two sorting programs is to develop a program similar to the SHELLSRT program that uses a bubble sort to sort the randomly created list of names. Once this is complete, you can compare the time it takes for a bubble sort and a Shell sort to sort arrays containing the same number of randomly arranged items.

If you want to explore the details of how the Shell sort operates, try creating a program similar to the BUBBLE program that sorts a very small array and displays on screen the changes that occur as the array is sorted.

PERFORMING SEARCH OPERATIONS

Stored data is of little value unless you can find what you need when you need it. The two sections that follow describe two methods of searching an array for a particular item.

USING A SEQUENTIAL SEARCH

As its name implies, a sequential search requires looking at each element of an array, in sequence, until the element you are searching for has been found. This kind of search can be very quick if the element you want is near the beginning of the list and quite slow if you are looking for an element at the end of a long list.

The SEQSRCH program shown in Figure 10.7 creates an array containing each of the uppercase letters of the alphabet by using the ASCII code values (65 through 90) for these letters. Once the array is complete, the following prompt asks you which letter you want to find in this list:

Search for what letter?

The letter you name is then passed as an argument to the Sequential-Search procedure, which uses a sequential search to find that letter in

```
REM SEQSRCH.BAS
'Demonstrates a sequential search of an array.

DECLARE SUB SequentialSearch (Array$(), ListLength%, Key$, Match%)
DIM Letter$(26)
DEFINT A-Z
CONST FALSE = 0, true = NOT FALSE
CLS

'Fill the array using ASCII codes for A-Z (65 -90)
FOR N = 1 TO 26
   Letter$(N) = CHR$(N + 64)
NEXT N

'Get the item to be searched for
INPUT "Search for what letter"; SearchItem$

'Search for the item
CALL SequentialSearch(Letter$(), 26, SearchItem$, Match)

'Display results
SELECT CASE Match
   CASE FALSE
      PRINT "No match was found"
   CASE ELSE
      PRINT SearchItem$; " is item"; Match; "on the list."
END SELECT

'-----------------SequentialSearch------------------
'Compare each item in list to Key$ until a match is found
'----------------------------------------------------
SUB SequentialSearch (Array$(), ListLength, Key$, Match)
   Match = FALSE
   FOR N = 1 TO ListLength
      IF Array$(N) = Key$ THEN
         Match = N
         EXIT FOR
      END IF
   NEXT N
END SUB
```

Figure 10.7: The SEQSRCH program listing

the array. If the letter is found in the array, the variable **Match** is set equal to the subscript of that item in the array. If no match is found, the **Match** variable remains equal to the constant value FALSE. The value of the **Match** variable is used to display the final results. A sample output screen is shown here.

> Search for what letter? C
> C is item 3 on the list.

USING A BINARY SEARCH

A binary search can be used to speed up a search procedure when you are searching a *sorted* list. A binary search begins by testing the midpoint of a range of values to see if it equals the search item. If the values are not equal, the binary search routine checks to see if the midpoint is greater or less than the search item. If the midpoint is less than the search item, the program then tests the midpoint of all the values that are larger than the original midpoint. If the midpoint is greater than the search item, the program tests the midpoint of the values that are smaller than the original midpoint. The binary search routine continues in this manner, cutting the number of items remaining to be searched in half with each pass through the search loop and testing the midpoint of the remaining values until a match is found.

To see how a binary search works, you can modify the SEQSRCH program you created in the previous section. Change the line that calls the Sequential Search procedure (about line 19) so that it now reads as follows:

> Call BinarySearch(Letter$( ), 26, SearchItem$, Match)

Then replace the SequentialSearch procedure with the BinarySearch procedure shown in Figure 10.8.

A good way to understand how a binary search works is to use QuickBASIC's debugging tools to step through this program and watch each of the variables used in the procedure. This will also give you a chance to see how array variables can be watched. Use the Add Watch command in the Debug menu to add each of the following variables to the Watch window: Match, BottomOfRange,

```
'---------------------BinarySearch--------------------
'Locate an item by dividing the array into sections
'-----------------------------------------------------
SUB BinarySearch (Array$(), ListLength, Key$, Match)
  Match = FALSE
  BottomOfRange = 1
  TopOfRange = ListLength
  DO UNTIL TopOfRange < BottomOfRange
    Midpoint = (TopOfRange + BottomOfRange) \ 2
    IF Array$(Midpoint) = Key$ THEN
      Match = Midpoint
      EXIT DO
    ELSEIF Array$(Midpoint) < Key$ THEN
      BottomOfRange = Midpoint + 1
    ELSE
      TopOfRange = Midpoint - 1
    END IF
  LOOP
END SUB
```

Figure 10.8: The BinarySearch procedure

TopOfRange, Midpoint, and Array$(Midpoint). Place a break point in the program just before the search procedure is called by moving to that position and pressing F9. When you run the program, execution will be interrupted at this point and you can use the F8 key to step through the sort procedure line by line.

In this example, which searches the 26 letters of the alphabet, even the longest possible search requires only five passes through the sorting loop. Compare this to the 26 passes that might be required using a sequential search, and you can see the potential advantages of a binary search.

SUMMARY

Arrays are lists of related data values that are stored using a common variable name. Each item on the list is identified by a subscript or subscripts placed in parentheses after the variable name. Space for array variables is reserved in memory with DIM statements. If you specify the dimensions of an array with fixed numeric values in the DIM statement, the array will be static. If you use variables to dimension an array, the array will be dynamic and as a result can change in size each time a program runs.

Like simple variables, array variables can either be used globally throughout a program or can remain local to one particular section of program code. To pass an array from the main module of a program to a procedure in the program, include the array in the argument list. It must be identified as an array in this list by an empty set of parentheses following the variable name.

Arrays are used in a broad range of programming applications, including sort and search operations that are a vital part of many data processing programs. This chapter introduced the bubble and Shell sorting algorithms and both sequential and binary search techniques.

In this chapter DATA statements were used as a means of storing data to be read into an array. A more common method of storing quantities of data is the use of data files. The creation and management of disk files for storing and retrieving data is the subject of the next two chapters of this book.

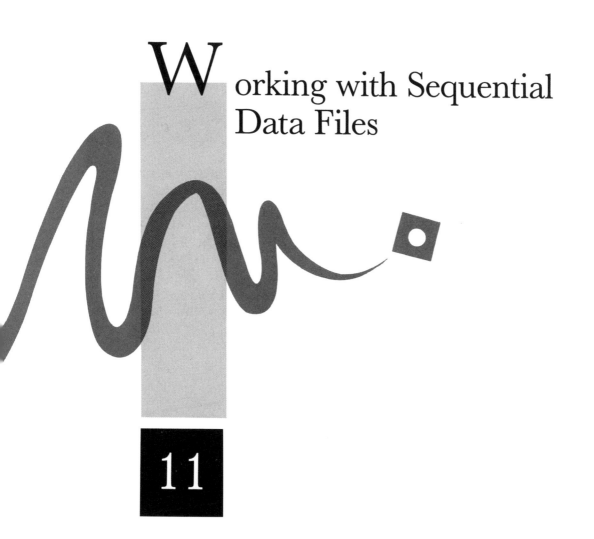

Working with Sequential Data Files

11

CHAPTER *11*

IN ORDER TO BE USEFUL FOR DATA HANDLING, a computer program must allow its users to store and retrieve data between program runs, a task accomplished by the creation of auxiliary data files used specifically for data storage. Unlike the information held only temporarily in the computer's electronic memory, information in a data file is stored permanently and can be retrieved at any time. And unlike the information coded directly into a program, information stored in an auxiliary data file can be updated by the individual who uses a program.

If you have used any of the familiar commercial computer software programs, such as word processors, electronic spreadsheets, or database managers, then you are familiar with the use of files to store and retrieve information. The manipulation of auxiliary data files is an essential part of most computer applications. All of the applications listed above allow the user to create new files and update existing files. Most software programs also enable a user to import or export data files to or from other computer applications. A solid understanding of the characteristics of auxiliary data files will help you write more flexible programs and will also allow you greater flexibility when you make use of existing computer software. In this chapter and the one that follows, you will learn how to write programs that create and update data files.

Data files use different strategies for storing data, depending on the nature of the task at hand. This chapter introduces *sequential* data files. The defining characteristic of sequential files is that new data must always be added to the *end* of these files. To retrieve data from a sequential file, it is necessary to search through the file item by item, starting at the beginning, until the desired information has been found. (A second type of file, known as a *random-access* file, is covered in Chapter 12.)

The WAGES program developed in the next sections of this chapter introduces the use of sequential data files. This program will be used to demonstrate how to

- Write a program that creates a sequential file and adds data to it;

- Examine the contents of a sequential file directly, using both the QuickBASIC environment and DOS commands;

- Write a program that retrieves and uses the data stored in a sequential file.

After learning these basic techniques, you will learn about a group of BASIC commands that will provide you with more flexibility in working with sequential files. These commands can be used to manage files from within your programs.

Finally, the PROGLIST program at the end of the chapter demonstrates the use of sequential files that have already been created by another application. In this case, the files used are text files of your own QuickBASIC programs.

WORKING WITH RECORDS AND FIELDS

Before you begin programming with data files, you should know a few fundamental file-management terms that are used to describe the organization of these files. Let's begin by picturing some familiar data-management systems. A phone book is a data-management system that arranges information alphabetically by last name. In this system, each entry occupies one line and name, address, and phone number are presented in a consistent order on each line. An encyclopedia also lists items in alphabetical order, but in this case, the length of each article and the nature of the information presented varies from entry to entry. Some data-management systems—like the desk, table, and floor space where this book is being written—appear to have almost no organizational structure at all. Like these differing systems, different computer data files employ varying degrees of internal structure.

The terms *record* and *field* are used to describe the structure of data files. When the contents of a file are divided into related units of information, these units are known as records. Each record may or may not be further subdivided into units known as fields. Using these terms to describe the phone book, we can describe each individual's phone listing as one record. Within each record we can identify three fields—name, address, and phone number.

In the sections that follow, you will develop a program called WAGES.BAS. This program uses keyboard input to build a data file containing a total of seven records. Each record has three fields: the name of a profession, and the average weekly wages for both men and women in that profession. These values are stored in a sequential file called WAGES.DAT. The program then retrieves the information in this file and uses it to create an on-screen table that displays all the values in the file, and also to calculate and display averages for men and women. This display is shown in Figure 11.1.

```
Profession                    Men        Women

Assembly Line Worker          311         198
Cashier                       330         240
High School Teacher           411         357
Lawyer                        660         502
Mechanic                      384         247
Sales Clerk                   239         167
Waiter                        229         149

Average                       366         265




Press any key to continue
```

Figure 11.1: The output of the WAGES program

CREATING AND WRITING TO A SEQUENTIAL DATA FILE

Adding information to a data file is referred to as *writing to* the file. The steps used to write data to a sequential file are summarized here.

Each step will be explained in detail in the sections that follow.

1. Open the file with an OPEN statement. Open the file FOR APPEND if you want to add information to the end of an existing file. Open the file FOR OUTPUT if you want to overwrite an existing file. Either statement can be used to create a new file.

2. Write information to the file using a WRITE # or a PRINT # statement.

3. Use a CLOSE statement to close the file.

The AddData procedure of the WAGES program demonstrates these three steps. Figure 11.2 shows the main module of the program and the AddData procedure. Notice that one program line—the one that calls the DisplayData procedure—has been turned into a remark statement by placing an apostophe at the beginning of the line. This technique allows you to run the program before you have added the DisplayData procedure to it. Later, when you have added this procedure, you can activate the CALL statement by removing that apostrophe from the line.

OPENING A FILE

The terms *input* and *output* refer to the direction of data movement with reference to the system's random access memory. Data values that are sent *out* *from* memory and *into* a data file are referred to as output.

The first executable statement in the AddData procedure is an OPEN statement. An OPEN statement is required before any file input or output (I/O) operations can be performed. When you are opening a sequential file, the OPEN statement includes the following information:

- A string value that contains the name of the data file being opened.

- A clause that describes the kind of I/O procedure (reading or writing to the file) that will follow.

- A file number that will be used to identify the opened file in subsequent program lines.

```
REM WAGES.BAS
'Using a sequential file to store wage data

DECLARE SUB DisplayData ()
DECLARE SUB AddData ()

'Add data to the file
CALL AddData

'Display the data and calculate averages
REM CALL DisplayData

END

'------------------------AddData----------------------------
'Opens the WAGES.DAT and adds new data entered from the keyboard
'---------------------------------------------------------------
SUB AddData

   'Open the file
   OPEN "WAGES.DAT" FOR APPEND AS #1

   'Get data and write it to the file
   CLS
   DO
     INPUT "Profession (Press Enter to stop): ", Profession$
     IF Profession$ <> "" THEN
       INPUT "Average weekly salary for men: ", Men
       INPUT "Average weekly salary for women: ", Women
       WRITE #1, Profession$, Men, Women
     END IF
     CLS
   LOOP UNTIL Profession$ = ""

   'Close the file after last name has been added
   CLOSE #1

END SUB
```

Figure 11.2: The WAGES.BAS main module and AddData procedure

There are two ways to open a sequential file when you want to write data to the file. The syntax for these two kinds of OPEN statements is shown here, along with a brief explanation of the effect of each statement:

- OPEN *file$* FOR OUTPUT AS *#n*—opens a new file with the specified file name. If the file already exists, the new data replaces any existing data.

- OPEN *file$* FOR APPEND AS *#n*—opens the specified file and adds new data to the end of the file, leaving existing data intact. If no such file exists, a file with this name is created.

In an OPEN statement, the *file$* specification can be any valid DOS file name (for example, FILENAME.EXT) or can include a complete file pathname (for example, C:\DATA\FILENAME.EXT). When no directory path is included, the program looks for and opens the file within the current default directory. The number *n* in an OPEN statement is an integer value that will be used to identify the file in subsequent program statements.

The OPEN statement in the AddData procedure reads as follows:

OPEN "WAGES.DAT" FOR APPEND AS #1

This statement opens the file named WAGES.DAT and identifies it as file #1. The first time you run the program, the WAGES.DAT file will be created in the default directory. The FOR APPEND clause means that during each subsequent run, new data will be added to the end of the existing file.

WRITING TO A FILE

The AddData procedure uses a WRITE # statement in order to transfer data from memory to the WAGES.DAT file. The WRITE # statement identifies the file that is to receive data by using the number assigned to that file in the OPEN statement. The AddData procedure uses three separate input statements to receive keyboard input for the three variables **Profession$**, **Men**, and **Women**. These three values combine to make one record in the WAGES.DAT file. This WRITE # statement writes each complete record to the file.

WRITE #1, Profession$, Men, Women

Enter the program as shown in Figure 11.2. Run the program and add the data for the first two records as shown here:

Profession (Press Enter to stop): Assembly Line Worker
Average weekly salary for men: 311
Average weekly salary for women: 198

Profession (Press Enter to stop): Cashier
Average weekly salary for men: 330
Average weekly salary for women: 240

After typing in these two records, press ◄┘ when the third input screen appears. This will terminate program execution. At this point there is no visible evidence that the program has accomplished anything, because the effects of the program are on your disk, rather than on screen. You will examine the contents of the file you just created shortly, but first look at the CLOSE statement that ends the AddData procedure. The next section explains the role of this statement.

CLOSING A FILE

The final step in working with a data file is closing the file. Closing a file serves two important purposes:

- QuickBASIC does not add information directly to your disk file. Instead, an area of memory known as a *file buffer* is reserved for each open file. When a statement that writes data to a file is executed, the data is transferred initially to this buffer. Only when the file buffer is full is the data actually transferred to the disk file. (This is done in order to save time because transferring data in memory is faster than performing disk operations.) Closing a file causes any remaining information in a file buffer to be written to the disk.

- When you are working with sequential files, you cannot read and write to a file simultaneously. If you have been writing data to a file, you must close it and then reopen it when you want to read data from this same file.

The close statement in the AddData procedure,

    CLOSE #1

identifies the file to be closed by number. A close statement can include a list of one or more file numbers, or it can be included alone. When no files are listed in a CLOSE statement, all open files will be closed. There are additional BASIC statements that close all open files. Three of these are summarized here:

RESET	Closes all open files.
CLEAR	Closes all open files and also reinitializes all program variables.

> END   Terminates program execution and closes all
>   open files.

Once a file has been closed, the file number that was used to identify it can either be reassigned to the same file or used to identify a different file.

Before continuing to build the WAGES program, let's take a look at the data file you have created.

VIEWING A SEQUENTIAL FILE

QuickBASIC sequential files use standard ASCII text format. This means that you can view the contents of these files directly from DOS, or you may choose to examine and modify the files using any one of a number of word processing programs. You can also create, view, and edit text files directly from within the QuickBASIC environment. The exercises that follow show you two ways to examine the contents of the WAGES.DAT file you just created.

WORKING WITH DATA FILES
WITHIN THE QUICKBASIC ENVIRONMENT

When you are working in the QuickBASIC View window, you can retrieve text files as well as program files, using either the *Open Program* or *Load File* commands in the File Menu. However, if you open a file using the *Open Program* command, the QuickBASIC smart editor continues to check each line of text for correct QuickBASIC syntax, making it awkward to work with files whose contents are not lines of QuickBASIC code. One of the options you have when you use the *Load File* command is to open a file as a document. Doing this turns off the smart editor and allows you to view and modify text as you would with any word processor. The following instructions describe how to load WAGES.DAT as a document file.

If you have been working with Easy Menus, change to the expanded menus with the *Full Menus* command in the Options menu before starting the exercise.

1. Save the WAGES.BAS program and use the New Program command to clear the view window.

2. Select the *Load File* command from the File menu. This will open the Load File dialog box.

3. Type *.* into the File name input area and press ⏎. As a result, the Files list will include all the files in the current default directory, rather than just those with the .BAS extension.

4. Press Tab to move the cursor to the Files list and select the WAGES.DAT file from this list.

5. Press Tab twice to move the cursor to the *Load As* area and use the → key to select the *Document* option. This option will turn off the QuickBASIC smart editor.

6. Press ⏎ to execute the command. The WAGES.DAT file contents will appear in the view screen as shown here:

> "Assembly Line Worker",311,198
> "Cashier",330,240

Once you have opened a document file, you can modify and save it using the same editing commands you use to work with Quick-BASIC program files.

If you want to view a text file without making changes to it, you can also do this directly from the operating system. The next exercise tells how.

USING THE DOS SHELL COMMAND

The *DOS Shell* command is also one of the features of the Quick-BASIC expanded File menu. This command allows you to execute DOS commands without requiring you to exit from QuickBASIC. When you activate the Dos Shell command, you will see the message

> **Type EXIT to return to QuickBASIC**

followed by the DOS command prompt. You can then use any DOS command or run any executable program (those with .BAT, .COM, and .EXE extensions). QuickBASIC, along with any work you have created using the QuickBASIC environment, remains in memory. When you want to return to the QuickBASIC Work screen, type **Exit** at the DOS command prompt.

⊚ The *Type EXIT...*
command appears
on screen only once. This
makes it easy to forget
that you are using the
DOS Shell command
from within the Quick-
BASIC environment. If
you forget to type **Exit**
and type **qb** instead, it is
possible, with sufficient
memory, to load Quick-
BASIC twice into mem-
ory. This somewhat
baffling occurrence can
make it appear that you
have lost the work that
you left in the Work
screen. To retrieve your
work, exit from the new
Work screen with the
regular Exit command
and then type **Exit** at the
DOS prompt to return to
the original Work screen.
As a rule, typing **qb** will
result in a "Program too
long to fit in memory"
message.

Try the following exercise to explore the DOS Shell command:

1. Select the *DOS Shell* command from the File menu.

2. Enter the command **TYPE WAGES.DAT** at the command prompt. The contents of this file are displayed on screen, followed by the command prompt.

3. Enter the command **DIR WAGES.∗** at the prompt. You can use the resulting directory list to see the amount of storage space that the WAGES.DAT file occupies on your disk.

4. Enter the command **EXIT** to return to the QuickBASIC Work screen.

The DOS Shell command provides you with a convenient way of viewing text files, looking up the date or size of a file, changing directories, or running short programs while your current work remains loaded in memory.

In the following section you will return to the WAGES program and add a procedure to it that uses the data in the WAGES.DAT file to create an on-screen display.

READING AND USING DATA STORED IN A SEQUENTIAL FILE

Retrieving stored information from a data file into memory is referred to as *reading* from the file. The steps used to read data from a sequential file are summarized below. They will be explained in detail in the sections that follow.

1. Open the file using an OPEN FOR INPUT statement.

2. Read information from the file using an INPUT #, a LINE INPUT #, or an INPUT$ statement. Items in sequential files are read from one *delimiter* to the next, and the EOF function is used to determine when the end of the file has been reached.

3. Close the file.

The DisplayData procedure shown in Figure 11.3 demonstrates these techniques by reading values from the WAGES.DAT file into memory and using these values to create the table shown in Figure 11.1.

Add this procedure to the WAGES program. Remove the apostrophe from the line in the program that calls this procedure and run the program. Add two additional items to the data file (refer to Figure 11.1) and then press ◄─┘ to continue with the program. You will see an on-screen table produced by the DisplayData procedure that includes the two records you just added, plus the two records that were already in the file. The following sections explain the actions of this procedure.

```
'-----------------------DisplayData----------------------
'Open the WAGES.DAT file and use values to create a table
'--------------------------------------------------------
SUB DisplayData

   'Display contents of the file
   PRINT
   PRINT "Profession"; TAB(30); "Men", "Women"
   PRINT

   'Open the file for input
   OPEN "WAGES.DAT" FOR INPUT AS #1

   'Get values until the end of the file is reached
   DO UNTIL EOF(1)
      INPUT #1, Profession$, Men, Women
      PRINT Profession$; TAB(30); Men, Women
      Count = Count + 1
      SumMen = SumMen + Men
      SumWomen = SumWomen + Women
   LOOP

   'Calculate and display average values
   PRINT
   PRINT "Average"; TAB(30); SumMen \ Count, SumWomen \ Count

   'Close the file
   CLOSE #1

END SUB
```

Figure 11.3: The WAGES.BAS DisplayData procedure

OPENING A FILE FOR INPUT

When you want to read information from a sequential data file into memory, you must first open the file using an OPEN statement using the syntax shown here:

OPEN *file$* FOR INPUT AS *#n*

In addition to specifying the name of the file and the file number it is being assigned, this statement indicates that the file will be used for input. The statement line that opens the WAGES.DAT file in the DisplayData procedure is

OPEN "WAGES.DAT" FOR INPUT AS #1

WORKING WITH DELIMITERS

Following the OPEN statement in the DisplayData procedure is a DO...LOOP that uses an INPUT # statement to read three values at a time from the data file, displays these values on screen, and keeps running totals for each of the two numeric values.

The WAGES.DAT file created by the AddData procedure is organized with one record on each line and includes punctuation marks that separate each field from its neighbor. Punctuation marks and individual lines serve an important purpose when data is read from a sequential file, acting as markers to indicate the end of one data item and the beginning of the next. Such markers are known as *delimiters*. The delimiters in the WAGES.DAT file were placed there automatically as a result of the WRITE # statement in the AddData procedure.

The delimiters used in a sequential file depend on whether the items in the file consist of string or numeric data. String values can be separated by double quotation marks ("), commas (,), or the code for the end of a line (CR-LF). (A WRITE # statement places double quotation marks around string values and also separates these values with a comma.) The CR-LF code is added at the end of each list of values added to a file with a WRITE # statement. Numeric values can be separated by commas (,), the presence of one or more blank spaces in a list of values, or a CR-LF.

READING DATA FROM A SEQUENTIAL FILE USING INPUT #

Data is read from the WAGES.DAT file with an INPUT # statement. The general syntax of an INPUT # statement is

INPUT #n, *variable1, variable2, ...*

As a result of an INPUT # statement, values are read from the data file and assigned to the variables named in the variable list.

The INPUT # statement in the DisplayData is shown here:

INPUT #1, Profession$, Men, Women

The first three items in the WAGES.DAT file are

"Assembly Line Worker",311,198

When the INPUT # statement is executed, "Assembly Line Worker", which is delimited by quotation marks, is assigned to the Profession$ variable. The numeric variable 311, which is delimited by commas, is assigned to the variable called Men. The next numeric value, 198, is assigned to the variable Women. This time a CR-LF marks the end of the data value. When the DO...LOOP repeats, the program continues to read values from the file, starting at the beginning of the next line and continuing in order until all values have been read. The EOF function, which is described next, is used in order to determine when the end of the file has been reached.

USING THE EOF FUNCTION

If an INPUT # statement tries to read past the end of a data file, an error message results. In order to avoid this message, you can use the EOF function to determine when the end of a file has been reached. The syntax of an EOF function is

EOF(*n*)

where *n* is the number of the file being read. When the end of the file is reached, the EOF function returns a true value (– 1). In the DisplayData procedure, the line

DO UNTIL EOF(1)

is used to ensure that the INPUT # statement does not attempt to read any values from the WAGES.DAT file after the end of that file has been reached.

Run the program again, adding the remaining records to the file. Your output should now match Figure 11.1. If you are interested in experimenting with this program, try the following modifications:

- Add a procedure that produces a written report using the data in the WAGES.DAT file.

- Rewrite the program so that it creates a new data file, with four values in each record. In addition to the three shown here, have the computer calculate the average weekly wage for all workers and include this value as the fourth field in each record.

MORE WAYS OF ADDING AND RETRIEVING DATA

The WAGES.BAS program uses a WRITE # statement to add data to the WAGES.DAT file and an INPUT # statement to read data from the file. Some additional commands for writing and reading from sequential files are covered next. Understanding these commands will help give you more control of sequential file management.

COMPARING WRITE # AND PRINT #

When you use WRITE # to add data values to a file, delimiters are added automatically, which is convenient when you want the information in the file to be read by the computer. However, because sequential files are ASCII text files, you might also want to create files meant to be displayed or printed rather than read into memory by the computer. For these applications, you can use a PRINT # statement. A PRINT # statement adds data to a file using the same rules of syntax that govern on-screen display when you use a PRINT statement.

To understand the difference between WRITE # and PRINT #, create and run the following short program, which uses these two methods to add the same data to two different files.

```
READ Today$, Age, First$, Last$
DATA "August 23, 1990",28,Jean,Smith
```

```
OPEN "WRITE" FOR OUTPUT AS #1
WRITE #1, Today$, Age, First$, Last$

OPEN "PRINT" FOR OUTPUT AS #2
PRINT #2, Today$, Age, First$, Last$

CLOSE #1, #2
```

After running the program, compare the data in the WRITE and PRINT files it creates. Look first at the WRITE file, which looks like this.

```
"August 23, 1990",28,"Jean","Smith"
```

Add the following lines to your program to read and display data from this file.

```
CLS
OPEN "WRITE" FOR INPUT AS #1
INPUT #1, Today$, Age, First$
PRINT Today$: PRINT Age: PRINT First$
CLOSE #1
```

Because of the delimiters that were added automatically to the file, the data is correctly read and displayed as

```
August 23, 1990
 28
Jean
```

Now examine the PRINT file to see the effect of the PRINT # statement. This file, shown below, contains no delimiting commas or quotation marks.

```
August 23, 1990     28     Jean     Smith
```

Instead, the data is spaced in columns. Columns such as this are ideal if you want to create a table to be read by a person, but the next exercise shows what happens if you try to have the computer read this data. Add these lines to your program.

```
PRINT
OPEN "PRINT" FOR INPUT AS #1
INPUT #1, Today$, Age, First$
PRINT Today$: PRINT Age: PRINT First$
CLOSE #1
```

When the computer reads the value for the string variable Today$, it searches for a delimiter, and, in this case, misinterprets the comma in the date, using it to mark the end of the first data value. This means that *1990* is left unread. When the numeric value for Age is read, the computer uses the space after 1990 as the next delimiter, and assigns this value to the Age variable. Finally, when the string variable First$ is read, the computer finds no delimiters until it reaches the end of the line, so all the remaining data is read into this variable. The resulting output is shown here:

```
August 23
  1990
28              Jean            Smith
```

Although the data in the PRINT file is quite readable to us, it is incorrectly read by the computer. On the other hand, the WRITE file is accurately read by the computer, but presents a dense, cluttered appearance.

USING LINE INPUT #

When you use INPUT # to read data from a file, any one of several delimiters is recognized. In contrast, the LINE INPUT # statement reads all of the information on one line regardless of the presence or absence of commas, quotation marks, and spaces. When LINE INPUT # is used, data is read one line at a time into a string variable. The syntax of a LINE INPUT # statement is

LINE INPUT #*n*, *StringVariable$*

If you use LINE INPUT # to read data from the WAGES.DAT file you created earlier, you can read the entire line of data for each record into a single variable, as shown here.

```
OPEN "WAGES.DAT" FOR INPUT AS #1
LINE INPUT #1 Record$
PRINT Record$
CLOSE #1
```

The first line of data, which corresponds to the first record in the file, is assigned to the Record$ variable, which is then displayed as

```
"Assembly Line Worker",311,198
```

LINE INPUT # is demonstrated in the PROGLIST program that concludes this chapter.

USING INPUT$ FOR FILE INPUT

Refer to Chapter 8 for information about using INPUT$ for keyboard input.

An additional way of reading data from a sequential file is with the INPUT$ function. You have seen how to use this function to get keyboard input. As with keyboard input, you can use INPUT$ to read a specified number of characters, in this case from a file rather than from the keyboard. When you use INPUT$ to read from a file, you must include the file number as well as the number of characters you want to read from the file. The syntax is shown here:

```
INPUT$(n, #Filenumber)
```

The value of the numeric expression n determines the number of characters to be read from the file, and *Filenumber* gives the number of the file that is being read.

To demonstrate this function, first create an ALPHABET file with each of the letters of the alphabet, either using the program shown here or by creating and saving the file using the View screen.

```
OPEN "ALPHABET" FOR OUTPUT AS #1
FOR Ascii = 65 TO 90
   Letter$ = CHR$(Ascii)
   PRINT #1, Letter$;
```

```
NEXT Ascii
CLOSE
```

Next, type and run this short program, which reads the file as two 13-character-long string values.

```
OPEN "ALPHABET" FOR INPUT AS #1
CLS
DO UNTIL EOF(1)
   DataIn$ = INPUT$(13, #1)
   PRINT DataIn$
LOOP
CLOSE
```

The output is shown here:

```
ABCDEFGHIJKLM
NOPQRSTUVWXYZ
```

Try modifying the program to read two characters at a time. Also see what happens when you try to read three or four characters at a time.

FILE-MANAGEMENT TECHNIQUES

In order to handle the files created by your programs, you should be familiar and comfortable with the DOS file-management commands. These commands allow you to perform such tasks as copying, renaming, and erasing files. If you are working with a hard disk, you should also know how to make and remove directories and how to work with directory paths. There are several BASIC commands similar to the DOS commands that perform these tasks. It is also possible to incorporate DOS commands into your programs. The next two sections describe commands that you can use to incorporate file management into your QuickBASIC programs.

USING THE SHELL STATEMENT

Using the SHELL statement allows you to incorporate DOS commands into your program. A SHELL statement can be followed by any valid command string. For example, the statement

    SHELL "Dir *.BAS"

will result in an on-screen display of all files with the .BAS extension. These lines would result in a directory listing of all .BAS files on the disk in the A drive:

    Drive$ = "Dir A:\"
    FileList$ = "*.BAS"
    SHELL Drive$ + FileList$

Although the command strings in these examples are provided in different ways, both examples use a standard DOS command. The SHELL command can also be used to run any executable program. If your disk contains an AUTOEXEC.BAT file, you could use the command

    SHELL "Autoexec"

to run this batch file from within a program.

If the SHELL statement is used alone, with no command string, the effect is identical to the effect of the DOS Shell command in the File menu. The person running the program will be presented with a DOS prompt from which any valid DOS command can be executed. Typing **Exit** at this prompt returns control to the program.

A SUMMARY OF BASIC FILE-MANAGEMENT COMMANDS

Programs that use data files are most useful to the user if they can perform tasks such as listing, erasing, and renaming files. You can use the BASIC commands described in the material that follows to incorporate file management into your QuickBASIC programs.

FILES *filespec$*   Lists all or some of the files in the current directory or in other directories on the disk.

The FILES command lists file names in column format. The file specification can include standard DOS wildcard symbols (? and *)

and can also indicate a directory path. The command shown here would list all files in the QB45 directory that begin with the letter A:

FILES "C:\QB45\A*.*"

When no path is indicated, the FILES command searches the correct directory for the specified files. When FILES is used without an argument, it displays all the files in the current directory.

KILL *filespec$*   Deletes files from a disk.

Like the file specification in the FILES command, the KILL command can include standard DOS wildcard symbols and can also indicate a directory path. Be careful when using wildcard symbols. The statement

KILL "*.*"

will delete all files in the current directory without displaying the familiar DOS message *Are you sure? (Y/N)*. If a KILL statement specifies a file that is not on the disk, program execution will be interrupted and an error message will be displayed.

NAME *oldfilespec$* AS *newfilespec$*—renames a file, or to moves a file to a new directory.

The file specifications in a NAME statement may or may not include a directory path. When no path is indicated, all changes take place in the current directory. The file named first is renamed using the name that follows the AS clause. The statement

NAME "OLDNAME" AS "NEWNAME"

renames the OLDNAME file, giving it the name NEWNAME. By including a directory path, you can use this command to move a file from one directory to another. This command moves the SALES file from the current directory to the DATA directory without changing the file name.

NAME "SALES" AS "\DATA\SALES"

Don't try the KILL "*.*" command unless you are working in a directory that contains no files you want to keep.

The NAME command cannot be used to transfer a file from one disk to another, however.

The three commands below all involve working with directories.

MKDIR *pathspec$*   Creates a new directory.

CHDIR *pathspec$*   Changes the default directory.

RMDIR *pathspec$*   Removes a directory from the disk.

The MKDIR, CHDIR, and RMDIR commands work like their DOS counterparts, although they cannot be shortened to MD, CD, and RD. The two statements

```
MKDIR "a:\junk"
```

and

```
SHELL "MD a:\junk"
```

are equivalent. Both will create a directory named JUNK on the disk in the A drive.

When a directory name is given with no path specification, the directory used will be a subdirectory of the current directory. For example, the command

```
CHDIR "Letters"
```

will change directories to the LETTERS subdirectory of the current directory. If this directory does not exist, program execution is interrupted and an error message is displayed. Error messages also result if you try to create a directory that already exists or remove a nonexistent or incorrectly identified directory. You'll learn more about handling error messages like this in Chapter 14.

THE PROGLIST PROGRAM

Some programs, like the WAGES program, are designed both to create and read disk files. Other useful programming applications are designed to handle files that already exist on the disk. PROGLIST is in the second category, and the files it uses are your own Quick-BASIC program listings.

You may have noticed that when you print programs with the QuickBASIC Print command, the printed output contains no margins. Long programs printed in this way can be hard to read. Using PROGLIST, you can print out your program files with top, bottom, and left-hand margins that are easily adjusted by changing constants in the program listing. The program even lets you use a remark statement to include a special code ('pa or 'PA) within your programs wherever you want printout to start on a new page.

In order to use PROGLIST, you must first save any program you want to print as *text*, rather than with the default QuickBASIC format. Once you've saved a file as text, it can be handled like any other sequential data file. PROGLIST reads each program line as a single record, with the CR-LF at the end of each line serving as a delimiter between records.

The PROGLIST program listing is shown in Figure 11.4. The main body of the program sets three constants, MAXLINES, TOP-MARGIN, and LEFTMARGIN to control the number of lines per page, the size of the top margin, and the size of the left-hand margin. One variable, Lines%, is declared as a SHARED variable. Lines% is used to keep track of the number of lines per printed page.

The first procedure called is the GetFile$ function, which requests the name of the file to be printed using the following prompt:

What file would you like to print?

In response to this prompt, the user can enter the name of any Quick-BASIC program that has been saved as a text file. The procedure checks to see if the .BAS extension was included in the user response, and adds it to the file name if it was omitted. The full file name is then returned to the program, and an OPEN statement opens the file for input.

The next procedure called is PrintListing. This procedure uses a LINE INPUT # statement to read the program, one line at a time. As each line is read, an IF...THEN structure checks to see if the line begins with 'pa (or 'PA). If this marker is present at the beginning of a line, the line is not printed and instead the NewPage procedure is called. NewPage advances the printer to the top of the next page,

```
REM PROGLIST.BAS
'Prints a program  with top and bottom margins on each page and
'starts new pages where 'PA are the first three characters on a line.

DECLARE FUNCTION GetFile$ ()
DECLARE SUB NewPage ()
DECLARE SUB PrintListing ()

'The global lines% variable keeps track of printed lines
COMMON SHARED lines%

'Set constants for margins and printed lines per page
CONST MAXLINES = 53, TOPMARGIN = 4, LEFTMARGIN = 6

'Get the name of a file to print
FileName$ = GetFile$

'Open that file for input as a sequential file.
OPEN FileName$ FOR INPUT AS #1

'Ready the printer.
PRINT : PRINT "Ready the printer and press any key to begin."
Ready$ = INPUT$(1)

'Create a top margin
FOR n% = 1 TO TOPMARGIN
  LPRINT
NEXT n%

'Print the file
CALL PrintListing

'Close the file
CLOSE #1

END

'pa
'Display program info and get the name of a file to print.
FUNCTION GetFile$
  CLS
  PRINT "This program can be used to print QuickBASIC programs."
  PRINT "Programs must First be saved as Text Files."
  PRINT
  INPUT "What file would you like to print"; ProgFile$
  'Add the .BAS extension if no extension was used
  IF INSTR(ProgFile$, ".") = 0 THEN
    ProgFile$ = ProgFile$ + ".BAS"
  END IF
  GetFile$ = ProgFile$
END FUNCTION

'Start a new page and reset the line counter
SUB NewPage
  LPRINT CHR$(12)                'Use a FF code to advance to paper
  FOR n% = 1 TO TOPMARGIN        'Create a top margin
    LPRINT
  NEXT n%
  lines% = 0                     'Reset the line counter
END SUB

'Print the file line by line using top margins and page advances
SUB PrintListing
  DO
    'Read a line of text from the program.
    LINE INPUT #1, TextLine$
```

Figure 11.4: The PROGLIST program listing

```
       'Print the line of text unless it begins with 'PA or 'pa
       IF UCASE$(LEFT$(TextLine$, 3)) = "'PA" THEN
          'Start new page
          NewPage
       ELSE
          'Print each line, advancing page after maximum lines per page
          LPRINT TAB(LEFTMARGIN); TextLine$
          lines% = lines% + 1
          IF lines% = MAXLINES THEN NewPage
       END IF
    LOOP WHILE NOT EOF(1)

       'Advance page when done
       LPRINT CHR$(12)
    END SUB
```

Figure 11.4: The PROGLIST program listing (continued)

prints blank lines to create a top margin, and resets the value of Lines% to zero.

If a program line does not begin with the page-advance marker, it is printed out, and the value of the Lines% variable is incremented by one. If the value of Lines% reaches the limit set by MAXLINES, the NewPage procedure is called.

Type in the program listing as it appears in Figure 11.4 and then save the file using the *Text–Readable By Other Programs* Format option. Print the program, first using the QuickBASIC Print command in the Files menu. Then try running the program, and enter *PRO-GLIST* in response to the prompt that asks you what file you want to print. This time the printed output that results will include top and left margins, and, because of the *'pa* marker, the printer will advance to a new page before printing the program procedures that follow this marker. Try using PROGLIST to print other programs, but remember that they must first be saved as text files. You might also want to experiment with changing the three constants, MAXLINES, TOP-MARGIN, and LEFTMARGIN, in order to find a page layout that suits your tastes.

SUMMARY

The use of data files gives your programs enormous flexibility for storing and retrieving data. Sequential data files are standard text files.

Individual elements in a sequential file are separated by delimiters, which are used by the computer when data is read from these files.

An OPEN statement must be used to open data files before any I/O operation takes place. With sequential files the OPEN statement must specify whether the file will be used for input or output. To open a file for output, use OPEN...FOR APPEND if you want to add data to the end of an existing file, and OPEN...FOR OUTPUT if you want to replace existing data. Once you open a file with either technique, you can add information to it using WRITE # or PRINT # statements. Using WRITE # creates a file that includes delimiters, while using PRINT # creates a file with an appearance that matches the screen output that would be produced using PRINT statements. To open a file for input, use an OPEN...FOR INPUT statement and then use INPUT #, LINE INPUT #, or INPUT$ to read data from the file, depending on the amount of material you want to read with each input statement.

Every open file must be closed before it can be used for a different kind of I/O operation and also before the end of program execution. CLOSE, RESET, CLEAR, and END are examples of commands that you can use to close your data files.

Working with data files also means performing a variety of operations involving file and directory management. BASIC commands for performing these tasks were summarized in this chapter. An alternative way of performing these tasks is with the SHELL command. This flexible and powerful statement allows you to invoke any DOS operation from within your programs.

In this chapter you have worked exclusively with sequential files. While these files have many useful applications, they are also limited because they must always be read in order from beginning to end. A second kind of data file, known as a random-access file, is not limited in this way. Random-access files are the subject of Chapter 12.

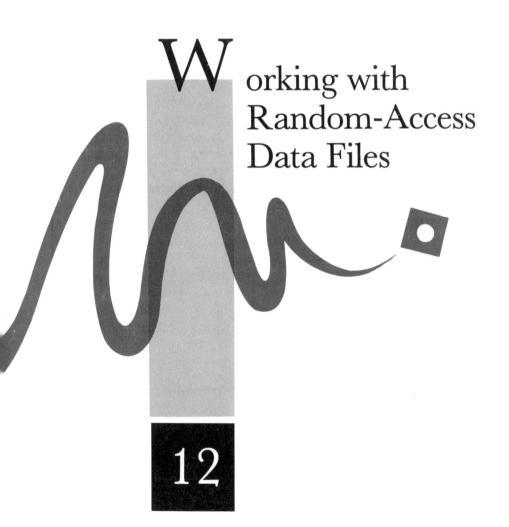

W orking with Random-Access Data Files

12

CHAPTER *12* ─────────────────

THIS CHAPTER INTRODUCES THE USE OF RANDOM-access data files for storing and retrieving data. As their name implies, random-access files allow you access to any record in a file at any time. The difference between sequential-access and random-access is somewhat analogous to the difference between listening to music on tape and listening to music on a record or a compact disc. Like a sequential-access file, a tape requires you to run through each part of the tape in order, which is perfectly satisfactory when you are interested in hearing an entire tape, but slow and awkward when you want to hear one particular song. Like a random-access file, records and discs allow you to select and listen to songs in any order.

Random-access files differ from sequential files in several important ways:

- The structure of a random-access file is fixed and must be carefully defined before you use the file. This structure describes the number and type of file in each record.

- Delimiters such as commas, spaces, and carriage returns are not used to separate items in a random-access file because the structure of a random-access file means that information can be found and identified based on its position in the file.

- Once a random-access file has been opened, it is possible both to read information *from* the file and write new information *to* the file.

- The records in a random-access file can be read directly into memory in any order by identifying each record by number.

- Existing records can be modified by identifying a record by number and writing new information to the targeted record.

- Random-access files use a *binary* format to store numbers. This more compressed format means that random access files use fewer bytes of storage space to store numbers, and also that these files cannot be viewed or modified directly as text.

Figure 12.1 shows an example of the structure of a random-access file. The file contains two string fields: a 10-character Name field, and an 8-character PhoneNumber field. The length of each record in this file is 18 bytes, and the length of the entire file is therefore equal to 18 multiplied by the total number of records in the file.

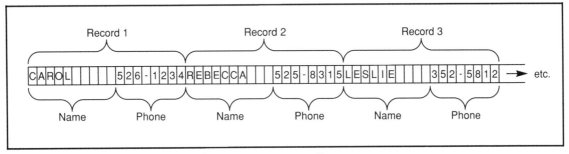

Figure 12.1: The arrangement of data in a random-access file

In general, sequential files are more useful when the records in the file are of variable length, when the contents of a file will not need to be altered once the file has been created, or when the file is a short, simple one and this simpler programming method is desirable to save program development time. Random-access files are useful when there will be frequent additions, deletions, and modifications to the file; when you want to be able to work with sorted records; and when online, rapid access to any record in a file is desired.

In the material that follows, you will learn how to create and work with random-access files.

A STEP-BY-STEP GUIDE TO USING RANDOM-ACCESS FILES

The steps used to create and use a random-access file are summarized below. The details of each step will be covered in the sections that follow.

1. Declare a composite, user-defined data-type by using a TYPE...END TYPE structure. This data-type describes the

QuickBASIC programming allows you to define the structure of a random-access file in two different ways, using either a FIELD statement or a TYPE statement. The TYPE statement is a newer and more flexible approach to handling random-access records and this newer technique will be used here.

size and type of each of the fields that make up a record in the file.

2. Declare a record variable to be of this user-defined type using a DIM or COMMON statement.

3. Use an OPEN statement to open a file for random access, specifying the name of the file, the number that will be used to identify this file, and the length of each record in the file.

4. Use the LOF and LEN functions to calculate the number of records in the file.

5. Add records to the file with a PUT statement.

6. Read records from the file with a GET statement that specifies the file number and the record number for the record you want to retrieve.

7. Update existing records by using a GET statement to retrieve the record, changing the desired fields, and using a PUT statement to write the new data to the same location in the file.

8. Use a CLOSE statement to close the file.

In the material that follows you will explore each of these eight steps as you build the FUNDS.BAS program. This program is the output of an imaginary high school's computer programming class. Because of a recent voter initiative, the Anytown School District has had to face severe budget restrictions. In order to save the computer and music programs in the schools, the district has embarked on a fund-raising campaign. Each school in the district has developed a fund-raising program, and FUNDS.BAS is a simplified database program that keeps track of these funds.

Figure 12.2 shows the module-level code of the FUNDS program. Begin by typing in this much of the program. It is explained below. Notice that four program statements toward the end of this listing have been turned into remark statements by using REM at the beginning of the line. Using this technique allows you to run the program before you create all of the procedures it will eventually include. As you create these procedures, remove the REM keyword from these lines.

```
REM FUNDS.BAS
'A program for a school district fund-raising project
'Demonstrates the use of a random access file

DEFINT A-Z

'Define a data type which describes the structure of each record
TYPE RecordType
   SchoolName AS STRING * 20
   Funds AS SINGLE
END TYPE

'Define a record variable which uses this data type
DIM SchoolRecord AS RecordType

'Procedure declarations
DECLARE SUB AddRecord (School AS RecordType)
DECLARE SUB DisplayRecords (School AS RecordType)
DECLARE SUB Update (School AS RecordType)

'Open a random-access file and indicate the length of each record
OPEN "FUNDS.DAT" FOR RANDOM AS #1 LEN = LEN(SchoolRecord)

'Calculate the number of records in the file
NumberOfRecords = LOF(1) \ LEN(SchoolRecord)

'Add a new record to the file
CLS
PRINT "Would you like to add a new school to the file (Y/N)? ":
Response$ = INPUT$(1)
IF UCASE$(Response$) = "Y" THEN CALL AddRecord(SchoolRecord)

'Display the records in the file
REM CALL DisplayRecords(SchoolRecord)

'Update an existing record
REM PRINT "Would you like to update a record (Y/N)? ";
REM Response$ = UCASE$(INPUT$(1)): PRINT Response$
REM IF Response$ = "Y" THEN CALL Update(SchoolRecord)

'Close the file
CLOSE #1

END
```

Figure 12.2: The module-level code of the FUNDS program

STEP ONE: DEFINING A NEW DATA-TYPE

See Chapter 3 for more information about QuickBASIC's five built-in data-types.

QuickBASIC provides you with five built-in data-types: SINGLE, DOUBLE, INTEGER, LONG, and STRING. The fields that make up a record in a random-access file will consist of some mixture of these five data-types. For example, if a company used a random-access file to store information about its employees, each record in the file might contain four fields: Name, Address, Phone, and Salary. String variables would be used to handle the first three items, while Salary would be handled as a numeric data-type.

Every different random-access file contains its own unique combination of field types. TYPE...END TYPE statements enable you to name and describe the data elements that make up each record in the file you are working with. The general syntax for a TYPE statement is

```
TYPE UserType
    ElementName AS Data-Type
    [ElementName AS Data-Type]
        .
        .
        .
END TYPE
```

UserType is the name you have chosen to use for the composite data-type you are describing. As part of the definition, each element in *UserType* is given a name and assigned a data-type. *Data-Type* can be any of QuickBASIC's built-in data-types, or another user-defined type. If the data-type is STRING, the length of the string element must also be specified. This is done by adding an asterisk followed by a numeric constant after the keyword STRING.

To understand the TYPE statement, see how it has been used in the FUNDS program. The program uses a random-access data file called FUNDS.DAT in order to store the names of the schools in Anytown, and the amount of money each school has raised. A user-defined data-type called RecordType is created as shown here:

```
TYPE RecordType
    SchoolName AS STRING * 20
    Funds AS SINGLE
END TYPE
```

This data-type describes the structure of each record in the FUNDS-.DAT file. The first element in each record is a 20-character-long string value called *SchoolName*. The second element is a single-precision value called *Funds*. Together they make up the new, user-defined data-type called RecordType.

STEP TWO: DECLARING
A VARIABLE WITH THE NEW DATA-TYPE

Once you have created a user-defined data-type, the next step is to declare a variable as having this new data-type. This is the variable you will use to read and write records to and from the data file. In the FUNDS program, the variable SchoolRecord is declared as having the user defined data-type. Once you have declared a variable as having the new data-type, you can work either with separate elements of the variable or with the entire variable. To identify separate elements within a composite variable, use a two-part name such as the one shown here:

SchoolRecord.SchoolName

This identifies the first element in the SchoolRecord variable. The suffix that follows the period must be one of the element names that you included in the TYPE statement that defined the record type. It follows that the second element in the SchoolRecord variable is identified as

SchoolRecord.Funds

To handle the entire variable, you use just the variable name, School-Record, without a period and suffix following it.

You can declare a variable in a DIM, DIM SHARED, or COMMON SHARED statement. The statement

DIM *VariableName* AS *RecordType*

Refer to Chapter 7 for more information about the difference between local and global variables; and the relationship between arguments and parameters.

declares a local variable called VariableName as having the user-defined data type called RecordType. In this next statement,

DIM SHARED *VariableName* AS *RecordType*

the variable is declared globally and will therefore be available to SUB and FUNCTION procedures as well as to the main module of the program.

Because the FUNDS program uses arguments to pass data from the module-level code to the SUB procedures, it declares a local record variable. This is done in the following program statement:

DIM SchoolRecord AS RecordType

The procedure declarations that follow this statement also specify that the parameter School, which is used in each of the program's three procedures, is also of the user-defined record type. If you omit these procedure declarations and then save the program, Quick-BASIC will automatically add procedure declarations such as this one at the beginning of the program:

DECLARE SUB AddRecord (School AS ANY)

The AS ANY clause is used because this declaration is added in a position in the program that precedes the definition of the Record-Type data-type. When AS ANY is used in a procedure declaration, no type checking occurs to ensure that arguments in procedure calls have the same data-type as their corresponding parameters in the called procedure.

STEP THREE: OPENING THE FILE

An OPEN statement can open an existing file for I/O operations, or create a new file if the file named in the OPEN statement does not already exist. Once you open a random-access data file, you can perform both read and write procedures with that file. A general form of the OPEN statement for working with random-access files is

OPEN *FileName$* **FOR RANDOM AS** *#FileNumber* **LEN** = *RecordLength*

FileName$ is the name of the file being opened and *FileNumber* is the number that will be used to identify this file in subsequent program lines. The FOR RANDOM clause identifies this as a random-access file. The LEN *clause* specifies the length of each record in a file. It is not necessary for you to calculate the length of each record. Instead, you can use the LEN *function* to return the length of the record variable you have already declared. To do this, you would replace LEN = *RecordLength* with LEN = LEN(*RecordVariable*). If you do not specify a record length in an OPEN statement, QuickBASIC sets a default record length equal to 128.

The following OPEN statement in the FUNDS program opens the FUNDS.DAT file for random access as file #1:

```
OPEN "FUNDS.DAT" FOR RANDOM AS #1 LEN = LEN(SchoolRecord)
```

STEP FOUR: CALCULATING THE NUMBER OF RECORDS IN THE FILE

When you are writing a record to a random-access file, you generally identify that record by number. If you don't specify a record number, the record you are adding to the file will automatically be added as the first record in the file, regardless of whether or not data is already stored in that location. In order to add information to the *end* of a random-access file, you must know how many records are already in the file. This figure is determined in the FUNDS program by dividing the length of the data file (LOF(1)) by the length of each record in the file (LEN(SchoolRecord)), as shown here:

```
NumberOfRecords = LOF(1) \ LEN(SchoolRecord)
```

In the next section you will see how to use the value of the variable NumberOfRecords to add new data to the FUNDS.DAT file.

STEP FIVE: ADDING RECORDS TO A RANDOM-ACCESS FILE

A PUT statement is used to write information to a random-access file. This statement can be used both to add new records to the end of a file and to alter existing records in the file. In the AddRecord procedure of the FUNDS program, it is used to add new records to the file. Add this procedure to your program as it is shown in Figure 12.3.

With the completed AddRecord procedure, you can now create the FUNDS.DAT file and add records to it. Run the program and the first prompt you see will be

Would you like to add a new school to the file (Y/N)?

```
DEFINT A-Z
'---------------------------AddRecord----------------------
'Adds new records to the FUNDS.DAT file
'-----------------------------------------------------------
SUB AddRecord (School AS RecordType) STATIC
  SHARED NumberOfRecords
  DO
    'Get data
    CLS
    INPUT "School Name: ", School.SchoolName
    INPUT "Funds raised: ", School.Funds

    'Calculate the record number for this record
    NumberOfRecords = NumberOfRecords + 1

    'Add data to the file
    PUT #1, NumberOfRecords, School

    PRINT : PRINT "Add another (Y/N)? "
    Continue$ = UCASE$(INPUT$(1))
  LOOP WHILE Continue$ = "Y"
END SUB
```

Figure 12.3: The AddRecord procedure of the FUNDS program

Press Y to call the AddRecords procedure and add the first record as shown here:

School Name: Anytown High School
Funds raised: 1500

The next prompt asks you if you want to

Add another (Y/N)?

Answer by pressing Y, and continue to add data for the first two or three schools listed in Figure 12.4.

Now study the AddRecord procedure to see how it added the values you just typed to the growing FUNDS.DAT file. The PUT statement in this procedure looks like this:

PUT #1, NumberOfRecords, School

The NumberOfRecords variable controls the position in the file where the new record will be placed. The value for NumberOf-Records is declared as a SHARED variable within the procedure definition. The School variable is a parameter that corresponds to the

```
Record #       School                   Funds Raised
   1           Anytown High School      $ 1,500.00
   2           King Jr. High            $   850.00
   3           Kennedy Jr. High         $   675.00
   4           Columbus school          $   450.00
   5           Roosevelt School         $   600.00
   6           Lincoln School           $   540.00

TOTAL                                   $  4,615.00

Would you like to update a record (Y/N)?
```

Figure 12.4: Displaying the Records in the FUNDS.DAT File

SchoolRecord argument and stores the information that makes up the new record. This important clause in the SUB statement

> School AS RecordType

establishes the data-type of the school variable.

The two INPUT statements shown here are used to get keyboard input for the two elements that make up the School variable.

> INPUT "School Name: ", School.SchoolName
> INPUT "Funds raised: ", School.Funds

Before this new information is written to the data file with the PUT statement, the value for NumberOfRecords is increased by one. This ensures that each new record will be added to the end of the existing file.

STEP SIX: READING RECORDS FROM A RANDOM-ACCESS FILE

The GET statement is used to read information from a random-access data file, as demonstrated by the DisplayRecords procedure of the FUNDS program. This procedure, shown in Figure 12.5, displays the contents of the file on screen. Add DisplayRecords to your

Because random-access files are not text files, you cannot examine the contents of these files within the View window, as you can do with sequential-access files.

program and remove the REM from the beginning of the line that calls this procedure from the main module of your program.

Run the modified program without adding any new schools to the file. The schools you have already added to the list should be displayed on screen, and the value for total funds raised should appear at the end of the list. This is accomplished by a loop that reads each record in turn from the FUNDS.DAT file, using the GET statement shown here:

GET #1, RecordNumber, School

As the loop repeats, the value for RecordNumber starts at one and increases by one until it reaches the total number of records. The values that are retrieved into the School variable for each record are then displayed on screen, along with that record's number. With each iteration of the loop, the value of the Funds field is added to the variable Total!, which keeps a running total of the funds raised. This total value is displayed after all the records have been read.

Run the program again, adding the remaining schools to the data file.

```
'-------------------------DisplayRecords----------------------
'Displays records and record numbers in an on-screen table
'-------------------------------------------------------------
SUB DisplayRecords (School AS RecordType)
    SHARED NumberOfRecords

    'Display the heading
    CLS
    PRINT "Record #", "School"; TAB(40); "Funds Raised"

    'Read and display each record, keeping track of total funds
    PRINT
    FOR RecordNumber = 1 TO NumberOfRecords
        GET #1, RecordNumber, School
        PRINT RecordNumber, School.SchoolName;
        PRINT USING "$#####,.##"; TAB(42); School.Funds
        Total! = Total! + School.Funds
    NEXT RecordNumber

    'Display the total
    PRINT
    PRINT "TOTAL";
    PRINT USING "$######,.##"; TAB(41); Total!
    PRINT
END SUB
```

Figure 12.5: The DisplayRecords procedure of the FUNDS program

STEP SEVEN: UPDATING EXISTING RECORDS

One of the most important characteristics of a random-access file is that it enables you to update any record in the file at any time. This technique is demonstrated by the Update procedure, shown in Figure 12.6. Add this procedure to your program and remove the REM statement from the beginning of the three lines following the line that reads

'Update an existing record

```
DEFINT A-Z
'-----------------------------Update--------------------------
'Uses record numbers to update specified records in the file
'-------------------------------------------------------------
SUB Update (School AS RecordType)
    SHARED NumberOfRecords
    DO
        'Find out which record to update
        INPUT "Please enter the record number: ", RecordNumber

        'Indicate if the record number is out of range
        IF RecordNumber > NumberOfRecords THEN
            PRINT "That record is out of range."

        'or update the file if the record number is OK
        ELSE
            'Get a new value for funds raised
            INPUT "What is the new value for funds raised"; School.Funds

            'Write the updated record to the file
            PUT #1, RecordNumber, School
            PRINT

            'Display the updated list
            CALL DisplayRecords(School)
        END IF
        PRINT "Change any more records (Y/N)? ";
        Continue$ = UCASE$(INPUT$(1)): PRINT Continue$
    LOOP WHILE Continue$ = "Y"
END SUB
```

Figure 12.6: The Update procedure of the FUNDS program

Run the program again, without adding any new schools to the list. After the list of schools has been displayed, respond to the prompt that reads

Would you like to Update a record (Y/N)?

by pressing Y. The next prompt will read

Please enter the record number:

If you enter a record number that is on the list, a GET statement reads that record into memory, and you are asked to enter a new value for the amount of funds raised. The value you enter is stored as School.Funds. The PUT statement shown here uses this value and the record number in order to update the file:

PUT #1, RecordNumber, School

After each update, the DisplayRecords procedure is called in order to display the updated file.

If you enter a record number that is not on the list, the program displays this message:

That record is out of range

To exit from the Update procedure, press N in response to the prompt that reads

Change any more records (Y/N)?

STEP EIGHT: CLOSING THE FILE

The final step in working with any program that uses data files is to close any open files. If you use a CLOSE statement with no file numbers, all open data files will be closed. Or, you can identify the files to be closed, as is done in this statement from the FUNDS program:

CLOSE #1

If you are working with more than one open file in a program and you use a CLOSE statement that specifies files by number, be sure to include the file numbers of all open files. A good backup is to place an END statement at the conclusion of any program that uses data files because one effect of an END statement is to close all open files.

Continue working with the FUNDS program until you feel comfortable with it and understand each of its procedures. If you want to experiment with modifying the file, you might try one of the following:

- Add a procedure that produces a printed report.

- Create a similar program that creates a data file with three fields in each record—school name, phone number, and funds raised.

- Modify the main module of the program so that the program is menu driven. The menu should include four choices that would allow you to add a record, update a record, display the records, or quit the program.

The next section shows you how you can organize information that is stored in a random-access file by using what is known as an *index*. You can continue on to this section now or return to it at some future point, if you prefer.

USING AN INDEX TO SORT RECORDS IN A FILE

An index is a way of ordering the material that is stored in random-access records. The records in these files are apt to be added in chronological order, but it is frequently useful to work with records arranged in some other way. An index organizes the records in a file according to a field known as a *key* field. If you want to see the list of schools in the FUNDS.DAT file arranged alphabetically, you can create an index that uses the SchoolName field as a key field. Using the Funds field as a key field would allow you to work with these records arranged according to the amount of funds raised.

An index can also improve a database program by making it easier for the user to locate a particular item. The update procedure used in the FUNDS program requires you to know the record number for the school you want to change. This is easy enough in this example because the entire file, including record numbers, can be viewed on screen simultaneously; but most databases are far too large to handle in this way. Typically the person using a program wants to find an item in a large list, and this user is likely to know the item by name rather than by record number. An index pairs the name the user knows for each record (the key field) with the record number for that record. The index is then sorted either alphabetically or numerically. The sorted index can be quickly searched for a particular key value. Once the value has been found, the record number that is paired with that value can be used to retrieve the entire record.

THE STRUCTURE OF THE FUNDSNDX PROGRAM

The FUNDSNDX program is a menu-driven program that uses an index in order to work with the information in the FUNDS.DAT file. This is the longest of the demonstration programs in this book. As you begin to work with larger programs, you may find it helpful to draw diagrams that show how the various parts of a program are related. These diagrams are known as *structure charts*. Figure 12.7 shows a structure chart of the FUNDSNDX program.

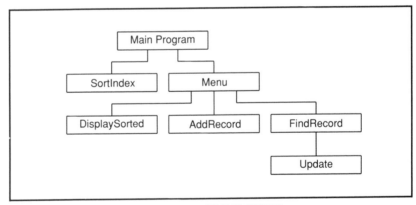

Figure 12.7: A structure chart for the FUNDSNDX program

The main body of the program defines and declares the data types. Unlike the FUNDS program, this program uses shared variables rather than arguments to pass data values to the program's procedure, and these variables are declared in the series of DIM SHARED statements. The next statements open the file and build an index using SchoolName as the key field. Once the index has been created, the program calls the SortIndex procedure, which sorts the elements in the index alphabetically according to school name. (The process of building and sorting the index is discussed in the following section of this chapter.) The Menu procedure, which is called next, displays the following choices:

(1) Display the contents of the file
(2) Add new schools to the file
(3) Update a school record
(4) Quit

If choice (1) is selected, the DisplaySorted procedure is called. This produces an alphabetically sorted list of the schools listed in the FUNDS.DAT file. If choice (2) is selected, the AddRecords procedure is called. This procedure adds records to the file and updates the index. If choice (3) is selected, the user is prompted to give a school name. This school name is searched for in the index array by the FindRecord procedure. If the name is found, the FindRecord procedure calls the Update procedure, which allows the user to update the value of funds raised for that school. Choice (4) terminates the menu loop, returning program control to the main body of the program. The last statement in the main body of the program closes the FUNDS.DAT file. The program listing is shown in Figure 12.8.

```
REM FUNDSNDX.BAS
'A menu driven program that uses an index to work with
'a random access file

'Define default data type and Boolean constants
DEFINT A-Z
CONST FALSE = 0, TRUE = NOT FALSE

'Define a record structure
TYPE RecordType
   SchoolName AS STRING * 20
   Funds AS SINGLE
END TYPE

'Define an index structure for school name
TYPE IndexType
   RecordNumber AS INTEGER
   SchoolName AS STRING * 20
END TYPE

'Declare procedures
DECLARE SUB AddRecords ()
DECLARE SUB DisplaySorted ()
DECLARE SUB FindRecord ()
DECLARE SUB Menu ()
DECLARE SUB SortIndex ()
DECLARE SUB Update (RecordNumber%)
```

Figure 12.8: The FUNDSNDX program listing

```
'Define record variable and index arrays
DIM SHARED SchoolRecord AS RecordType
DIM SHARED NumberOfRecords
DIM SHARED Index(1 TO 25) AS IndexType

'Open the random-access file
OPEN "FUNDS.DAT" FOR RANDOM AS #1 LEN = LEN(SchoolRecord)

'Calculate the number of records
NumberOfRecords = LOF(1) \ LEN(SchoolRecord)

'Create an index by reading each record in the file
'and assigning values to the Index array
FOR N = 1 TO NumberOfRecords
  GET #1, N, SchoolRecord
  Index(N).RecordNumber = N
  Index(N).SchoolName = SchoolRecord.SchoolName
NEXT N

'Sort the index
CALL SortIndex

'Display the main menu
CALL Menu

'Close the file
CLOSE #1
END

'-----------------------AddRecords----------------------
'Adds new records to the end of the FUNDS.DAT file
'-------------------------------------------------------
SUB AddRecords
  DO
    'Get Data and add it to the file
    CLS
    INPUT "School Name:  ", SchoolRecord.SchoolName
    INPUT "Funds raised:  ", SchoolRecord.Funds
    NumberOfRecords = NumberOfRecords + 1
    PUT #1, NumberOfRecords, SchoolRecord

    'Add this record to the end of the present index.
    Index(NumberOfRecords).RecordNumber = NumberOfRecords
    Index(NumberOfRecords).SchoolName = SchoolRecord.SchoolName

    PRINT : PRINT "Add another (Y/N)? "
    Continue$ = UCASE$(INPUT$(1))
  LOOP WHILE Continue$ = "Y"

  'Sort the altered file
  CALL SortIndex
END SUB

'-------------------------DisplaySorted---------------------
'Uses the index to Display records alphabetically by school name
'-------------------------------------------------------
SUB DisplaySorted
  CLS
  PRINT "School"; TAB(25); "Funds Raised"
  PRINT
  FOR I = 1 TO NumberOfRecords
    RecordNumber = Index(I).RecordNumber
    GET #1, RecordNumber, SchoolRecord
    PRINT SchoolRecord.SchoolName;
    PRINT USING "$#####,.##"; TAB(25); SchoolRecord.Funds
    Total! = Total! + SchoolRecord.Funds
```

Figure 12.8: The FUNDSNDX program listing (continued)

```
    NEXT I
    PRINT
    PRINT "TOTAL";
    PRINT USING "$######,.##"; TAB(24); Total!
    LOCATE 23, 1: PRINT "Press any key to continue"
    DO
       Anykey$ = INKEY$
    LOOP WHILE Anykey$ = ""
END SUB
'---------------------------FindRecord-----------------------
'Uses a binary search of the index to locate a school's record
'-----------------------------------------------------------
SUB FindRecord
    CLS
    'Get name of school to search for
    INPUT "School to Update: ", School$

    Match = FALSE
    BottomRecord = 1
    TopRecord = NumberOfRecords
    DO UNTIL TopRecord < BottomRecord
       'Start the search in the middle of the index
       Middle = (TopRecord + BottomRecord) \ 2

       'Trim the school name it the index to the number of
       'characters in the School$ string.
       LookFor$ = LEFT$(Index(Middle).SchoolName, LEN(School$))

       'Look for a match and set a new midpoint if one is not found
       IF LookFor$ = School$ THEN
          Match = Middle
          EXIT DO
       ELSEIF Index(Middle).SchoolName < School$ THEN
          BottomRecord = Middle + 1
       ELSE
          TopRecord = Middle - 1
       END IF
    LOOP

    'Use results of search to update the file
    IF Match THEN
       RecordNumber = Index(Match).RecordNumber
       CALL Update(RecordNumber)
    'or indicate if that record was not found
    ELSE
       PRINT "No school with that name was found"
       PRINT "Press any key to continue"
       DO
          Anykey$ = INKEY$
       LOOP WHILE INKEY$ = ""
    END IF
END SUB
'-----------------------------Menu---------------------------
'Displays the menu and responds to the user choice
'-----------------------------------------------------------
SUB Menu
    'Display Menu and get a choice
    DO
       'Display choices
       CLS
       PRINT TAB(30); "FUND RAISING MENU"
       PRINT
       PRINT TAB(20); "Select a menu item by pressing a number"
       PRINT : PRINT
       PRINT TAB(21); "(1) Display the contents of the file"
```

Figure 12.8: The FUNDSNDX program listing (continued)

```
          PRINT TAB(21); "(2) Add new schools to the file"
          PRINT TAB(21); "(3) Update a school record"
          PRINT TAB(21); "(4) Quit"

          'Get a menu choice and call the appropriate procedure
          Choice$ = INPUT$(1)
          SELECT CASE Choice$
            CASE "1"
              CALL DisplaySorted
            CASE "2"
              CALL AddRecords
            CASE "3"
              CALL FindRecord
          END SELECT
        LOOP UNTIL Choice$ = "4"

      END SUB

      '-----------------------------SortIndex-----------------------
      'Uses a Shell sort to sort the index by school name
      '-------------------------------------------------------------
      SUB SortIndex
        Interval = NumberOfRecords \ 2
        DO WHILE Interval > 0
          Limit = NumberOfRecords - Interval
          DO
            Swapmade = FALSE
            FOR I = 1 TO Limit
              IF Index(I).SchoolName > Index(I + Interval).SchoolName THEN
                SWAP Index(I), Index(I + Interval)
                Swapmade = I
              END IF
            NEXT I
            Limit = Swapmade
          LOOP WHILE Swapmade
          Interval = Interval \ 2
        LOOP
      END SUB

      '-----------------------------Update--------------------------
      'Retrieve and update a record located by the FindRecord procedure
      '-------------------------------------------------------------
      SUB Update (RecordNumber)
        'Get the record
        GET #1, RecordNumber, SchoolRecord

        'Display curent value for funds raised and get a new value
        PRINT "Current Funds Raised: "; SchoolRecord.Funds
        PRINT
        INPUT "New Funds Raised: ", SchoolRecord.Funds

        'Write the updated record to the file
        PUT #1, RecordNumber, SchoolRecord
      END SUB
```

Figure 12.8: The FUNDSNDX program listing (continued)

BUILDING AND SORTING AN INDEX

The second of the two TYPE structures in the FUNDSNDX program defines a composite data-type with two elements—RecordNumber and SchoolName. The following statement

DIM SHARED Index(1 TO 25) AS IndexType

declares the Index array as having up to 25 elements, each composed of a record number and a school name. Values are assigned to this array by this FOR...NEXT loop.

```
FOR N = 1 TO NumberOfRecords
  GET #1, N, SchoolRecord
  Index(N).RecordNumber = N
  Index(N).SchoolName = SchoolRecord.SchoolName
NEXT N
```

The resulting values for each of the two elements in the Index array are shown here:

	RECORDNUMBER	*SCHOOLNAME*
Index(1)	1	Anytown High School
Index(2)	2	King Jr. High
Index(3)	3	Kennedy Jr. High
Index(4)	4	Columbus School
Index(5)	5	Roosevelt School
Index(6)	6	Lincoln School

Once this array has been created, it is sorted with a Shell sort by the SortIndex procedure.

See Chapter 10 for more information about using and sorting arrays.

The sorted index array now contains an alphabetical list of the school names, and each element in the new array includes the original record number, which can be used to find the school in the FUNDS.DAT file. The elements in the sorted index are shown here:

	RECORDNUMBER	*SCHOOLNAME*
Index(1)	1	Anytown High School
Index(2)	4	Columbus School
Index(3)	3	Kennedy Jr. High
Index(4)	2	King Jr. High
Index(5)	6	Lincoln School
Index(6)	5	Roosevelt School

For more informa-
tion about conduct-
ing a binary search, refer
to Chapter 10.

In order to print an alphabetically arranged list of the records in the FUNDS.DAT file, the DisplaySorted procedure uses the sorted index to retrieve record 1 first, then record 4, and so on until the entire file has been read and displayed.

The index also allows the person using the program to call up a record by using the school name. Because the index is arranged alphabetically, a binary search of the school names can be performed to determine quickly if a particular school is on the list, and, if so, to which record number this name corresponds. Before trying to match keyboard input with data that has been read from a random-access file, a program must trim off any trailing spaces that have been included in string values. This is done here by matching only the first characters in the SchoolName field with the school name being searched for. This matching also allows the user to enter a school as either *Lincoln School* or simply *Lincoln.*

Notice that the AddRecords procedure adds a new element to the Index array to correspond to each new record that is added to the file, and then re-sorts the index before returning program control to the main body of the program. When you are working with an index, it is very important to keep the index sorted and up to date whenever any changes are made to the contents of the indexed file. Failure to do so can result in particularly baffling and hard-to-trace program bugs.

SUMMARY

Random-access files allow you the flexibility of working with any record in a file, regardless of its place in the file. This is accomplished by first defining the structure of each record in the file with a TYPE...END TYPE statement. The data type you define this way can then be used to handle the input and output of records in the file. Random access files are opened with an OPEN...FOR RANDOM... statement. Once a file is open, you can read records from the file with a GET statement and write new records, or update existing records, with a PUT statement.

Indexes are a common technique for organizing records in a random-access file. An index pairs the values in one key field of the file with each record's record number. This paired list can then be sorted and used to search the file for a particular record, or to display the records in sorted order.

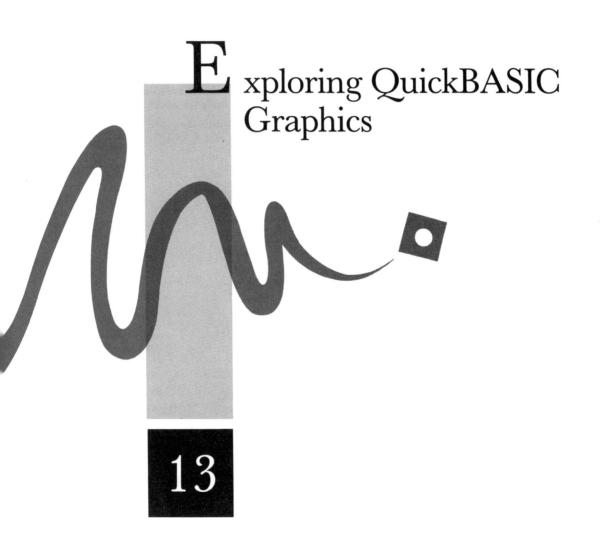

E xploring QuickBASIC Graphics

13

CHAPTER *13* ⎯⎯⎯⎯⎯⎯⎯⎯⎯⎯⎯⎯⎯⎯⎯⎯

THE USE OF SHAPES, COLORS, AND PATTERNS CAN make your programs more dynamic and more fun to work with. In this chapter, you will be introduced to QuickBASIC graphics programming. You'll learn how to work with graphic screen modes and how to draw a variety of shapes on screen. The sample application that completes this chapter uses graphics commands to create on-screen graphs of linear and quadratic equations.

In order to use QuickBASIC graphics commands on a system with a Hercules graphics card, you must run the QuickBASIC utility program, MSHERC.COM, *before* you enter the Quick-BASIC environment. Find the program on your hard disk or on the Utilities 2 disk and run it by typing *msherc* at the DOS command prompt.

To use the QuickBASIC graphics commands, your computer must have graphics capability provided by any one of the following graphics cards: Hercules graphics adapter, Color Graphics Adapter (CGA), Enhanced Graphics Adapter (EGA), Video Graphics Array (VGA), or Multicolor Graphics Array (MCGA). In addition, your monitor must support pixel-based graphics. Monochrome monitors can be used for most of the examples shown in this chapter, but many additional graphics techniques allow you to work with the full range of colors available with a color monitor and graphics adapter.

⎯⎯⎯⎯⎯⎯⎯ *SELECTING A SCREEN MODE* ⎯⎯⎯⎯⎯⎯⎯

The screen output you have produced up to this point has all used *text format* for character display. Using text format, you are limited to the display characters that have an ASCII code. Each ASCII character is created within a fixed amount of screen space, known as a *character box*. The text output screen is made up of a grid of rows and columns of these character boxes. The available number of rows and columns varies from system to system, but a typical screen contains 25 rows and 40 columns. It is this grid that you use when you position text with a LOCATE statement.

For graphic output, however, the screen is divided into a much finer grid. Graphics grids are made up of individual *picture elements* or *pixels*.

Examine the characters on your screen, and you can see that each character display is produced by the illumination of many of these tiny pixels. The number of pixels in the grid determines the clarity or *resolution* of your graphic output. Graphics commands allow you to use these pixels to create an infinite variety of shapes and forms.

In order to use QuickBASIC's graphics commands in your programs, you must first include a SCREEN statement. The purpose of a SCREEN statement is to select from among several different *screen modes* that control the appearance of both graphic and text output. The screen mode you select will depend on the following factors:

- Your system hardware.

- The resolution you want for graphic output.

- The number of rows and columns you want for text output.

- The size and resolution you desire for each text character.

- The range of color choices you would like to have available.

QuickBASIC's screen modes are summarized in Table 13.1. Use the *Hardware Supported* column to determine which screen modes you can use with your system.

The resolution you get in your graphics output is a function of the number of pixels that make up the graphics grid. This information is provided in the column in Table 13.1 labeled *Graphics Grid*. The first figure given is the number of pixels that make up a horizontal row on your screen, and the second figure given is the number of pixels in each vertical column. For example, Screen Mode 9, with a pixel grid of 640 x 350, provides greater resolution than Screen Mode 1, with a 320 x 200 grid, but this screen is available only if you have an EGA or a VGA board.

Many programs combine both graphic and text output in the Output screen. The column labeled *Text Format* in Table 13.1 describes the dimensions of the text grid. The figures given are the number of character boxes in each row, followed by the number of these rows in each column. Screen Mode 1, which places text output in only 40 columns, produces much broader characters than does Screen Mode 2, which uses 80 columns for this purpose.

Table 13.1: Summary of QuickBASIC Screen Modes

SCREEN MODE	HARDWARE SUPPORTED	GRAPHICS GRID	TEXT FORMAT(S)	CHARACTER BOX SIZE(S)	NUMBER OF COLORS
0	All listed	None	*	8 × 8	16–64 *
1	CGA, EGA, VGA, MCGA	320 × 200	40 × 25	8 × 8	16
2	CGA, EGA, VGA, MCGA	640 × 200	80 × 25	8 × 8	16
3	Hercules	720 × 348	80 × 25	9 × 14	Monochrome
4	Olivetti	640 × 400	80 × 24	8 × 16	16
7	EGA, VGA	320 × 200	40 × 25	8 × 8	16
8	EGA, VGA	640 × 200	80 × 25	8 × 8	16
9	EGA, VGA	640 × 350	80 × 25	8 × 14	16–64
10	EGA, VGA	640 × 350	80 × 25 80 × 43	8 × 14 8 × 8	Monochrome
11	VGA, MCGA	640 × 480	80 × 30 80 × 60	8 × 14 8 × 8	256K
12	VGA	640 × 480	80 × 30 80 × 60	8 × 16 8 × 8	256K
13	VGA, MCGA	320 × 200	40 × 25	8 × 8	256K

CGA = Color Graphics Adapter
EGA = Enhanced Graphics Adapter
VGA = Video Graphics Array
MCGA = Multicolor Graphics Array
* Varies depending on the hardware available

In addition to controlling the size of your text characters, you can also control the resolution of text characters. The resolution of text display depends on the number of pixels used to form each character. This information is provided in the column labeled *Character Box Size*.

The final column in Table 13.1 describes the maximum number of different colors available with each of the different screen modes.

To select a screen mode, use a SCREEN statement that specifies the number of the screen mode you want to work with. For example,

```
SCREEN 2
```

selects Screen Mode 2. As you work through this chapter, experiment with each of the screen modes supported by your system in order to see how the features described in Table 13.1 affect the appearance of your screen output.

CREATING BASIC SHAPES

Simple elements like points, lines, rectangles, and circles are the building blocks for a variety of kinds of output. In addition to drawing pictures with them, you can use them to create visual displays that make information easier to understand, such as line graphs (points and lines), bar graphs (rectangles), and pie charts (circles). The BASIC commands for producing these simple elements are explained in the material that follows.

POSITIONING POINTS ON THE SCREEN

The simplest form of graphic output is controlled by the PSET and PRESET commands. Each of these commands controls the appearance of a single pixel. The basic syntax of a PSET statement is

```
PSET (x, y)
```

where x and y are numeric values that locate the position of a point on the screen. The horizontal position is indicated by x, the first coordinate, while the vertical position is indicated by the y coordinate. (This is the reverse of the order used in a LOCATE statement, where row precedes column.) The coordinates of the upper left-hand corner are (0,0), and the coordinates of the lower right-hand corner are the maximum values determined by the screen mode that has been selected. Figure 13.1 shows the coordinates of the center and corners of two different QuickBASIC screens.

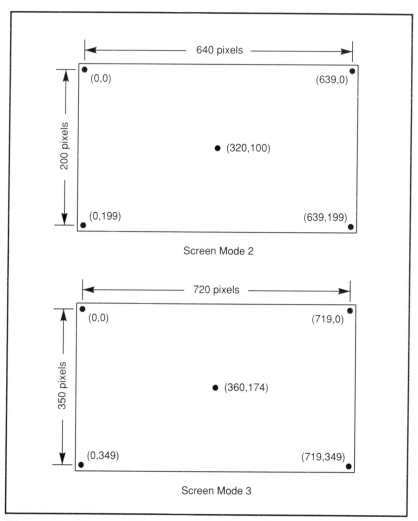

Figure 13.1: Using coordinates to locate pixels in Screen Modes 2 and 3

Try out the PSET command with the following short program. Replace the remark statement in line five with a SCREEN statement that identifies a screen mode supported by your system.

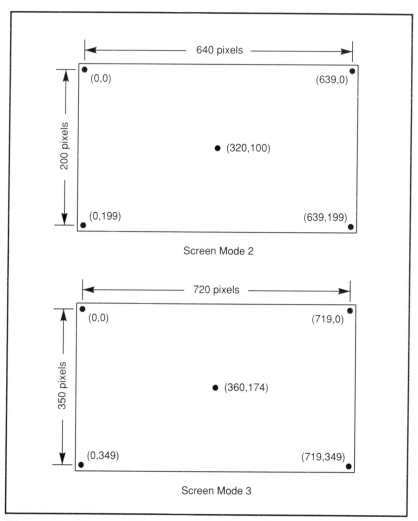
Before running any of the sample programs in this chapter, be sure you have included a SCREEN statement that selects a screen mode that is supported by your system hardware. Refer to Table 13.1 for more information about screen modes.

```
CLS
INPUT "Enter a value for x: ", x
INPUT "Enter a value for y: ", y
CLS
```

```
'Insert a SCREEN statement here
PSET (x, y)
FOR x = x + 10 TO x + 20
   PSET (x, y)
NEXT x
```

The program requests values for the x and y coordinates of a PSET statement. The output will be a graphics screen that draws a point at the position marked by these coordinates and, immediately to the right, a short horizontal line that will help you locate this point.

PRESET works just like PSET, but uses the background color rather than the foreground color when placing a point. This means you can use PRESET to "erase" points that have been placed on screen by a PSET command.

DRAWING LINES

The size and proportion of figures created by the sample programs in this chapter will vary somewhat, depending on the screen mode you choose. Figures shown here were produced using Screen Mode 3.

The LINE statement is a flexible graphics command that can be used to draw both lines and rectangles. In its most basic form, a LINE statement specifies the two endpoints of a line using two sets of coordinates as shown here:

```
LINE (x1, y1)-(x2, y2)
```

The resulting output is a line connecting these two points. The following program draws three lines, each starting in the upper left-hand corner of the screen.

```
'Insert a SCREEN statement here
LINE (1, 1)-(1, 200)          'Vertical line
LINE (1, 1)-(640, 200)        'Diagonal line
LINE (1, 1)-(640, 1)          'Horizontal line
```

Figure 13.2 shows the output of this program.

USING RELATIVE COORDINATES   Line statements can be modified to include only a hyphen and a single coordinate pair, as shown here:

```
LINE -(x, y)
```

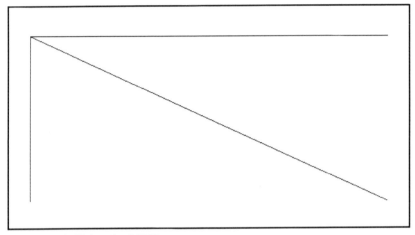

Figure 13.2: Using the LINE statement

In this case, a line is drawn from the last plotted point to the point specified by coordinates *x* and *y*. The program shown below uses this technique to draw a triangle. The output is shown in Figure 13.3.

```
'Insert a SCREEN statement here
LINE (200, 100)-(300, 150)
LINE -(250, 30)
LINE -(200, 100)
```

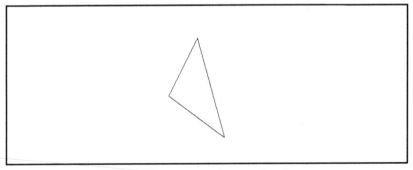

Figure 13.3: Using LINE statements to draw a triangle

USING THE STEP OPTION   An additional graphing tool, the STEP option, allows you to draw lines and place points on the graphics grid by using relative positions rather than specifying absolute coordinates. For example, the statement

```
LINE (50, 50)-STEP(0, 50)
```

describes a vertical line that starts at (50,50), and ends at a point with this same x coordinate, and a y coordinate that is 50 pixels beyond the original value of y. The statement above is equivalent to

```
LINE (50, 50)-(50, 100)
```

The STEP option can also be used in statements that omit the first coordinate pair. In this case the change in position is relative to the most recently plotted point. When combined, the pair of statements shown here are also equivalent to each of the two LINE statements shown above.

```
PSET (50, 50)
LINE -STEP(0, 50)
```

DRAWING BOXES

Although it is possible to draw rectangles by drawing a series of four lines, an easier technique uses the B or BF option within a LINE statement, with the syntax shown here.

```
LINE (x1, y1)-(x2, y2), Color, B[F]
```

When a LINE statement is used this way, $(x1, y1)$ and $(x2, y2)$ indicate diagonally opposite points to be used in the construction of a rectangle. The B option results in a rectangle drawn in outline only, while BF draws a rectangle and then fills it with the current foreground color. The foreground color is indicated by a numeric value for *Color*. If no value for *Color* is given, the current foreground color is used. Even if you omit this item, both commas that precede B or BF must be included in the LINE statement. The program shown here draws two boxes, one in outline, and one filled with color using the default foreground color. The program output is shown in Figure 13.4.

```
'Insert a SCREEN statement here
'Drawing a box
LINE (10, 10)-(100, 100), , B
'Drawing a full box
LINE (100, 100)-(200, 200), , BF
```

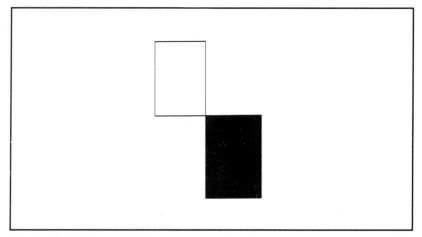

Figure 13.4: Using a LINE statement to draw boxes

If you are using an EGA or a VGA color monitor, you can run the following program with screen modes 7, 8, or 9. This program displays a diagonal pattern of boxes, each filled with a different color. Both the placement and color of each box are determined by the value of the variable, x. The SLEEP statement slows down the display to add a small element of suspense to the program output.

```
'Using color in a box
SCREEN 7
CLS
FOR x = 0 TO 16
    LINE (x * 15, x * 10)-STEP(20, 20), x, BF
    SLEEP 1
NEXT x
```

DRAWING CIRCLES

The CIRCLE statement is a graphics command that draws circles with a specified center and radius. The statement

CIRCLE (*x*, *y*), *Radius*

draws a circle with a center at point (x, y). The length of the radius is given by the value *Radius*.

The program shown here uses a CIRCLE statement within a FOR...NEXT loop to produce the series of concentric circles shown in Figure 13.5.

```
'Insert a SCREEN statement here
FOR Radius = 10 TO 100 STEP 10
    CIRCLE (200, 100), Radius
NEXT Radius
```

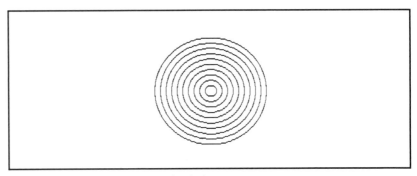

Figure 13.5: Drawing concentric circles

CIRCLE statements can also be used to draw arcs and ellipses. The complete syntax of a CIRCLE statement includes many optional clauses, as shown here:

CIRCLE [STEP] (*x*,*y*),*Radius*[,[*Color*][[*Start*][,[*Stop*][*Aspect*]]]]

A full circle (360°) is approximately equal to 6.28 radians. See the section on trigonometric functions in Chapter 9 for more information about converting degree measurements to radians.

The values for *Start* and *Stop* are used for drawing arcs and wedges. They are angles, measured in radians, which indicate the starting and stopping points for an arc. When the radian measure is given as a negative value, the CIRCLE statement will also draw a line from the center of the circle to this end of the arc. *Aspect* is a ratio used for drawing ellipses. It describes the ratio of the vertical radius of the ellipse to its horizontal radius. These features are demonstrated by the three program lines shown here, which produce the output shown in Figure 13.6:

Don't use -0 when you want to draw a vertical line as one edge of a pie-shaped wedge. Instead, use a very small negative value such as $-.0001$.

```
'Insert a SCREEN statement here
CIRCLE (100, 100), 70, , 1.57, 3.14    'Arc
CIRCLE (200, 100), 70, , -1.57, -3.14  'Wedge
CIRCLE (150, 150), 70, , , , 5 / 25    'Ellipse
```

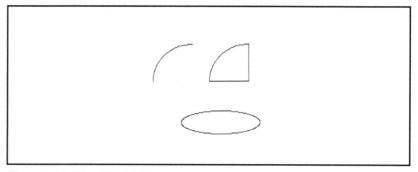

Figure 13.6: The CIRCLE statement: variations on a theme

WORKING WITH THE GRAPHICS VIEWPORT

By default, graphics output fills the entire monitor screen, and uses a coordinate system that places the point (0, 0) in the upper left-hand corner of the screen. Two statements, VIEW and WINDOW, allow you to select how much screen to use for your graphics output and which coordinates you want to use to define the corners of the output area.

The area of your monitor screen that is used for displaying program output is called the *viewport.* A VIEW statement defines the size of the viewport by using the coordinates of its upper left-hand corner and its lower right-hand corner. For example, the full screen in Screen Mode 2 extends from (0, 0) to (640, 200). To define a viewport that uses only the top half of this screen for output, you would use this VIEW statement:

```
VIEW (0, 0)-(640,100)
```

It is also possible to customize the coordinate system you use within the graphics viewport by means of a WINDOW statement that specifies the coordinates that will identify the upper-left and lower-right corners in subsequent program statements. These new coordinates can be specified with any single-precision values. The WINDOW statement below redefines the coordinates of the full screen, so that the vertical and horizontal values both range from 10 to − 10. As a result, the point with coordinates (0, 0) will be situated in the *center* of the newly defined viewport. This is demonstrated by the three program lines shown below. When you run the program, the two LINE statements draw lines that cross in the center of the screen.

```
WINDOW ( − 10, 10)-(10, − 10)
LINE (0, 10)-(0, − 10)
LINE ( − 10, 0)-(10, 0)
```

If you add the following VIEW statement *before* the WINDOW statement, the coordinates given in the WINDOW statement will mark the corners of the smaller viewport defined by the VIEW statement.

```
VIEW (0, 0)-(200, 100)
```

Run the program again, and you will see a smaller cross. Although this cross is centered in the new viewport, it is no longer centered on your monitor screen.

Using WINDOW statements greatly simplifies the task of presenting data in visual form. Such a statement is used in the GRAPH program that concludes this chapter.

THE GRAPH PROGRAM

The GRAPH program is an application employing many of the commands covered in this chapter. This graph-drawing program gives the user a choice of drawing the graph of a linear equation (of the form $y = mx + b$) or a quadratic equation (of the form $y = ax^2 + bx + c$), on a standard set of axes. The program listing is shown in Figure 13.7.

```
REM GRAPH.BAS
'Graphing linear and quadratic equations

CONST FALSE = 0, TRUE = NOT FALSE

DECLARE SUB GraphLine ()
DECLARE SUB CreateAxes ()
DECLARE SUB GraphQuadratic ()

'Select a screen statement that works on your system
'SCREEN 2          'CGA, EGA, VGA, or MGA
'SCREEN 3          'Hercules
'SCREEN 9          'EGA or VGA

WINDOW (-40, 30)-(40, -30)

DO
   'Display menu and get a choice
   CLS
   PRINT "Press a number to indicate your choice."
   PRINT
   PRINT "(1) Graph a linear equation"
   PRINT "(2) Graph a quadratic equation"
   PRINT "(3) Quit"
   Choice$ = INPUT$(1)

   'Respond to the choice
   SELECT CASE Choice$
     CASE "1": CALL GraphLine
     CASE "2": CALL GraphQuadratic
     CASE "3": Done = TRUE
     CASE ELSE: BEEP
   END SELECT
LOOP UNTIL Done

END

'-------------------------CreateAxes-------------------------
'Draw an x-axis and a y-axis with unit markings and labels
'-----------------------------------------------------------
SUB CreateAxes
   CLS

   'Draw the x and y axes
   LINE (-30, 0)-(30, 0)               'x axis
   LINE (0, -30)-(0, 30)               'y axis

   'Mark off units on x axis
   FOR n% = -30 TO 30
     LINE (n%, -.5)-(n%, .5)
   NEXT n%

   'Mark off units on y axis
   FOR n% = -30 TO 30
     LINE (-.5, n%)-(.5, n%)
   NEXT n%

   'Label each axis
   LOCATE 1, 42: PRINT "y"
   LOCATE 12, 70: PRINT "x"
END SUB
```

Figure 13.7: The GRAPH program listing

```
'------------------------GraphLine-----------------------
'Draw the graph a a linear equation
'-----------------------------------------------------------
SUB GraphLine
  CLS
  PRINT "To draw the graph of a linear equation of the form:"
  PRINT
  PRINT " y = mx + b"
  PRINT
  INPUT "Enter a value for m (the slope)       :", m
  INPUT "Enter a value for b (the y-intercept) :", b

  CALL CreateAxes

  'Calculate its endpoints and graph the line.
  y1 = m * -30 + b
  y2 = m * 30 + b
  LINE (-30, y1)-(30, y2)

  'Label the graph

  VIEW PRINT
  LOCATE 24, 60
  PRINT "y = "; m; "x + "; b

  'Pause before clearing the screen
  LOCATE 1, 1: PRINT "Press any key"
  DO UNTIL INKEY$ <> ""
  LOOP
  CLS
END SUB

'-----------------------GraphQuadratic-----------------------
'Draw the graph of a quadratic equation
'-----------------------------------------------------------
SUB GraphQuadratic
  CLS
  PRINT "To draw the graph of a quadratic equation of the form:"
  PRINT
  PRINT " y = ax^2 + bx + c"
  PRINT
  INPUT "Enter a value for a :", a
  INPUT "Enter a value for b :", b
  INPUT "Enter a value for c :", c
  CALL CreateAxes

  'To speed the process, use whole number increments to
  'find the first integer value of x for which y is on graph
  FOR x = -30 TO 30 STEP 1
     y = a * x ^ 2 + b * x + c
     IF ABS(y) <= 30 THEN EXIT FOR
  NEXT x

  'Start graphing where x is one less than this value
  FirstX = x - 1
  'Calculate the value of y at this point to use as limiting value later
  FirstY = a * FirstX ^ 2 + b * FirstX + c

  'Calculate and graph coordinate pairs
  FOR x = FirstX TO 30 STEP .1
     y = a * x ^ 2 + b * x + c
     PSET (x, y)
     IF ABS(y) > ABS(FirstY) THEN EXIT FOR
  NEXT x
```

Figure 13.7: The GRAPH program listing (continued)

```
'Label the graph
VIEW PRINT
LOCATE 24, 50
PRINT "y = "; a; "x^2 +"; b; "x +"; c

'Pause before clearing the screen
LOCATE 1, 1: PRINT "Press any key"
DO UNTIL INKEY$ <> ""
LOOP
CLS
END SUB
```

Figure 13.7: The GRAPH program listing (continued)

The first executable line of the program defines Boolean constants for TRUE and FALSE. This is followed by three procedure declarations. After the procedure declarations, the listing shown here includes remark statements that indicate three screen modes that can be used to run this program. Select a screen mode that is supported by your system, and include that SCREEN statement (*without* the apostrophe shown in Figure 13.7) in your program.

The next program statement is a WINDOW statement that redefines the coordinates of the viewport's corners, so that the coordinates for x range from – 40 to 40, and the coordinates for y range from – 30 to 30. The DO...LOOP that follows generates the menu shown here:

Press a number to indicate your choice.
(1) Graph a linear equation
(2) Graph a quadratic equation
(3) Quit

A SELECT CASE structure handles keyboard input. If choice 1 is selected, the GraphLine procedure is called, and if choice 2 is selected the GraphQuadratic procedure is called. Choice 3 results in a change of value for the Boolean variable, **Done**, which controls repetition of the DO...LOOP. Pressing any key other than 1, 2, or 3 produces a BEEP. The program continues to repeat this menu display until the user selects choice 3.

The GraphLine procedure begins with a set of INPUT prompts. These prompts are shown here, along with sample input values.

To draw the graph of a linear equation of the form:

y = mx + b

Enter a value for m (the slope)   :2
Enter a value for b (the y-intercept)   : – 3

Once these values have been entered, the CreateAxes procedure is called. This procedure uses two LINE statements to create the vertical (y) and horizontal (x) axes. Then, two separate FOR...NEXT loops create a series of short lines that mark off the units on each axis. Finally the axes are labeled with x and y. When this is done, program control returns to the Graphline procedure. The two program statements

y1 = m * –30 + b
y2 = m * 30 + b

calculate the endpoints for the line to be drawn. Once these endpoints have been determined, a LINE statement is used to draw the line. A label is added to the graph with these three program statements:

VIEW PRINT
LOCATE 24, 50
PRINT "y = "; m; "x +"; b

As it is used here, VIEW PRINT allows you to add text to the viewport without disturbing the graph that has been drawn. Figure 13.8 shows the finished output.

The GraphQuadratic procedure is very similar to the GraphLine procedure, but rather than drawing a single straight line, the procedure uses a series of dots placed by PSET statements to draw the curved graph of a quadratic equation. These dots are set at intervals of x equal to 0.1 units. The location of each dot is calculated separately within a FOR...NEXT loop. This loop could begin with x = – 30 and end at x = 30, but this would mean calculating many values beyond the range of axes created in the CreateAxes procedure—wasted time worth eliminating. In order to speed the process, the procedure first tests values of x at intervals of one to find the first integer value for x that produces a value for y that

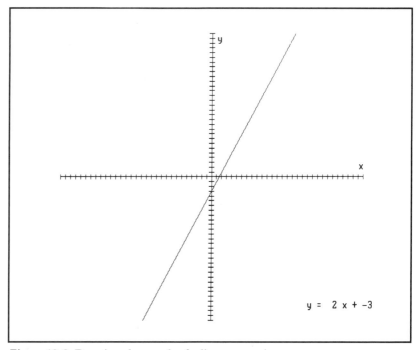

Figure 13.8: Drawing the graph of a linear equation

is on the graph. By starting graphing at the value of x one smaller than this, you can ensure that all values of y will be displayed, without having to calculate a large number of values whose absolute value is greater than the limit of 30 set by the WINDOW statement. As each point is plotted, the program continues to check to see if y has exceeded the range of the graph. This checking is done by comparing each successive value of y to the value of y (FirstY) where graphing began. When the absolute value of y exceeds this first value, an EXIT FOR statement is used to stop the graphing process.

The input screen produced by the GraphQuadratic procedure is shown here with sample input values:

To draw the graph of a quadratic equation of the form:

    y = ax^2 + bx + c

Enter a value for a   : – 0.5

```
Enter a value for b       :2
Enter a value for c       :10
```

The graph produced when these values are entered is shown in Figure 13.9.

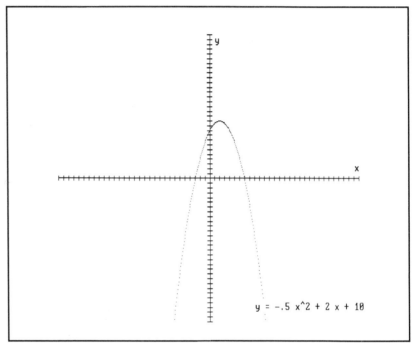

Figure 13.9: Drawing the graph of a quadratic equation

Try running the program with the values given here and then experiment with other values.

SUMMARY

Incorporating graphics output in programs can make them more useful and enjoyable. Any program that uses the graphics command statements must first include a SCREEN statement that selects one of QuickBASIC's graphic screen modes. These screen modes are summarized in Table 13.1.

Graphics commands covered in this chapter are briefly summarized here:

SCREEN	Selects a screen mode.
PSET	Positions and illuminates a single pixel.
PRESET	Resets a pixel to the background color.
LINE	Draws both lines and boxes.
CIRCLE	Draws circles, arcs, pie-shaped wedges, and ellipses.
VIEW	Defines limits to the graphics viewport.
WINDOW	Redefines the coordinates used to locate graphic output.

Use the online Index and Table of Contents to explore details of QuickBASIC's graphic commands that were not discussed in this chapter.

R efining Your Programming Technique

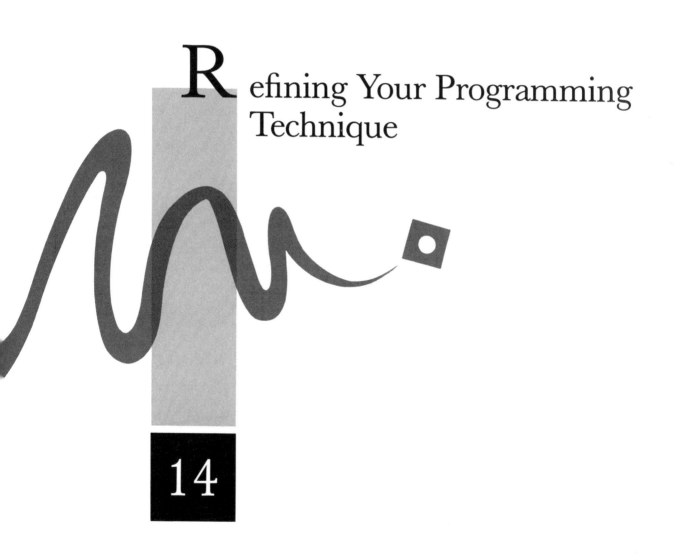

14

CHAPTER **14** _____

AS YOU SPEND MORE TIME DEVELOPING PROGRAMS, you will probably notice that many routines can be used in the same way over and over again in a variety of programming applications. The first part of this chapter shows you QuickBASIC techniques for building new programs using pieces of existing programs, thereby avoiding unnecessary repetition during program development. You will also learn about *quick libraries*. Creating and using a quick library enables you to expand the QuickBASIC programming language to include procedures that meet your individual programming needs.

Most programs work well enough when the person who developed them is at the keyboard. A far more interesting and more important challenge for the programmer is to write programs that work smoothly when a novice is in control. The second part of this chapter shows you how to create error-handling routines in your programs. These routines will help the users of your programs avoid the confusion and frustration that arise when a program behaves in an unexpected way.

STRATEGIES FOR BUILDING LARGER PROGRAMS

All of the programs shown in this book so far have been created as separate, individual files built from the ground up. But all new programs do not have to be created in this way. This chapter will introduce you to several ways of using parts of existing programs to build new programs. These include:

- Moving or copying SUB and FUNCTION procedures from one program to another.

- Building programs by combining two or more programs into a single unit, without altering the integrity of the original program files.

- Developing your own *library* of procedures and then using the procedures from this library much as you now use the built-in BASIC statements and functions.

To demonstrate these techniques, the exercises that follow use the FUNDS.BAS program developed in Chapter 12. This program requires keyboard input of numeric data, but, as it stands now, the program cannot handle numeric input that includes commas or dollar signs. In order to improve the program, you will add to it the NumberFilter procedure that was created as part of the FILTERFN program in Chapter 9. This procedure filters unwanted characters from numeric input. Adding it to the FUNDS.BAS program makes that program more flexible and easier to use.

MOVING PROCEDURES

One useful programming technique moves or copies SUB and FUNCTION procedures from one program to another. You will use this technique later to copy the NumberFilter procedure from the FILTERFN program to a newly created program that will contain only this procedure.

To move procedures from one program to another, use the SUBs command in the View menu, following the steps outlined here. Note that there is a difference between copying and moving a procedure and that you can do *either* one *or* the other.

1. Open the *source* file; this is the file containing the procedure you want to move.

2. If the *destination* file (the file you want to move the procedure to) already exists, load it into memory using the *Load File* command in the File menu; or, if no destination file exists, create one using the *Create File* command in the File menu.

3. Activate the *SUBs* command from the View menu. This command will open the SUBs dialog box. Working within this dialog box, highlight the name of the procedure you want to move, and then trigger the *<Move>* command. Next, select a destination file from the list of files in the resulting display.

4. If you want to *copy* the procedure (that is, add it to the destination file without changing the source file), use the *Unload* command in the File menu to unload the source file *without* saving the changes you made to this file, and then save the destination file with the *Save* or *Save As* command.

5. If you want to *move* the procedure (that is, remove it from the original source file and leave it in the destination file only), use the *Save All* command from the File menu to save the changes, and then use the *Unload* command to unload one of the files.

In the exercise that follows, you will copy the NumberFilter procedure from the FILTERFN program to a newly created file called FILTER2.BAS, which is an example of a *procedures-only* program. Although a procedures-only program cannot run on its own, it can be a useful building block for developing new programs that can use the SUB and FUNCTION procedures it contains. You'll use FILTER2 in a later exercise that demonstrates how to combine separate modules into a single program.

1. Open the FILTERFN program. (Refer to Chapter 9 for the program listing.)

2. Activate the *Create File* command from the File menu. A dialog box will open with a *Name:* input area. Type FILTER2 and press ⏎ to create a new module with this name. The View screen will clear, and you will see FILTER2.BAS in the Title bar. Although FILTERFN is no longer in view, it is still loaded into memory.

3. Select the *SUBs* command from the View menu (or use the F2 shortcut key) to see a display of the currently loaded files. This display is shown here:

    FILTERFN.BAS
      NumberFilter
    FILTER2.BAS

4. Highlight NumberFilter, and then press Alt+M to activate the *<Move>* command from the list of actions at the bottom of the dialog box.

5. A new dialog box will open, asking you to choose a destination module. Select FILTER2 from the list of loaded files and press ←⎯.

6. You will be returned to the original SUBs dialog box with the structure shown here, reflecting the change you just made.

   FILTERFN.BAS
   FILTER2.BAS
     NumberFilter

   Check to be sure FILTER2.BAS is highlighted and press ←⎯ to return to the Work screen. The View window will be empty because this newly created program contains only the NumberFilter procedure and does not yet include any module-level code.

7. Save the FILTER2 program by using the *Save* command in the File menu. (When several programs are loaded simultaneously, this command saves the program that is currently in the active window.) After the Save command has been executed, a FUNCTION declaration will appear in the View window.

8. To unload the FILTERFN.BAS program without saving the change you just made to this program, activate the *Unload File* command from the File menu and select FILTERFN.BAS from the list of loaded files. Press ←⎯ and you will see a message that reads

   File has been modified since last saved. Save it now?

   Select <*No*> to unload the file without altering its original contents.

9. The Unload File dialog box will open, asking you to choose a new main module for your program. FILTER2.BAS is the only remaining module in memory. Press ←⎯ to select it as the main module. (You'll learn what is meant by *main module* in the next exercise.)

10. Add remark statements to identify this new program, so that the View window contains the following lines:

    ```
    REM FILTER2.BAS
    'A procedure-only module
    DECLARE FUNCTION NumberFilter! (StringValue$)
    ```

11. Use the *Change* command in the Search menu to find each occurrence of NumberFilter and replace it with Number-Filter!. By specifically identifying NumberFilter as a single-precision number in this way, you can incorporate this program into programs that have declared some other default data-type.

12. Save the completed module using the *Save* or *Save As* command and clear the View window.

The program you have just created can now be loaded into memory whenever you are developing a program that asks for numeric input from the keyboard. The techniques you'll need in order to do this are the subject of the next section.

WORKING WITH MULTIPLE MODULES

It is possible to build a program in QuickBASIC by loading several programs files into memory simultaneously. Once a program has been loaded, any of its procedures can be called by any of the other loaded programs. Each individual file is called a *module*, and the module that contains the first executable statement of a program is called the *main module*. Using separate program modules for different parts of a program offers several advantages:

- Modules help you avoid repetitive programming tasks because frequently used procedures do not need to be rewritten and debugged every time you write a program. Related procedures can be saved in a single module, and then you need only load that module into memory in order to use any of the procedures it contains.

- Modules help with program development because it is easier and less frustrating to develop, test, and debug individual procedures separately and then add them to a larger program only after you are sure they work correctly.

- Modules can help simplify program maintenance. If you want to update a procedure that you use in several different programs, you need change only the one module that contains the procedure. Once this change is made, all programs that use this module will reflect the change.

To build a program using more than one module, start with the main module in the View window and then add additional modules to it, using the *Load File* command in the File menu. Once the composite program is working properly, save it using the *Save All* command in the File menu. One effect of this command is to save all the changes you have made to all of the currently loaded files. A second effect is the creation of a new file on your disk, a file that will use the same name that you gave your main module but will have a .MAK, rather than a .BAS, extension. The .MAK file contains a list of all the files that were loaded when the Save All command was executed. As long as this file remains on your disk in the current directory, all of the included files will be loaded automatically each time you open the main module. If you compile the composite program by using the *Make EXE File* command, all of the loaded files will be combined to create a single .EXE file.

In order to practice building a program from separate modules, you will modify the FUNDS program (See Chapter 12, Figures 12.2–12.6), as outlined below. Each step is explained in detail in the exercises that follow. You will:

- Modify the FUNDS program so that it calls the NumberFilter procedure and then save the modified program as FUNDS2.BAS.

- Load the FILTER2 module, containing the NumberFilter procedure, into memory.

- Save the composite program so that each time you load FUNDS2, the FILTER2 module will be loaded with it.

Using the *Save* or *Save As* commands will result in the creation of a .MAK file only if the main module is in the active window. These two commands will also save *only* those changes made to the module in the active window. The *Save All* command creates the .MAK file regardless of which module is in the active window and saves all changes made to all loaded modules.

MODIFYING THE FUNDS PROGRAM The following steps
modify the FUNDS program so that it can use the NumberFilter
procedure:

1. Open the FUNDS.BAS program. (Refer to Chapter 12 to
   see the listing for this program.)

2. Modify the module-level code of the program so that it
   matches Figure 14.1. New or altered lines have been marked
   with a '* at the end of the line.

```
REM FUNDS2.BAS                                       '*
'A modification fo the FUNDS.BAS program             '*
'This program uses a loaded file (FILTER2.BAS)       '*
'in order to filter numeric input.                   '*
'Changes are indicated by '* at the end of a line '*

DEFINT A-Z

'Define a data type which describes the structure of each record
TYPE RecordType
  SchoolName AS STRING * 20
  Funds AS SINGLE
END TYPE

'Define a record variable which uses this data type
DIM SchoolRecord AS RecordType

'Procedure declarations
DECLARE SUB AddRecord (School AS RecordType)
DECLARE SUB DisplayRecords (School AS RecordType)
DECLARE SUB Update (School AS RecordType)
DECLARE FUNCTION NumberFilter! (StringValue$)        '*

'Open a random-access file and indicate the length of each record
OPEN "FUNDS.DAT" FOR RANDOM AS #1 LEN = LEN(SchoolRecord)

'Calculate the number of records in the file
NumberOfRecords = LOF(1) \ LEN(SchoolRecord)

'Add a new record to the file
CLS
PRINT "Would you like to add a new school to the file (Y/N)? ":
Response$ = INPUT$(1)
IF UCASE$(Response$) = "Y" THEN CALL AddRecord(SchoolRecord)

'Display the records in the file
CALL DisplayRecords(SchoolRecord)

'Update an existing record
PRINT "Would you like to update a record (Y/N)? ";
Response$ = UCASE$(INPUT$(1)): PRINT Response$
IF Response$ = "Y" THEN CALL Update(SchoolRecord)

'Close the file
CLOSE #1

END
```

Figure 14.1: The main module of the FUNDS2 program

```
'----------------------------AddRecord----------------------
'Adds new records to the FUNDS.DAT file
'-----------------------------------------------------------
SUB AddRecord (School AS RecordType) STATIC
  SHARED NumberOfRecords
  DO
    'Get data
    CLS
    INPUT "School Name: ", School.SchoolName
    LINE INPUT "Funds raised: ", FR$          '*
    School.Funds = NumberFilter!(FR$)         '*

    'Calculate the record number for this record
    NumberOfRecords = NumberOfRecords + 1

    'Add data to the file
    PUT #1, NumberOfRecords, School

    PRINT : PRINT "Add another (Y/N)? "
    Continue$ = UCASE$(INPUT$(1))
  LOOP WHILE Continue$ = "Y"
END SUB

'-------------------------DisplayRecords--------------------
'Displays records and record numbers in an on-screen table
'-----------------------------------------------------------
SUB DisplayRecords (School AS RecordType)
  SHARED NumberOfRecords

  'Display the heading
  CLS
  PRINT "Record #", "School"; TAB(40); "Funds Raised"

  'Read and display each record, keeping track of total funds
  PRINT
  FOR RecordNumber = 1 TO NumberOfRecords
    GET #1, RecordNumber, School
    PRINT RecordNumber, School.SchoolName;
    PRINT USING "$#####,.##"; TAB(42); School.Funds
    Total! = Total! + School.Funds
  NEXT RecordNumber

  'Display the total
  PRINT
  PRINT "TOTAL";
  PRINT USING "$######,.##"; TAB(41); Total!
  PRINT
END SUB

'----------------------------Update------------------------
'Uses record numbers to update specified records in the file
'-----------------------------------------------------------
SUB Update (School AS RecordType)
  SHARED NumberOfRecords
  DO
    'Find out which record to update
    INPUT "Please enter the record number: ", RecordNumber
    'Indicate if the record number is out of range
    IF RecordNumber > NumberOfRecords THEN
      PRINT "That record is out of range."

    'or update the file if the record number is OK
    ELSE
      'Get a new value for funds raised
      LINE INPUT "What is the new value for funds raised"; FR$  '*
      School.Funds = NumberFilter!(FR$)                         '*

      'Write the updated record to the file
      PUT #1, RecordNumber, School
      PRINT
```

Figure 14.1: The main module of the FUNDS2 program (continued)

```
            'Display the updated list
            CALL DisplayRecords(School)
        END IF
        PRINT "Change any more records (Y/N)? ";
        Continue$ = UCASE$(INPUT$(1)): PRINT Continue$
    LOOP WHILE Continue$ = "Y"
END SUB
```

Figure 14.1: The main module of the FUNDS2 program (continued)

    3. Modify the AddRecord procedure by replacing the single line

        INPUT "Funds raised: ", School.Funds

    with these two lines:

        LINE INPUT "Funds raised: ", FR$
        School.Funds = NumberFilter!(FR$)

    4. Modify the Update procedure by replacing the single line

        INPUT "What is the new value for funds raised: "; School.Funds

    with these two lines:

        LINE INPUT "What is the new value for funds raised: "; FR$
        School.Funds = NumberFilter!(FR$)

    5. Save the modified program as FUNDS2 using the *Save As* command.

LOADING MULTIPLE MODULES INTO MEMORY   You now have two completed modules, FILTER2.BAS and FUNDS2.BAS, which are ready to be combined to form a single program capable of filtering numeric input. Once you combine these two modules, you will be ready to run the composite program. These final steps are described next. (If you have cleared the Work screen, open the FUNDS2 program before proceeding.)

    1. With the FUNDS2 program open in the View window, use the *Load File* command in the File menu to load the FILTER2.BAS program into memory.

2. Press F2 to see the loaded modules and their procedures. The dialog box will display the following program structure:

```
FUNDS2.BAS
   AddRecord
   DisplayRecords
   Update
FILTER2.BAS
   NumberFilter
```

Press Esc to return to the View window.

3. Run the program. To test to see if the newly added Number-Filter procedure is working, answer the question, "Would you like to add a new school to the file (Y/N)?" by pressing Y, and then enter the information shown here:

```
School Name: Emerson School
Funds Raised: $1,234

Add another (Y/N)? N
```

The program should proceed to add and display this record accurately because the NumberFilter procedure will strip the dollar sign and comma from the value entered for Funds Raised.

4. Save the new program using the *Save All* command. Each time you open the FUNDS2 program from now on, the FIL-TER2 module will be loaded into memory automatically.

When you print a program that contains more than one module, you can use the Print command in the File menu to choose whether to print only the module that is in the active window, or all the modules that are used in the program. The default Print command prints only the current module. To print all the modules in the program, select the *All Modules* option from the Print dialog box before proceeding with the Print command.

PROCEDURE DECLARATIONS IN MULTIPLE-MODULE PROGRAMS

In order to create the composite FUNDS2 program in the preceding exercise, you had to add an additional procedure declaration to

Metacommands are a special group of QuickBASIC program commands that are placed after a REM statement. Unlike most commands in a REM statement, however, metacommands direct the handling of your program when it is compiled. QuickBASIC meta-commands are always preceded by a dollar sign.

the main module of the new program. When you save a single module program, procedure declarations are added automatically to your program listing. However, the QuickBASIC smart editor will *not* add procedure declarations for procedures that are not part of a program's main module. One way to handle this limitation is to type in any necessary declarations (as you did with FUNDS.BAS) each time you add a procedures-only module to a program you are developing. If you are adding a module with many procedures, however, this can be a time-consuming activity, and, in addition, typing declarations introduces an additional source of potential mistakes.

QuickBASIC provides you with an alternative way of including these procedure declarations in your program—the use of an *include* file. An include file is a text file containing program lines that are read into your program wherever you have placed an $INCLUDE meta-command that identifies the file to be included. Include files are typically identified with a .BI extension.

The syntax for an $INCLUDE metacommand is shown here:

REM $INCLUDE: *'FileName'*

When this command is encountered, the QuickBASIC compiler temporarily stops processing your program file and instead processes the file indicated by *FileName*. Once all the statements in this file have been executed, program control returns to the line following the one with the $INCLUDE metacommand. When you create an .EXE file, the contents of the include file are substituted for the $INCLUDE command and incorporated directly into the finished program. An included file *cannot* contain SUB or FUNCTION procedures.

You can avoid typing declarations statements altogether by letting QuickBASIC generate these statements in the module that contains the procedures, using the commands in the Edit menu to copy them to the clipboard, and then retrieving them into a newly created include file.

You can create an include file that allows you to avoid the necessity of retyping procedure declarations each time you load a procedures-only file. For each procedures-only file you create, create a separate include file that contains the appropriate procedure declarations and use $INCLUDE to add these declarations to any program that uses that module. (You will work with $INCLUDE later, as part of the creation of a quick library.)

CREATING A QUICK LIBRARY

A second way of incorporating previously written procedures into your programs is by making and using a *quick library*. A quick library is a collection of procedures that have already been written and compiled and can be loaded into memory whenever you load Quick-BASIC from the operating system. By creating quick libraries, you can define and create your own "personalized" programming commands and use these commands whenever the library is loaded into memory. Quick library procedures are faster to load and require less disk space than procedures saved as modules, but because quick libraries do not use source code, you can no longer read and modify their procedures once you have created a library.

To create and use a quick library:

1. Build a procedures-only module that contains procedures that you frequently use. For convenience, also create an include file at this time with procedure declarations for all the procedures in the module.

2. With the module in the View window, use the *Make Library* command in the Run menu to create a quick library file. This file will be identified with a .QLB extension.

3. To use the library, load it into memory when you first load QuickBASIC by typing /**L** and the library name after you have typed **qb**. For example, to load a library named SAMPLE.QLB, you would load QuickBASIC with the following command line:

    QB /L SAMPLE.QLB

4. Use an include file to add procedure declarations to your program, and then use your quick library commands as you would use QuickBASIC built-in statements and functions.

These techniques are demonstrated in the exercises that follow.

CREATING THE DISPLAY PROGRAM The DISPLAY program shown in Figure 14.2 is a short module consisting of three procedures that control some aspect of the appearance of screen output: The Bold procedure produces high intensity output, the Center procedure positions output in the center of the screen, and the CenterBold procedure produces centered and bold display. Type in the program and save it as DISPLAY.BAS.

In the next exercise, you will use this file to create a quick library.

```
REM DISPLAY.BAS
'Three procedures for controlling screen output

SUB Bold (Text$)
   COLOR 15, 1
   PRINT Text$;
   COLOR 7, 1
END SUB

SUB Center (Text$)
   PhraseLength = LEN(Text$)
   Position = (80 - PhraseLength) \ 2
    PRINT TAB(Position); Text$
END SUB

SUB CenterBold (Text$)
   PhraseLength = LEN(Text$)
   Position = (80 - PhraseLength) \ 2
   COLOR 15, 1
   PRINT TAB(Position); Text$
   COLOR 7, 1
END SUB
```

Figure 14.2: The DISPLAY program listing

CREATING AND LOADING THE SCREEN QUICK LIBRARY
In order to create a quick library that contains the procedures in the DISPLAY program, follow these steps:

1. With the DISPLAY program on screen, select the *Make Library* command from the Run menu.

2. Enter the name

   SCREEN

   where you see "Quick-Library File Name:".

3. Select the *<Make Library and Exit>* option and then wait while the file is compiled and the new library is created. Messages describing this process will appear on screen, and when the process is complete you will be returned to the DOS command prompt.

The library you have just created is stored on your disk as SCREEN.QLB. An additional file called SCREEN.LIB is also created as part of the process. This file contains the same code as the SCREEN.QLB file, but in a different form. The .LIB file must be present whenever you create stand-alone programs using the procedures in a QuickBASIC quick library.

In order to use the quick library you just created, load Quick-BASIC with the following command line:

```
QB  /L  SCREEN.QLB
```

Before you use this new library, create an include file that contains DECLARE statements for each of its procedures, as described next.

CREATING AN INCLUDE FILE FOR THE PROCEDURES IN THE SCREEN LIBRARY   One way to create an include file is to use the *Create File* command in the File menu. This command allows you to choose from a list of three document types, the characteristics of which are summarized here:

Module	The smart editor checks these files for BASIC syntax, and files are not saved as text unless you specify this with a *Save As* command.
Include	The smart editor checks for BASIC syntax, and files are saved as text files.
Document	The smart editor is turned off, and files are saved as text files.

In the steps that follow, you'll use the *Create* command to make an include file to be used when you use the SCREEN.QLB quick library.

1. Activate the *Create File* command in the File menu. Type the name

   ```
   SCREEN.BI
   ```

   in the files input area and select *Include* as the file type. Press ◀┘ to return to the View window.

2. Type in the three procedure declarations shown here.

DECLARE SUB Center (text$)
DECLARE SUB Bold (text$)
DECLARE SUB CenterBold (text$)

3. Save the file with any of the save commands in the File menu.

USING THE SCREEN.QLB QUICK LIBRARY   Whenever you
load the SCREEN library, you can call any of its procedures in your
program, but you should first include appropriate declaration statements. The TESTMENU program shown in Figure 14.3 is a short
sample program that uses the procedures in the SCREEN library. In
order to include the declarations in the SCREEN.BI file, the following statement has been included.

'$INCLUDE: 'SCREEN.BI'

If you want to use
procedures in a
quick library, remember
to load the library into
memory whenever you
first enter QuickBASIC.
If you forget, you will get
"procedure not defined"
error messages when you
run a program that uses
procedures in the library.

```
REM TESTMENU.BAS
'Uses procedures defined in the SCREEN.QLB quick library

'Use an $INCLUDE metacommand to include procedure declarations
' $INCLUDE: 'SCREEN.BI'

'Display a sample menu
CLS
PRINT : PRINT : PRINT
CenterBold "SAMPLE MENU"
Center "Bold keys indicate key choices"
PRINT
PRINT SPACE$(30);
Bold "1. F"
PRINT "irst choice"
PRINT SPACE$(30);
Bold "2. S"
PRINT "econd choice"
```

Figure 14.3: The TESTMENU program

Type in the program as it appears in Figure 14.3. It is possible to
view the three lines of code that make up the SCREEN.BI file by
using the *Included Lines* command in the View menu. As a result of
this command, the included lines are displayed in bold at the point in
your program where you have placed the $INCLUDE command.
To remove these lines from the display, repeat the *Included Lines*
command.

Run the program. It produces the following simplified menu display, using the procedures in the SCREEN quick library:

SAMPLE MENU
Bold keys indicate key choices

1. First choice
2. Second choice

The menu selections shown here have no real effect; their purpose is only to demonstrate the *use* of the three quick library procedures: Bold, Center, and CenterBold.

HANDLING RUN-TIME ERRORS

The program development *techniques* described so far in this chapter are important only to the individual who is creating a program. Modules and quick libraries exist solely for the convenience of the program developer; the end user does not see (or care) how a program is written. The program *refinements* we are about to look at, however, are extremely important to the end user, and, although they make program writing more complicated, they can make your programs easier to use—a goal of utmost importance.

Anyone using QuickBASIC soon becomes familiar with the variety of error messages that appear either as your write your program or as a program runs. Some error messages prevent a program from running at all. These are known as *compile-time* errors. Syntax errors fall into this category. A second group of errors causes interruption of a program during its execution. These are *run-time* errors. Compile-time errors must be corrected by the program developer, while run-time errors may be confronted by the end user. Examples of run-time errors include trying to print when the printer isn't ready, or trying to open a file with a bad file name. If you are running a program from within the QuickBASIC environment, a run-time error results in the display of an error message in a dialog box. After the box is cleared, you are returned to your program code. If a run-time error occurs during execution of a compiled .EXE program file, an error message like the one shown below appears on screen, and program execution is interrupted.

Error *n* in module *module-name* at address *segment-offset*

The value *n* identifies the error using a code number, the *module-name* is the name of the module in which the error occurred, and *segment-offset* identifies the area of memory where the error occurred.

Error messages like these help to give computers a bad name. To new, anxious users, these messages are frightening and intimidating; and even old pros may watch in horror as they realize that open files have not been closed and valuable data has been lost.

Run-time errors result from a variety of causes, but well-written programs anticipate and avoid a very high percentage of them by including error-handling routines within the programs. The BASIC language provides tools specifically designed for this purpose.

CREATING AN ERROR-HANDLING ROUTINE

In order to prevent run-time errors from interrupting program execution, you can include error-handling routines in your program. With these in place, run-time errors result in the activation of the error-handling routines rather than forcing program execution to halt.

The general steps used in creating error-handling routines are summarized below. They will be explained in detail in the material that follows.

- Activate error trapping with an ON ERROR statement. ON ERROR statements must include a line label that identifies the section of code that contains the error-handling routine.

- Place the line label in the *module-level* code of your program in a position where it will not be reached during normal program execution.

- Follow the line label with a series of statements that take appropriate actions to help the user correct the source of the error and continue program execution.

- Complete the routine with a RESUME statement that identifies the line at which program execution should continue.

- Turn off error trapping with an ON ERROR GOTO 0 statement. (This is necessary only if you do not want the same error-handling routine to remain in effect throughout your program.)

THE ON ERROR GOTO STATEMENT

Error trapping is activated with an ON ERROR statement having the following syntax:

ON ERROR GOTO *LineLabel*

> Because zero has a special meaning in ON ERROR statements, never use *0* as a line label to identify an error-handling routine.

LineLabel is a numeric or character line label that identifies the location of an error-handling routine. Should any run-time error occur after this ON ERROR statement has been executed, program flow will be directed to the statement identified by this line label. Although ON ERROR statements can be placed anywhere in the module-level code or the SUB and FUNCTION procedures of a program, the line label that identifies the error-handling routine must be located in the module-level code.

Error trapping can be subsequently deactivated by placing this statement in your program:

ON ERROR GOTO 0

GENERATING AND CORRECTING A RUN-TIME ERROR

The following short program generates a run-time error because the unconditional DO..LOOP causes the READ statement to read beyond the last item in the DATA statement.

```
CLS
DO
  READ item$
  PRINT item$
LOOP
DATA 1,2,3,4,5
```

Type in the program and then run it. After the five data items have been displayed, the program will be abruptly interrupted and a dialog box with the message

Out of DATA

will appear, and the *READ item$* statement where the error occurred will be identified as the current statement. Press Esc to close the dialog box. (To see how the same error is handled when it occurs in an .EXE program, use the *Make EXE* command in the Run menu to make an .EXE file, and then exit to the system and run this version of the program.)

Figure 14.4 shows a modification of this program designed to handle the run-time, out-of-data error. Error trapping is activated by the following statement:

ON ERROR GOTO ErrorTrap

The ErrorTrap routine has been placed after the program's END statement so that it will be executed only when a run-time error occurs. The routine consists of the following two lines:

EndOfData = TRUE
RESUME NEXT

```
REM FIXERROR.BAS
'Using an error trapping routine to avoid a run-time error

CONST FALSE = 0, TRUE = NOT FALSE
ON ERROR GOTO ErrorTrap

CLS
DO
  READ item$
  IF EndOfData THEN EXIT DO
  PRINT item$
LOOP
DATA 1,2,3,4,5
END

ErrorTrap:
EndOfData = TRUE
RESUME NEXT
```

Figure 14.4: Trapping an Out of DATA error

EndOfData is a Boolean variable that is used to control the iterations of the DO..LOOP. The RESUME NEXT statement returns program execution to the line *following* the statement at which the error occurred. In this case the line is an IF...THEN statement that responds to the altered value of EndOfData by exiting from the loop without any further attempts to read data.

The RESUME statement that ends an error-handling routine returns program flow to the correct position for a successful return to normal program execution. RESUME statements are described in the next section.

THE RESUME STATEMENT

A RESUME statement can return control from an error-handling routine in three different ways:

RESUME	Returns the program to the *same* line that caused the error, and the program attempts once more to execute this line.
RESUME NEXT	Returns the program to the *line following* the one that caused the error.
RESUME *LineLabel*	Returns the program to the line identified by *LineLabel*. The line label identified cannot be contained within a procedure, so this technique can be awkward and should be avoided whenever error trapping occurs within a procedure.

The program shown in Figure 14.5 uses both a RESUME and a RESUME NEXT statement. The error-handling routine in this program is designed to handle an LPRINT command given when the printer is not ready. The Trap routine allows two possible responses: (1) A SELECT CASE structure uses RESUME if the user wants to correct the error and reattempt the printer command; (2) RESUME NEXT is used if the user wants to proceed with the program without printing.

```
'Comparing RESUME and RESUME NEXT

ON ERROR GOTO Trap
LPRINT "HI"
END

Trap:
  CLS
  PRINT "The printer is not ready."
  PRINT "Press C to continue."
  PRINT
  PRINT "(Any other key will cancel the print operation.)"
  Response$ = INPUT$(1)

  SELECT CASE Response$
    CASE "C", "c"
        RESUME
    CASE ELSE
        RESUME NEXT
  END SELECT
```

Figure 14.5: Comparing RESUME and RESUME NEXT

Type in the program and try running it with your printer off to see how it performs.

WORKING WITH ERROR CODES

Appendix D con-
tains a table of run-
time errors and their code
numbers.

The error-handling routines in the programs you just created made assumptions about what specific error caused a program to be interrupted. While this may be sufficient for some simple programs, it is often the case that any one of a number of run-time errors could occur at a given point during program execution. In order to handle such possibilities, each error is identified with an *Error Code*. When an error has occurred, the ERR function can be used to return the code number for that error, and this returned value, in turn, can be used to control the actions of an error-handling routine.

The ERRCODE program shown in Figure 14.6 demonstrates the use of error codes. This program asks the user to input the name of a disk drive or directory path and then lists the contents of that disk or directory. Two different errors are anticipated:

- A request has been made to read from a disk that is not ready because no disk is in place, the door is open, or a similar error has occurred. This results in error code 71 (Disk not ready).

- A directory name was typed in incorrectly, or identified a directory not on the specified disk. This results in error code 53 (File not found).

A SELECT CASE structure is combined with the ERR function in order to handle these two possibilities. The RESUME statement directs the program to return to the GetDirectory line label at the end of the error-handling routine.

Type in the program and test it by running it with both valid and invalid disk drive and path specifications.

```
REM ERRCODE.BAS
'Using error codes to identify which run-time error occured.

ON ERROR GOTO BadDirectory

CLS
PRINT "To see a list of files, enter a disk drive or path."
PRINT "Press Enter to view the default directory."
PRINT
GetDirectory:
  INPUT "Drive or Directory: ", PathSpec$
  IF PathSpec$ = "" THEN
    FILES
  ELSE
    FILES PathSpec$ + "\*.*"
  END IF

END

BadDirectory:
SELECT CASE ERR
  CASE 71        '71 is the error code for Disk not ready
    PRINT "That Disk drive is not ready."
    PRINT "Be sure a disk is in place and the door is closed."
    RESUME GetDirectory
  CASE 53        '53 is the error code for File not found
    PRINT "That directory name was not found."
    PRINT "Try again, or press Enter to see current directory."
    RESUME GetDirectory
END SELECT
```

Figure 14.6: The ERRCODE program listing

SUMMARY

QuickBASIC provides a variety of techniques you can use to build programs from existing sections of program code. Using the QuickBASIC menus, you can move procedures from one program module to another. By moving existing procedures, you can create procedures-only modules that can be loaded into memory when you write new programs, allowing the new programs to call the existing procedures. Making a quick library allows you to create already compiled code containing the procedures you use most frequently.

These procedures can be used any time you load the library into memory using a QuickBASIC command line prompt. An additional technique for putting programs together from existing code is the use of include files. These files contain sections of code that can be incorporated into your program by using the $INCLUDE metacommand. Include files are useful for including procedure declarations in the main module of multiple-module programs and in programs that call quick library procedures.

Error-handling routines are a programming refinement that will help your programs run smoothly under a wide variety of circumstances. Using error-trapping techniques, you can develop routines that handle run-time errors that might otherwise interrupt program execution. Error trapping is activated using an ON ERROR statement that directs program execution to a section of code identified by a line label. The statements that follow the label allow your program to respond to run-time errors in a manner that avoids program termination.

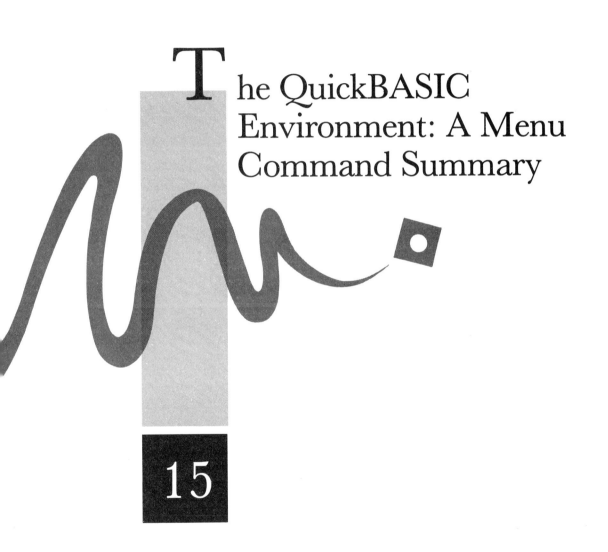

The QuickBASIC
Environment: A Menu
Command Summary

15

CHAPTER **15** ────────────────────

THIS CHAPTER REVIEWS THE USE OF QUICKBASIC'S
pull-down menus. The first three sections contain general information about using the menus. The remainder of the chapter is a menu-
by-menu summary of each of the commands available with the Full
Menus option. Where shortcut key alternatives are available, they
are included in the section heading.

──────────── *CONVENTIONS USED IN*
DISPLAYING QUICKBASIC MENUS ────

The QuickBASIC pull-down menus use the following display
conventions:

- If a command name is followed by three dots (...), activation
  of this command is always followed by a dialog box requesting more detailed instructions. Commands without these
  dots execute immediately (unless more information is
  required by the circumstances in effect when you choose the
  command).

- Some commands can be activated only after certain prior
  conditions have been met and are unavailable at other times.
  On color monitors, commands that are currently available
  are displayed in high-intensity video, while unavailable commands have a low-intensity, "ghosted" appearance. On
  monochrome monitors, the display of available commands
  will always include one highlighted letter (which can be used
  to activate that command), while unavailable commands are
  displayed with no highlighted letter.

- Toggle commands—those that are used both to select a setting and return to its alternative—are marked with a bullet
  (•) when the condition they describe has been selected.

HOW TO ACTIVATE QUICKBASIC MENU COMMANDS

To activate a command from the *keyboard*:

1. Press **Alt** to activate the Menu bar.

2. Choose a menu by pressing the highlighted letter in that menu's name (or use cursor-control keys to select a menu and then press ←.)

3. Activate the command by pressing the highlighted letter in that command's name (or use the cursor-control keys to select the command and then press ←.)

To activate a command using a *mouse*:

1. Move the mouse cursor to the title of the menu you want to select and click the left mouse button.

2. Move the mouse cursor to the name of the command you want to select and click the left mouse button.

HOW TO USE QUICKBASIC DIALOG BOXES

Activating any menu command whose name is followed by three dots will result in the appearance of a dialog box that lets you choose from among a variety of options. Dialog boxes may contain one or more of the following:

Text Box	An input area for typing in text from the keyboard.
List Box	An input area that allows you to select an item from a list of possible choices.
Command List	A list of possible action choices, such as <OK> to continue with a command, <Cancel> to cancel a command, and <Help> to receive more information about a command.

If you are using a keyboard for input, you can use either of these two methods to move the cursor to a text box, list box, or an item in the command list:

- Use the Tab key to move sequentially through the possible choices, or use Shift+Tab to move in the reverse direction.

OR

- Press Alt to display highlighted key choices. While still holding the Alt key, press the key that is highlighted in the input area or command choice you wish to select.

To select a text box, list box, or command choice using a *mouse*:

- Move the mouse cursor to the item you want to select and click the left mouse button.

THE FILE MENU

The File Menu contains commands for creating new files, saving files, retrieving files, and combining existing files. This menu also includes commands for printing files and exiting QuickBASIC.

THE FILE MENU: NEW PROGRAM

Use the *New Program* command to clear the View window when you are ready to create a new program. All currently loaded files will be removed from memory.

The following two items are not affected by the New Program command:

- The contents of the Immediate window are not erased.

- Material that has been placed in the clipboard using the Cut or Copy editing commands remains in memory.

If all loaded modules have been saved in their current form, no further action is required after you activate the New Program command. However, if modifications have been made since the last save

The term *module* is used to describe any individual disk file containing program code. A completed program can consist of one or more separate modules.

command, a dialog box will open allowing you to choose from the following three action choices: (1) Save all modifications before the screen and memory are cleared; (2) abandon the modified version of the loaded file or files and clear the screen and memory; or (3) cancel the New Program command and return to the Work screen as it was when you invoked the command.

THE FILE MENU: OPEN PROGRAM

Use the *Open Program* command to load an existing program from disk into memory. Any current work is cleared from the View screen and memory (as with the New Program command) prior to loading the new program.

The Open Program command dialog box contains three input areas:

File Name   This is a text box that can be used to select an individual file by name, or to indicate which files you want to see listed in the Files list. Use this box to select:

- *A particular file by name* (e.g., MENUDEMO). If the file is a BASIC program, the .BAS file extension need not be included. QuickBASIC will look for the named file in the current directory. To open a file in a different disk directory, you can include a directory path as part of the file specification (e.g., C:\MQB\FUNDS).

- *A particular group of files for display* in the Files list. (For example, type ***.*** to display all files in the current directory or ***.MAK** to display only those files with a .MAK extension.)

- *A disk or directory path* whose files you want to view in the Files area. (For example, type **A:** to display the program files in the A drive, or **C:\qb45*.*** to display all files in the QB45 directory.)

Files

This is a list box containing an alphabetical list of files. After moving the cursor to the Files list, select a file either with the direction keys or by pressing a letter to move the cursor to the first file on the list that begins with that letter. Unless you have specified otherwise (with the File Name or Dirs/Drives input areas), the Files list will include all the .BAS files in the current directory.

Dirs/Drives

This is a list box that allows you to use the direction keys to select from among the listed drives and directories. Use the two dot (..) option to see a list of directories contained in the parent directory of the current default directory.

If you select the Open Program command when a program currently in the View window has had modifications made to it since it was last saved, a dialog box will open allowing you to either save the modifications, open the new program without saving these modifications, or cancel the Open Program command.

THE FILE MENU: MERGE

Before you attempt to merge a program file, be sure it has been saved as a text file.

Use the *Merge* command to insert the entire contents of a *text* file into a currently loaded file. The original file will remain on screen, and the file you choose from the Merge dialog box will be added to it. Module-level code will be inserted at the current cursor position, while SUB and FUNCTION procedures will be inserted at the end of the file, arranged alphabetically along with any procedures that were part of the original file.

Refer to the Open Program command for information about the input areas in the Merge dialog box.

THE FILE MENU: SAVE

Use the *Save* command to replace a file on your disk with a modified version of the same file. When the file on screen has previously been saved, no dialog box appears, and the Save command saves modifications to the file using the name and format you have already given the file. However, if you are working with an unsaved and untitled program, a Save dialog box will open, allowing you to select a name, format, and disk or directory destination for the file. Refer to the Save As command below for more information about these options.

THE FILE MENU: SAVE AS

Use the *Save As* command to save a file to disk. Unlike the Save command, this command always opens a dialog box. The three input areas in this box are summarized here:

File Name	Type in a file name here. A directory path can be included if you want to save a file to a directory other than the current directory. If no file extension is included, a .BAS extension will automatically be added to the file.
Dir/Drives	Select a disk or directory destination from this list box. If no selection is made, the file will be saved in the current directory.
Format	Two file formats are available: (1) The default QuickBASIC format saves files using a fast, compact format that can be read and edited only within the QuickBASIC environment; (2) text format saves your file as an ASCII text file, allowing it to be read into any environment capable of handling ASCII files. Text files are also necessary for certain QuickBASIC applications, such as creating include files or merging files.

Use the Save As command when you want to keep several versions of a file, giving a new name to each new version, or when you want to alter a file format. Because this command is always accompanied by a dialog box, you can also cancel its action before proceeding, a feature that makes it both more prudent and less convenient than the instantaneous Save command.

THE FILE MENU: SAVE ALL

Use the *Save All* command when you are working with multiple-module programs. The command will save all changes that have been made to all loaded modules. A .MAK file will also be saved that links the parts of the loaded program, and, as a result, all the loaded files will automatically be reloaded into memory whenever you re-open the main module. Like the Save command, the Save All command saves your work instantly, opening a dialog box only if you are working with an untitled file. Be aware that any changes you make to loaded modules will affect all programs that use those modules.

THE FILE MENU: CREATE FILE

Use the *Create File* command to create a new file, without removing existing work from memory. The dialog box that opens allows you to choose from among the three file types summarized here:

Module   Use this to create program code in QuickBASIC format, with syntax checking in effect. (This is the default QuickBASIC file type.) When you use Create File to add a new module to a program, the new module will automatically be added to the .MAK file linking the parts of that program.

Include   Use this to create program code in text format, with syntax checking in effect. Unlike modules, include files are not added to the .MAK file that links program modules. To add an include file to a program, use QuickBASIC's $INCLUDE metacommand.

Document   Use this to create a document file with no syntax checking in effect. Like include files, document files are not added to the .MAK file that links program modules. Use document files to create or modify data files or other files that are not written in BASIC code.

THE FILE MENU: LOAD FILE

Use the *Load File* command when you want to load more than one file into memory simultaneously. Three input areas—File Name, Files, and Dirs/Drives—are identical to those used to open a program file. (Refer to the Open Program command for more information.) An additional command choice allows you to load the file as a Module, Include, or Document file. These file types are described above.

Use the Load File command to build multiple-module programs. To move different parts of a multiple program into the View window, use the SUBs command in the View window (or press F2). Save multiple-module programs using the Save All command.

THE FILE MENU: UNLOAD FILE

Deleting Files: QuickBASIC menus include no command for removing existing files from your disk. You can do this by working in the immediate window and using a *KILL* command followed by quotation marks and then the name of the file you want to delete. (For example: KILL "junkfile".) Currently open files cannot be deleted in this way.

Use the *Unload File* command when you are working with multiple-module programs and you want to remove a file from memory. The Unload File dialog box displays all currently loaded files. Use the cursor-control keys to highlight the file you want to unload. When you remove a program module from memory, it will also be removed from the .MAK file when you use the Save All command, and as a result, it will no longer be loaded into memory when the main module is reopened.

THE FILE MENU: PRINT

Use the *Print* command to print out all or part of any currently loaded file. The following three choices are always presented in the Print dialog box:

Selected Text	Use this choice to print only that text you have previously highlighted by simultaneously holding down the Shift key and using cursor-control keys.
Active Window	Use this to print the contents of the currently active window. This is useful if you want to print a particular procedure in a program. You can also print the contents of the Immediate window with this command.

Current Module   Use this to print an entire program
module, including all SUB and
FUNCTION procedures. Procedures are
printed alphabetically after the
module-level code.

In addition to these three options, a fourth print option is available only when Full Menus have been selected:

All Modules   Use this to print all of the separate files
that make up a multiple-module program.
Each module is followed by the procedures
which are part of that module. The main
module is printed first, followed by
additional modules arranged in
alphabetical order.

THE FILE MENU: DOS SHELL

Use the *DOS Shell* command to leave QuickBASIC temporarily and execute operating system commands, without unloading the QuickBASIC program or affecting any of your current work in the QuickBASIC environment. Return to QuickBASIC by typing **exit** ◄─┘ at the DOS command prompt.

THE FILE MENU: EXIT

Use the *Exit* command to leave QuickBASIC and return to the operating system. If you have saved your work and/or cleared the screen prior to activating the Exit command, no further actions are necessary. If you have made modifications to any file or files currently in memory, a dialog box will open that presents three choices: (1) Save the changes and then exit QuickBASIC; (2) return to DOS without saving the changes; or (3) cancel the command and return to the Work screen as it was when you invoked the command. This dialog box ensures that you will not inadvertently leave the QuickBASIC environment without saving your most recent work.

THE EDIT MENU

The Edit menu contains commands that enable you to build and modify your programs efficiently. Many Edit commands involve *selecting* text and then moving sections of selected text to an area of memory called the *clipboard*. The selection process and the use of the clipboard are reviewed next, followed by a summary of each of the Edit menu commands.

THE EDIT MENU: SELECTING TEXT

QuickBASIC edit commands allow you to delete, copy, and move whole sections of text. Before using these commands you must mark, or *select*, the block of text you want to work with. Selected text is displayed in reverse video.

To select a block of text:

While selected text is displayed in reverse video, pressing any ordinary character key has the effect of permanently deleting the selected text and replacing it with what you have typed. Text deleted in this way *cannot* be retrieved.

1. Move your cursor to the beginning of the section you want to mark.

2. Hold down the *Shift* key and simultaneously use the cursor-control keys to move to the end of the section you want to mark.

The selected text will be displayed in reverse video. Once you have selected text, you can proceed with the Edit menu's Cut, Copy, Paste, and Clear commands. If you decide not to continue with one of these commands, pressing any of the cursor control keys unselects the marked text and returns it to its normal appearance.

THE EDIT MENU: USING THE CLIPBOARD

QuickBASIC sets aside an area of memory known as a *clipboard* for temporary storage of material that you want to move or copy. Several commands, summarized here, move text into the clipboard. Once you have moved text to the clipboard, you can use the Paste command to copy this material to the current file at the cursor location. Notice that some, but not all, delete commands move deleted text to the clipboard, making it possible to undo some delete commands.

The following actions all move text into the clipboard:

- Selecting the Copy command in the Edit menu
- Selecting the Cut command in the Edit menu
- Erasing a line of text with Ctrl+Y

The following two delete commands *do not* move the deleted text to the clipboard:

- Selecting the Clear command in the Edit menu
- Erasing a word with Ctrl+T

Whenever you execute a command that sends material to the clipboard, it replaces what was already there. Otherwise, the contents of the clipboard remain unchanged, even if you clear the current work from the View screen.

THE EDIT MENU: UNDO = ALT+BACKSPACE

Undo will only undo alterations that have affected a single line of text.

Use the *Undo* command if you have changed a line of text and decide you want to restore the line to its original appearance, rather than keep the changes you made. The Undo command works only if you have not yet moved the cursor off the altered line. This command is of no use if you have typed a *new* line of text and then altered it without ever moving your cursor from the line, because in this case Undo will restore the blank line that was present initially.

THE EDIT MENU: CUT = SHIFT+DEL

The *Cut* command removes a selected section of text from the screen and places it in the clipboard, where it remains until replaced by a subsequent command. This command cannot be activated if no text has been selected. The Cut command has two important uses: deleting blocks of text from a program, and moving text from one part of a program to another.

To delete text from your program:

1. Select a section of text. (See *Selecting Text* above.)

2. Choose the Cut command from the Edit menu (or press Shift+Del).

Text deleted in this way can be retrieved as long as the contents of the clipboard remain unaltered.

To move text from one part of a program to another:

1. Select a section of text. (See *Selecting Text* above.)

2. Choose the Cut command from the Edit menu (or press Shift+Del).

3. Move the cursor to the position at which you want to place the text and use the Paste command (Shift+Ins) to insert the text.

THE EDIT MENU: COPY = CTRL+INS

Use the Copy and Paste commands to copy useful sections of code from QuickBASIC's online Help screens and sample programs directly into programs that you are developing.

Use the *Copy* command to make a copy of a section of code and move it to other parts of the same program or to a different program. The Copy command moves a copy of a selected section of text to the clipboard without removing it from its original position. This text remains in the clipboard and can be copied to new locations repeatedly, until the contents of the clipboard are replaced by new material. The Copy command cannot be activated if no text has been selected.

To copy text from one part of a program to another:

1. Select a section of text. (See *Selecting Text* above.)

2. Choose the Copy command from the Edit menu (or press Ctrl+Ins).

3. Position the cursor where you want to put the copy, and use the Paste command (Shift+Ins) to insert the text.

THE EDIT MENU: PASTE = SHIFT+INS

Use the *Paste* command to insert the contents of the clipboard into the currently loaded file. The Paste command cannot be activated if the clipboard is empty.

Be sure that no text is highlighted when you activate the Paste command unless you want that text to be replaced. If you inadvertently replace selected text with the contents of the clipboard during a Paste operation, the lost text cannot be retrieved unless it has been saved to a disk file.

The Paste command can be used either to *add* the contents of the clipboard to a file without altering existing text, or to use the contents of the clipboard to *replace* a selected section of text. These two alternatives are accomplished as follows:

- If no text is selected, the contents of the clipboard are placed at the cursor position between items of existing text. Inserted text is placed to the *right of and below* the current cursor position.

- If a section of text has been highlighted prior to the Paste action, the contents of the clipboard will *replace* the highlighted text.

THE EDIT MENU: CLEAR = DEL

Material deleted with the Clear command cannot be retrieved unless it has been saved to a disk file.

Use the *Clear* command to delete selected sections of text from the screen *without* placing the text in the clipboard. This is useful if you want to preserve the present contents of the clipboard for use in a future Paste command.

THE EDIT MENU: NEW SUB

Typing **SUB** or **FUNCTION** followed by the procedure name is a quick, alternative way to create a new procedure. You can include parameters in the SUB statement when you use this method.

Use the *New SUB* command to create and name a new SUB procedure. Choosing this command opens the New SUB dialog box with a text box for the Name of the new procedure. Type the name of the new procedure in this box and then press ←┘. The contents of the active window will change to contain the SUB and END SUB statements for this procedure, with the procedure name in the Title bar. Don't include parameters in the text box when you open a procedure with the new SUB command. Add these to the SUB statement after you are returned to the View window.

THE EDIT MENU: NEW FUNCTION

If a section of text has been selected prior to invoking the New SUB and New FUNCTION commands, the selected text will automatically be entered as the new procedure name.

Use *New FUNCTION* to create and name a new FUNCTION procedure. Choosing this command opens the New FUNCTION dialog box with a text box for the Name of the new procedure. Type the name of the new procedure in this box and then press ←┘. The contents of the active window will change to contain the FUNCTION and END

FUNCTION statements for this procedure, with the procedure name in the Title bar. Don't include parameters in the text box when you open a procedure with the new FUNCTION command. Add these to the FUNCTION statement after you are returned to the View window.

THE VIEW MENU

The View menu contains commands that help you work with the various parts of a developing program: SUB and FUNCTION procedures, discrete modules, include files, and document files.

THE VIEW MENU: SUBS = F2

The *SUBs* command is a multipurpose command that allows you to manipulate the procedures and—in the case of multiple-module programs, the modules—that make up a program. The SUBs dialog box includes a list box that displays the structure of all loaded modules and allows you to select any of the procedures or modules listed. Having selected an item from this list, you can choose from the following command options:

Edit in Active	Displays the selected item in the active window.
Edit in Split	Divides the View window into two sections. The top section displays the contents of the original View window, while the bottom section displays the selected item. (Techniques for manipulating a split View window are described under the Split command, below.)
Delete	Deletes the selected item.
Move	Moves a selected procedure from one module to another.

THE VIEW MENU: NEXT SUB = SHIFT+F2

Use the *Next SUB* command to cycle the procedures in your program one at a time into the active window, in alphabetical order.

Each time you use this command, the active window will display the next procedure in your program. If the last procedure in your program is in the active window, pressing Shift+F2 will display the first procedure in your program. The keystroke combination Ctrl+F2 cycles through the procedures in reverse order.

THE VIEW MENU: SPLIT

The *Split* command divides the View window into two work areas. When you first invoke the split command, the two work areas will each contain the same section of your program. To select a different section of your program for display in one of these two areas:

1. Use F6 or Shift+F6 to change the active window.

2. Use the SUBs command (F2) to select a section of your program to display in the active window.

The commands described here for controlling the size of an active window work with Help screens and the Immediate window as well.

The following commands can be used to change the relative sizes of the windows in your work screen:

Alt+Plus(+)	Increases the size of the active window by one line.
Alt+Minus(−)	Decreases the size of the active window by one line.
Ctrl+F10	Makes the active window occupy the full Work screen. Repeating the command returns the screen to its original configuration.

THE VIEW MENU: NEXT STATEMENT

Use the *Next Statement* command when program execution has been interrupted before completion. This command shows you the line that would have been executed next had the program continued. If you move the cursor around in a suspended program, you can use this command to return to the point where the program was interrupted.

THE VIEW MENU: OUTPUT SCREEN = F4

Use *Output Screen* when you are working with the QuickBASIC Work screen and you want to switch to view the Output screen. Once you have viewed the Output screen, return to the Work screen by repeating the Output Screen command.

THE VIEW MENU: INCLUDE FILE

Include files that are loaded into memory with the Include File command are *not* linked to your program with a .MAK file when you use the Save All command.

The *Include File* command can be activated only when a currently loaded program contains a statement with an $INCLUDE metacommand. Use this command when you want to modify the include file. The Include File command loads the include file into memory and displays it in the active window without removing other files from memory. Once you have modified the file, return to your program using the SUBs command (F2).

THE VIEW MENU: INCLUDED LINES

The *Included Lines* command is a toggle that is useful only when a loaded module contains an $INCLUDE metacommand. When Included Lines has been selected, the contents of the include file will be displayed in your program in high-intensity video in place of the $INCLUDE statement, but the included lines are displayed this way for viewing purpose only. If you try to modify any of these lines, a dialog box will open that allows you to choose to display and edit the included file in the View window. (If you accept this option, the effect is the same as using the Include File command described above.)

THE SEARCH MENU

The commands in the search menu include search operations, which allow you to move quickly and efficiently through large files; and search-and-replace operations, which allow you to make rapid and thorough modifications to items that occur at several locations in a file. The term *target text* is used here to refer to the item you want to find in a search operation.

THE SEARCH MENU: FIND

Once you open the Find dialog box, pressing ⏎ will immediately initiate the search. Be sure you have correctly specified your desired search conditions before you press ⏎.

Use the *Find* command to find a particular word, phrase, or mathematical expression in the file (or files) you are working with. A search initiated with this command will search a file, starting at the current cursor position, and move the cursor to the next occurrence of the target text in your file. If the text is not found between the current cursor position and the end of the file, the search will continue, starting at the beginning of the file, until the entire file has been searched. If a match is found in another part of your program (in either a procedure or module), that part of your program is moved into the active window. If no match is found, the cursor is returned to its original position.

The Find dialog box includes the following items:

Find What	Use this text box to specify the target text for the search. You can type the target text here, or use either of the following techniques to have the text entered automatically into this box: (1) Place the cursor on a target word before invoking the Find command; or (2) hold down the Shift key and use the cursor-control keys to select a target phrase or expression before invoking the Find command.
Match Upper/Lowercase	Selecting this option restricts the search to sections of text that exactly match the case of the target text as it is displayed in the Find What input area. For example, if this option is selected, "Print" would not be identified as a match for "PRINT".
Whole Word	Selecting this option means that a search will not identify a target

| | string if it is incorporated into a longer word. For example, a whole word search for PRINT will not stop at LPRINT. |
| Search | This input area allows you to specify the scope of the search. You may choose to search the contents of the active window only, the current module (including all of its SUB and FUNCTION procedures), or—if more than one module is loaded—all the modules in memory. |

THE SEARCH MENU: SELECTED TEXT = CTRL+BACKSLASH(\)

The *Selected Text* command allows you to perform a quick search for selected text. Select text by holding the Shift key down while you use the cursor-control keys to mark the target text for the search. Activate the command by using the Search Menu or by pressing Ctrl+\. No dialog box opens, and only the *active window* is searched for the selected text.

THE SEARCH MENU: REPEAT LAST FIND = F3

Use *Repeat Last Find* as a quick way to repeat the most recent search operation. This command uses no dialog box. If you have just performed a Find or a Change command, the Repeat Last Find command searches for the target text as you defined it in the prior command. If no target text was defined in a prior command, the Repeat Last Find command searches for the word at the cursor.

THE SEARCH MENU: CHANGE

Use *Change* to find and alter every occurrence of a character, word, phrase, or mathematical expression. The Change dialog box includes two text input areas:

<table>
<tr><td>Find What</td><td>As in the Find command, this box defines the target text, but to have the text entered automatically into this input area you must select the target text (by holding down the Shift key and using cursor-control keys to highlight the text) prior to invoking the Change command.</td></tr>
<tr><td>Change To</td><td>Type the desired replacement for the target text in this box. If this box is left empty, the target text will be systematically erased.</td></tr>
</table>

The Change dialog box includes the following three options, which work as they do when you use the Find command: Match Upper/Lowercase, Whole Word, and Search. The dialog box shows four command choices: <Find and Verify>, <Change All>, <Cancel>, and <Help>. The first two are explained here.

<table>
<tr><td><Find and Verify></td><td>Selecting this option allows you to confirm each modification individually. Each time the target text is found, you will be given the following four choices: (1) Change (make the change and continue the operation); (2) Skip (don't make the change and continue the operation); (3) Cancel (don't make the change and stop the operation at this point); and (4) Help (display on-screen information about the Change command).</td></tr>
<tr><td><Change All></td><td>Selecting this option means that all changes are made automatically without any pause for confirmation.</td></tr>
</table>

Use **Tab**, not ←, to move from the Find What input area to the Change To input area. Pressing ← initiates the Change operation. Do not press ← before you have completely defined all of the Change conditions.

Think twice before initiating a Change All command. This choice can frequently result in changes that you did not anticipate and that are difficult to correct. Always make a practice of saving your file to disk before initiating a Change All change.

THE SEARCH MENU: LABEL

Use the *Label* command to find program statements that you have identified with a line label. The dialog box that opens contains the same choices as the Find dialog box. The Find Label command will automatically add a colon to whatever you enter into the Find What input area. For example, if you initiate a Find Label search for *ErrorHandler*, the search will locate the line label *ErrorHandler:*.

THE RUN MENU

The Run menu contains commands that allow you to initiate program execution, create stand-alone programs, and create QuickBASIC quick libraries.

In descriptions of the Run menu, the term *current statement* is used when program execution is interrupted before the program is completed. The current statement is the statement that was executing when program execution was suspended.

THE RUN MENU: START = SHIFT+F5

The effect of the Start command is equivalent to using the Restart command followed by the Continue command.

The *Start* command runs the currently loaded program, beginning at the first executable line. Use this command whenever you want to ensure that a program starts at the beginning. If a program has been interrupted before completion (by a run-time error, Ctrl+Break, a Watchpoint, or a Breakpoint), the Start command runs the program from its first executable line, regardless of where execution was interrupted.

THE RUN MENU: RESTART

Use *Restart* if you want to clear the effects of a program whose execution has been interrupted by a run-time error, Ctrl+Break, a Watchpoint, or a Breakpoint. The Restart command reinitializes all variables and resets the current statement to the first executable line in your program, but does *not* initiate program execution.

THE RUN MENU: CONTINUE = F5

The *Continue* command causes a suspended program to continue with the current statement. Use this command in combination with Ctrl+Break, Watchpoints, and Breakpoints to run and study a program in segments rather than all at once. You can also use the Continue command when run-time errors interrupt program execution. After correcting the line containing the error, use Continue to proceed with program execution without restarting the program. (However, some editing changes *require* you to restart your program. The QuickBASIC editor recognizes such a change and displays a dialog box that notifies you that you will have to restart your program after making the change.)

The Continue command will start program execution at the beginning of your program if it has not yet been run, if it ran to completion on its most recent run, or if you have reset the program with the Restart command.

THE RUN MENU: MODIFY COMMAND$

*Modify COMMAND$* is useful for advanced users who are developing and debugging programs that use the COMMAND$ function. These programs allow the user to type in command line information when they invoke the program. To debug these programs, use Modify COMMAND$ to test program response to various command line possibilities without leaving the QuickBASIC environment.

THE RUN MENU: MAKE EXE FILE

Use the *Make EXE* file command to make versions of your programs that you can run directly from the operating system without loading them into QuickBASIC. These files are given an .EXE extension and can be executed by typing the part of the file name that precedes this extension at the DOS command prompt. (For example, you can run a program called TUTOR.EXE by typing *tutor* at the DOS prompt.)

The Make EXE dialog box includes the following items:

Produce Debug Code   Selecting this option produces a program that reports the following debugging information if errors occur at run time: Arithmetic overflow errors are identified, and array bounds and line locations are given. You must also use this option if you want an .EXE program to respond to Ctrl+Break. Using Debug Code will make your program file larger, and the program may take longer to run.

EXE Requiring BRUN45.EXE   Programs created with this option are much smaller files, but will run only if a copy of the file BRUN45.EXE provided with your distribution diskettes is available at run time.

Stand-Alone EXE file   Programs created with this option can stand alone. These files directly incorporate the routines of the BRUN45.EXE module, making them larger but slightly faster than programs that use this module at run time.

The PACKING.LST text file on the Utilities 2 distribution disk contains an inventory and brief description of each of the files provided to you with your QuickBASIC software.

The following files, provided with your QuickBASIC distribution diskettes, must be available in the current directory or in your search path in order to execute the Make EXE File command: BC.EXE, LINK.EXE, BRUN45.LIB, and BCOM45.LIB.

THE RUN MENU: MAKE LIBRARY

Use *Make Library* to create a QuickBASIC quick library from the currently loaded module. A quick library is a compiled collection of user-defined procedures. Quick libraries are given a .QLB extension and must be loaded into memory using the /L option as part of the

QB command line you use when you first load QuickBASIC. (For example, type **QB /L SAMPLE.QLB** to load a library called *sample*.)

THE RUN MENU: SET MAIN MODULE

Use *Set Main Module* when you are working with multiple-module programs and you want to select a different main module for the program. Changing the main module changes the flow of program control; the first statement executed in a multiple-module program is always the first executable statement of that program's main module.

THE DEBUG MENU

The Debug menu contains commands that allow you to study your program in detail as it executes. Many of the Debug menu commands require using QuickBASIC's Watch window, and for that reason the material that follows includes

- General information about the QuickBASIC Watch window;
- A summary of each of the commands in the Debug menu;
- A description of some debugging techniques not covered by the Debug menu commands.

WORKING WITH QUICKBASIC'S WATCH WINDOW

The Watch window is an area of the QuickBASIC Work screen that you can use to watch the values of selected variables and expressions in your program as they change during program execution. If program execution is interrupted by a Watchpoint or Breakpoint (described below) or by Ctrl+Break or a run-time error, the Watch window displays the values of all watched variables or expressions at that point in program execution. If a program runs to completion, the Watch window displays the final value of all watched items. Use the Restart command in the Run menu to reset all watched items to their initial values (either zero or the null string).

The values of procedure-level variables or expressions are not available if program execution stops during execution of module-level code, and, similarly, module-level variables or expressions are not available if program execution stops during execution of a procedure-level statement. (This is true even if a variable has been declared as global in a SHARED statement.) If the value of a variable is not available, it is identified as *<Not watchable>* in the Watch window.

THE DEBUG MENU: ADD WATCH

You use the *Add Watch* command to add new variables or expressions to the Watch window in one of two ways. You can open a dialog box and type in the item you want to watch:

1. Activate the Watch window to open the Add Watch dialog box.

2. Type the variable or expression you want to watch in the input area of this dialog box.

3. Press ⏎ to add this item to the Watch window.

The second method requires that you select text before activating the Add Watch command. Do this by holding down the Shift key while you use the cursor-control keys to highlight the item you want to watch. To use this method,

1. Select the variable or expression you want to watch.

2. Activate the Add Watch command. The item you selected will be added immediately to the Watch window without the appearance of the Add Watch dialog box.

The Instant Watch command(Shift + F9) is an additional quick and easy way to add variables to the Watch window.

THE DEBUG MENU: *INSTANT WATCH = SHIFT+F9*

Use the *Instant Watch* command when program execution has been interrupted to see the value of a variable or expression that is not yet displayed in the Watch window. To use Instant Watch to display a *variable*:

1. Position the cursor on the variable you want to watch.

2. Select Instant Watch from the Debug menu (or press Shift+F9). A dialog box will open that displays the current value of that variable.

3. Either press ◄─┘ to add the variable to the Watch window or press Esc to close the Instant Watch dialog box without adding the variable to the Watch window.

To use Instant Watch to display an *expression*:

- Select the expression to watch by pressing Shift and using the cursor-control keys, and then proceed with steps 2 and 3 as described above.

The Instant Watch dialog box will not display the final value of a variable or expression after program execution has been completed—instead the message <Not available> will appear. If you want to know the final value of a variable or expression, you must add it to the Watch window before you run the program.

THE DEBUG MENU: WATCHPOINT

The *Watchpoint* command allows you to set a condition for suspending program execution. This condition can be defined using a relational statement (e.g., X > 9) or a Boolean variable. (Refer to Chapter 6 for more information about Boolean variables.) When the relational statement is true (or when the Boolean variable reaches a non-zero value), program execution will be interrupted.

To use a Watchpoint in your program:

1. Activate the Watchpoint command.

2. Type an expression into the text box of the Watchpoint dialog box.

3. Press ◄─┘. The expression will appear in the Watch window followed by either <TRUE> or <FALSE>, depending on

whether the expression is true or false at the time you add it to your program.

4. Run your program. When the expression becomes true, program execution will be interrupted. (If you wish to continue program execution from this point, press F5 for normal execution or use F8 to proceed one line at a time.)

If you prefer, you can select an expression from your program by holding down the Shift key and using the cursor-control keys to highlight the expression. If you activate the Watchpoint command after selecting an expression, it will be added to the Watch window directly, without the appearance of the Watchpoint dialog box.

THE DEBUG MENU: DELETE WATCH

Use the *Delete Watch* command to remove an item from the Watch window by following these steps:

1. Activate the Delete Watch command. A dialog box opens containing a list of all items currently in the Watch window.

2. Use the cursor-control keys to select an item from the list.

3. Press ◄┘ to remove this item from the Watch window and close the Delete Watch dialog box.

THE DEBUG MENU: DELETE ALL WATCH

Activating the *Delete All Watch* command immediately clears all items from the Watch window.

THE DEBUG MENU: TRACE ON

The *Trace On* command is a toggle command that allows you to study the sequence of events that occurs during program execution. After you select this command, a bullet (•) will appear in front of the command name in the Debug menu. (Repeating the command turns Trace off and removes the bullet from the menu.)

If you set Trace On before running a program, it has the following two effects:

- When you run your program, it will execute in slow motion. Your program code will remain on screen, and each statement will be highlighted as it is executed.

- The computer will continuously keep track of the most recently executed 20 lines of code.

This command enables you to watch the flow of your program at a slower pace. You can interrupt the program by using Breakpoints, Watchpoints, or Ctrl+Break. At the point of interruption, use the following keys to review the last 20 statements that have been executed:

Shift+F8 and Shift+F10 are effective only if you have traced a history of program execution by using either the Trace On or the History On command.

Shift+F8   Retraces your progress backward through the program by moving the cursor to the previously executed line.

Shift+F10   Moves the cursor forward through the stored sequence of executed commands.

Moving the cursor with these two commands allows you to study the flow of your program, but does not affect the current statement. If you continue program execution, the next statement to be executed will be the statement at which the program was interrupted.

THE DEBUG MENU: HISTORY ON

The *History On* command causes the computer to keep track of the last 20 lines of code that are executed during program execution. (History On works like the Trace On command described above, but History On does not affect the normal speed of program execution.) Turn this toggle command on when you want to keep a record of the sequence of command execution in a program operating at normal speed.

THE DEBUG MENU: TOGGLE BREAKPOINT = F9

Use the *Toggle Breakpoint* command to suspend program execution at any specified point or points during program execution. To set a breakpoint:

1. Move the cursor to the statement at which you want program execution to be suspended.

2. Select the Toggle Breakpoint command or press the F9 shortcut key. A band across the screen will mark the breakpoint line.

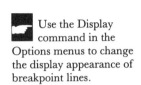 Use the Display command in the Options menus to change the display appearance of breakpoint lines.

When you run a program that contains a breakpoint, the program will stop when it reaches the marked line, and you will be returned to the Work screen, which will indicate that the breakpoint line is now the current statement. At this point you can study the items in your Watch window, continue program execution line-by-line with the F8 key, continue program execution at normal speed with the Continue command (F5), or make modifications and restart the program. If you set Trace On or History On, you can also use Shift+F8 and Shift+F10 to review the order of execution of the 20 statements that preceded the breakpoint.

To remove an individual breakpoint, place the cursor on the breakpoint line and repeat the Breakpoint command (F9). To remove all breakpoints, use the Clear All Breakpoints command.

THE DEBUG MENU: CLEAR ALL BREAKPOINTS

Activating the *Clear All Breakpoints* command immediately clears all breakpoints from your program.

THE DEBUG MENU: BREAK ON ERRORS

Use the *Break On Errors* command to find and correct the source of run-time errors in your program. This toggle command works with programs that contain an error-handling routine. When the Break On Errors option is selected, a bullet (•) appears before the command name in the Debug menu, and the following two conditions are established:

- If a run-time error occurs, QuickBASIC will suspend the program before the associated error-handling routine has been executed. The cursor will be on the line label specified in the ON ERROR statement.

- The History On command is activated, and thus you can back up to the program statement that triggered the error by pressing Shift+F8.

THE DEBUG MENU: SET NEXT STATEMENT

Use the Next State-ment command in the View menu to *find* the current statement in a suspended program. Use the Set Next Statement to *change* the current state-ment in a suspended program.

The *Set Next Statement* command is active only when program execution has been suspended. This command allows you to rerun a section of code or to skip over a section of code by selecting the program line you want QuickBASIC to begin with when program execution is resumed. To use the Set Next Statement command:

Remember that skipping over sec-tions of program code can introduce errors that might not occur if the program had executed in normal fashion.

1. Run your program and use Breakpoints, Watchpoints, or Ctrl+Break to suspend program execution.

2. Move the cursor to any position in the line you would like to be executed next.

3. Activate the Set Next Statement command. The screen display will change to reflect the fact that this is now the current statement.

4. Use the Continue command (F5) or the Step command (F8) to continue program execution from this point.

ADDITIONAL DEBUGGING TECHNIQUES

Some QuickBASIC debugging techniques are not available by activating commands in the Debug menu. The following function keys are used in debugging operations and have no equivalents in the pull-down menus:

F7   Pressing F7 causes a program to execute up to the line containing the cursor. Program execution is then suspended, with the cursor line as the current statement. In a previously suspended program, F7 runs the program starting at the current line and stopping at the line on which you have placed the cursor.

F8   Pressing F8 allows you to run your program one step at a time. In a suspended program, F8 executes the current statement. When a statement produces screen output, the output screen flashes momentarily. Use the Output Screen command (F4) to view this screen, and again to return to the Work screen.

F10 Like F8, this key allows you to run your program one step at a time, but unlike F8 (which executes each individual line in all FUNCTION and SUB procedures) F10 executes only the module-level code one line at a time. FUNCTION and SUB procedures are executed in their entirety, as a single step, without being moved into the View window.

The Immediate window can also be a valuable tool for program development and debugging. Debugging techniques using the immediate window include

- *Running individual program procedures*: To do this, execute a CALL statement from the Immediate window. If necessary, you can also use the Immediate window to set variable values and open files before testing the procedure.

- *Changing the value of variables:* Use assignment statements to alter the value of a variable in a suspended program.

- *Simulating run-time errors:* Type **ERROR** followed by an error code value to display the dialog box for that error. (Refer to Appendix D for a list of error messages.)

THE CALLS MENU

The Calls menu contains only the *Calls* command. This command is useful for debugging large, complex programs in which you have included nested procedures several layers deep. (A nested procedure is one that has been called by another procedure.) When program execution is suspended during execution of a procedure, the Calls menu displays a list of procedures. At the top of the list is the procedure that was being executed at the time the program was suspended—this is the *active* procedure. Beneath the name of the active procedure is the name of the procedure that called it (or the name of the program module if the suspended procedure was called from module-level code.) The list continues, showing the name of all procedures (up to eight) involved in reaching the point of program suspension and ending with the name of the program module that called the initial procedure.

For example, if the MULTIPLY.BAS program shown in Chapter 9 were interrupted during execution of the Good procedure, the Calls list would look like this:

```
Good
Multiplication
MULTIPLY.BAS
```

This list shows that the module-level code of the MULTIPLY program called the Multiplication procedure, which in turn called the Good procedure.

Highlighting a procedure on the calls list and pressing ⏎ brings that procedure into the View window. Highlighting a procedure and pressing F7 causes the program to execute up to the highlighted procedure.

THE OPTIONS MENU

The Options menu contains a variety of commands allowing you to customize the QuickBASIC program to suit your needs and tastes. Changes made with the Options menu are stored in a file called QB.INI and will remain in place between QuickBASIC work sessions. QB.INI is created when you first use the Options menu and updated with subsequent changes. If QB.INI is not present, QuickBASIC uses its original default settings.

THE OPTIONS MENU: DISPLAY

The *Display* command controls three display features of the QuickBASIC Work screen: colors, scroll bars, and tab stops. The Display dialog box has two input areas.

The first input area is titled *Colors*. Use this area to select the background and foreground colors used for displaying normal text, breakpoints (set with the Breakpoint command) and the current statement (the line about to be executed in a suspended program). A sample of the default display of each is shown, followed by two list boxes. These boxes show you the foreground and background colors that work with your monitor. As you highlight different items on these lists, the default display changes instantly, allowing you to evaluate the results. Pressing ↵ accepts the changes and returns you to the Work screen.

The second input area is titled *Display Options*. The first display option, Scroll Bars, is a toggle. The scroll bars along the right and bottom edge of the View window are used with a mouse to scroll sections of text through the display area. Turn this toggle off if you are not using a mouse. The second option, Tab Stops, allows you to select the number of spaces that will be indented when you use the Tab key. Pressing ↵ accepts the display Option settings and returns you to your Work screen.

THE OPTIONS MENU: SET PATHS

QuickBASIC will also find files if they are in a directory path that you created with a DOS PATH statement, and using the Set Paths command will not alter these paths.

The *Set Paths* command allows you to specify a search path for each of four file types: executable files (.EXE or .COM extensions), include files (.BI or .BAS extensions), library files (.LIB or .QLB extensions), and help files (.HLP extension). If you installed Quick-BASIC on a hard disk using the Easy Setup routine, the default location of all of these file types is the C:\QB45 directory. Four text boxes in the Set Paths dialog box allow you to type in directory paths for each of these four file types.

THE OPTIONS MENU: RIGHT MOUSE

The right button on a mouse can have one of two possible effects in the QuickBASIC environment, and the *Right Mouse* command allows you to select which of these effects occurs. The Right Mouse dialog box presents the following two options:

Context-sensitive Help   When this is selected, pressing the right mouse button gives you information about the item at the mouse cursor location. (This is equivalent to the keyboard F1 key.)

Execute up to this line

When this is selected, pressing the right mouse button executes the currently loaded program up to the mouse cursor position. (This is equivalent to the keyboard F7 key.)

THE OPTIONS MENU: SYNTAX CHECKING

Syntax Checking is a toggle command that allows you to enable and disable the QuickBASIC smart editor. When the editor is active, each time you move the cursor off a line, it is checked for correct BASIC syntax and, if the syntax is incorrect, an error message is displayed. When the editor is active, it will also format lines by displaying BASIC keywords in capital letters. When the editor is disabled, no syntax checking takes place, nor are any alterations made to the text as you entered it.

THE OPTIONS MENU: FULL MENUS

The *Full Menus* command allows you to choose between Quick-BASIC's Full menus and the abbreviated Easy menus. When Full menus are selected, a bullet (•) appears next to the Full Menus command and all of QuickBASIC's menu options are available. If this bullet is absent, the menu display is limited to a subset of the choices available with Full menus. By simplifying the number of available choices, Easy menus can help beginners work efficiently within the QuickBASIC environment. When Easy menus are selected, loading QuickBASIC results in the display of a welcome message. Pressing Esc clears this message.

THE HELP MENU

The Help menu provides you with the means to consult Quick-BASIC's extensive online help. The online help consists of a series of

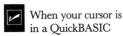 When your cursor is in a QuickBASIC help screen, you can use the Print command to print the complete contents of the active window.

Help screens connected by command headings called *hyperlinks* and indicated by a set of triangles (◄ and ►) on either side of each hyperlink heading. The Help screens fall into three categories.

- *General information screens* are those that are displayed initially when you invoke one of the help commands. These screens provide you with fundamental information about Quick-BASIC commands. They also include hyperlink headings that you can use to display additional Help screens.

- *Details* Help screens contain detailed descriptions of Quick-BASIC language commands. These screens can be displayed by positioning your cursor on the *Details* hyperlink of a currently displayed help screen and pressing F1 (or pressing ◄┘).

Use the Copy and Paste commands from the Edit menu to copy sections of code from the QuickBASIC Example screens to your programs.

- *Example* help screens show programming examples that demonstrate the use of the BASIC language commands. These can be displayed by positioning your cursor on the *Example* hyperlink of a currently displayed help screen and pressing F1 (or pressing ◄┘).

As you work with online help, you will frequently display a sequence of several different Help screens. If you want to retrace your steps and review any of the previously displayed screens,

- Press **Alt+F1** to view the preceding Help screen. Pressing Alt+F1 moves the display backward through a sequence of up to 20 screens.

- Press **Ctrl+F1** to move forward through this same sequence of screens.

THE HELP MENU: INDEX

The online index is an alphabetical list of BASIC programming keywords. To use the index,

1. Activate the Index command in the Help menu.

2. Press a letter of the alphabet to display the section of the index that contains terms starting with that letter.

3. Use the cursor-control keys and/or Tab and Shift+Tab to select the item you want to know more about.

4. Press F1 (or ←┘) to display the general Help screen about that item.

5. Use the hyperlinks to find out more about that item and related topics.

In addition to containing all BASIC statements and functions, the index includes the following six general topic headings:

Data Types

Expressions and Operators

Logical Operator Truth Table

Modules and Procedures

Operator Precedence Rules

Variable Scope Rules

THE HELP MENU: CONTENTS

The Help menu table of contents displays a list of topics about the QuickBASIC environment and the BASIC programming language. This list is reproduced in Figure 15.1. Selecting an item on the list will result in an on-screen display of information about that topic. Use the hyperlinks to learn more about this and related topics.

THE HELP MENU: TOPIC = F1

Activating the Topic command or pressing F1 results in the display of context-sensitive information about items in the QuickBASIC Work screen. The on-screen display that results depends on the location of your cursor when you invoke the command:

- If you are working with the QuickBASIC menus, pressing F1 displays information about the highlighted menu item.

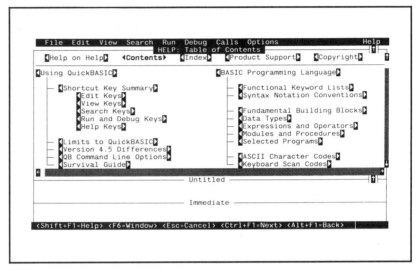

Figure 15.1: The online Table of Contents

- If your cursor is on a BASIC language keyword, pressing F1 displays the general Help screen concerning that keyword.

- If your cursor is on a variable or procedure name in your program, pressing F1 displays information about where and how you have used that item in your program.

THE HELP MENU:
HELP ON HELP = SHIFT+F1

Activating the *Help on Help* command (or pressing Shift+F1) displays a summary of the techniques you can use to get the most out of QuickBASIC's online help.

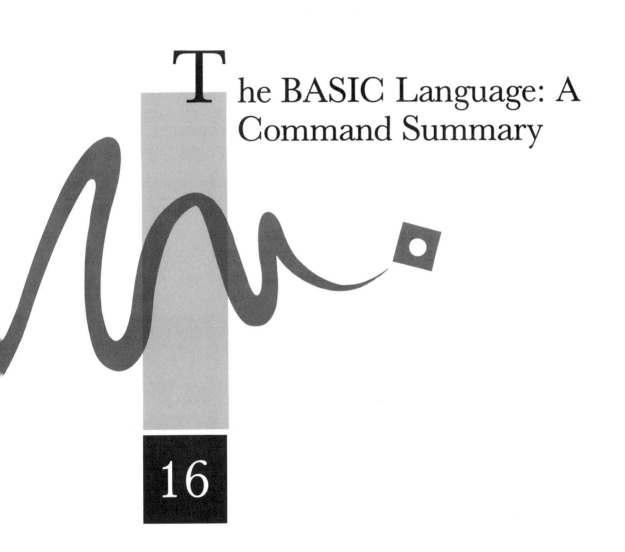

The BASIC Language: A Command Summary

16

CHAPTER **16**

THIS CHAPTER BRIEFLY SUMMARIZES THE BASIC
language commands covered in this book. In syntax statements,
brackets—[ ]—are used to enclose optional clauses. Parentheses—( )—
are used where you must include parentheses as part of your statement
syntax. Italics indicate specific items that you must provide within the
statement. Italicized terms ending with the word *List* represent a list of
one or more items separated by commas. A display in curly brackets—
{Item1 | Item2}—indicates that you should use one of the items con-
tained within the brackets.

ABS Function

Syntax: ABS(*NumericExpression*)

Description: Returns the absolute value of a numeric expression.

ASC Function

Syntax: ASC(*StringExpression*)

Description: Returns the ASCII code number of the first character
in the string expression.

ATN Function

Syntax: ATN(*NumericExpression*)

Description: Returns the radian measure of the angle whose tangent is equal to the numeric expression.

BEEP Statement

Syntax: BEEP

Description: Sounds the computer's speaker.

CALL Statement

Syntax 1:   CALL *ProcedureName*[(*ArgumentList*)]

Syntax 2:   *ProcedureName* [*ArgumentList*]

Description: Transfers program control to the named procedure. Variable arguments in the argument list are passed to procedure parameters by reference. Constants and expressions in the argument list are passed to procedure parameters by value.

CHDIR Statement

Syntax: CHDIR *PathSpecification*

Description: Changes the current default disk directory. The path specification must be a string expression.

CHR$ Function

Syntax: CHR$(*CodeNumber*)

Description: Returns the character whose ASCII code number is given in the argument.

CINT Function

Syntax: CINT(*NumericExpression*)

Description: Rounds the numeric expression given in the argument to the nearest integer and returns that value.

CIRCLE Statement

Syntax:
CIRCLE[STEP] (*x,y*),*Radius*[,*Color*][,[*Start*][,[*End*][,*Aspect*]]]]

Description: A graphics command for drawing circles, arcs and ellipses. The coordinates (*x,y*) mark the center of the circle with the given radius. *Start* and *End* are measured in radians and indicate starting and stopping points for drawing an arc. *Aspect* gives the aspect ratio of an ellipse. If you use some, but not all, of the final four arguments, include commas as place holders for the unused arguments.

CLOSE Statement

Syntax: CLOSE [[#]*FileNumber* [,[#] *FileNumber*]...]

Description: Closes the files specified in the argument list. If no argument is given, all open files are closed.

CLS Statement

Syntax: CLS {0 | 1 | 2}

Description: Clears the screen. The three optional arguments have the following effects: Using 0 clears both text and graphics, using 1 clears only the graphics viewport, and using 2 clears only the text viewport.

COLOR Statement

Syntax:

SYNTAX	SCREEN MODE
COLOR [*Foreground*][,[*Background*][,*Border*]]	0
COLOR [*Background*][,*Palette*]	1
COLOR [*Foreground*][,*Background*]	7-10
COLOR [*Foreground*]	12-13

Description: Selects display colors for the current graphics or text screen. Syntax and effect depend on the current screen mode.

COMMAND$ Function

Syntax: COMMAND$

Description: Returns a string value showing the command line used to invoke a program.

COMMON Statement

Syntax: COMMON [SHARED] *VariableList*

Description: Declares variables to be shared between program modules and/or procedures. If SHARED is included, variables are shared with all SUB and FUNCTION procedures within each program module.

CONST Statement

Syntax: CONST *ConstantName* = *Item* [,*ConstantName* = *Item*]...

Description: Gives constant names to string or numeric expressions. Once defined, constants remain the same throughout a program. Constants defined in module-level code are global, while constants defined in SUB or FUNCTION procedures are local to that procedure.

COS Function

Syntax: COS(*RadianAngleMeasure*)

Description: Returns the cosine of the angle given in the argument. Angle measurements must be given in radians.

DATA Statement

Syntax: DATA *Item1* [,*Item2*]...

Description: Supplies a list of data items to be read by a READ statement.

DATE$ Function

Syntax: DATE$

Description: Returns the current operating system date as a string value.

DATE$ Statement

Syntax: DATE$ = *StringExpression*

Description: Sets the string expression equal to the current operating system date.

DECLARE Statement

Syntax:
DECLARE {FUNCTION | SUB} *ProcedureName* [([*ParameterList*])]

Description: Declares the names of procedures used in a program, and invokes argument type checking to ensure that items in the argument correspond correctly to items in the parameter list.

DEF FN Statement

Syntax 1: DEF FN*NameOfFunction* [(*ParameterList*)] = *Expression*

Syntax 2: DEF FN*NameOfFunction* [(*ParameterList*)]

.

.

.

FN*NameOfFunction* = *Expression*

.

.

.

END DEF

Description: Defines and names a single line or multiline function. Functions defined in this way always begin with FN. DEF FN definitions must be placed in your program where they will be executed before the defined functions are used.

DEFDBL Statement

Syntax: DEFDBL *LetterRange* [,*LetterRange*]...

Description: Sets default data-type to double-precision values for those variables that begin with the letters included in the letter range or ranges.

DEFINT Statement

Syntax: DEFINT *LetterRange* [,*LetterRange*]...

Description: Sets default data-type to integer values for those variables that begin with the letters included in the letter range or ranges.

DEFLNG Statement

Syntax: DEFLNG *LetterRange* [,*LetterRange*]...

Description: Sets default data-type to long integer values for those variables that begin with the letters included in the letter range or ranges.

DEFSNG Statement

Syntax: DEFSNG *LetterRange* [,*LetterRange*]...

Description: Sets default data-type to single-precision values for those variables that begin with the letters included in the letter range or ranges.

DEFSTR *Statement*

Syntax: DEFSTR *LetterRange* [,*LetterRange*]...

Description: Sets default data-type to string values for those variables that begin with the letters included in the letter range or ranges.

DIM *Statement*

Syntax: DIM [SHARED] *Variable* [(*Subscripts*)] [AS *DataType*]

Description: Declares the name, data-type, and size of an array. DIM statements can also be used to establish the data-type of simple variables and can be used to declare both simple variables and arrays as global. If more than one variable or array is defined in a DIM statement, use commas to separate each item.

DO...LOOP *Statements*

Syntax 1: DO

       .

       .

       .

       LOOP [{WHILE | UNTIL} *BooleanExpression*]

Syntax 2: DO [{WHILE | UNTIL} *BooleanExpression*]

       .

       .

       LOOP

Description: The keywords DO and LOOP enclose a block of statements to be repeated. If no conditions are included in either the DO or LOOP statements, the block will either repeat endlessly or until conditions described in an IF ... THEN EXIT DO statement are met. If WHILE is used to set conditions for terminating the loop, the loop will continue to execute while a condition is true. If UNTIL is used to set conditions for terminating the loop, the loop will continue to execute until a condition is true.

END Statement

Syntax:
END [{DEF | FUNCTION | IF | SELECT | SUB | TYPE}]

Description: Used without argument, an END statement terminates execution of a program and closes any open files. Used with an argument, an END statement ends execution of a particular procedure or block.

EOF Function

Syntax: EOF(*FileNumber*)

Description: Tests for the end-of-file condition. Returns a true (– 1) value when the end of the file specified is reached.

ERASE Statement

Syntax: ERASE *ArrayName* [,*ArrayName*...]

Description: If an array is static, ERASE reinitializes the elements of the array. If an array is dynamic, ERASE deallocates the array, making more memory available if needed.

ERR Function

Syntax: ERR

Description: Returns the error code (an integer value) of the last error that occurred.

ERROR Statement

Syntax: ERROR *IntegerExpression*

Description: Simulates the occurrence of the error with the code given in the argument.

EXIT Statement

Syntax: EXIT {DEF | DO | FOR | FUNCTION | SUB}

Description: Terminates execution of the function, loop, or procedure it is placed within.

EXP Function

Syntax: EXP(*NumericExpression*)

Description: Returns the value of *e* raised to the power given in the argument (*e* is a mathematical constant approximately equal to 2.718282). The numeric expression in the argument must be less than or equal to 88.02969.

FILES Statement

Syntax: FILES (*FileSpecification*)

Description: Displays a list of files. Use the file specification argument to indicate drive, directory path, and/or files to be listed. For example FILES "A:*.BAS" will list all BASIC program files on the A drive. If no path is given, files in the current default directory are listed.

FIX Function

Syntax: FIX(*NumericExpression*)

Description: Returns the integer portion of the numeric expression, dropping all digits after the decimal point.

FOR...NEXT Statement

Syntax: FOR *CounterVariable* = *Start* TO *Stop* [STEP *Increment*]

      .

      .

      .

      NEXT [*CounterVariable*]

Description: Repeats a set of instructions. At the first iteration, the counter variable is set equal to the *Start* argument. With each subsequent iteration it is increased or decreased according to the value of the *Increment* argument. Execution of the loop continues until the counter variable reaches the value given by *Stop*. If no increment is given, the counter variable is increased by one with each iteration. Nested FOR...NEXT loops can use a single NEXT statement such as: NEXT *Counter1*, *Counter2*, ...

FUNCTION *Statement*

Syntax: FUNCTION *FunctionName* [*ParameterList*] [STATIC]

.
.
.

FunctionName = *Expression*

.
.
.

END FUNCTION

Description: Creates a user-defined function and declares the parameters of that function (if any). The body of the procedure is used to define the function. The value returned by the function is the expression that is set equal to the function name somewhere within the procedure definition.

GET *Statement*

Syntax: GET [#]*FileNumber* [,[*RecordNumber*][,*Variable*]]

Description: Reads a record from the random-access file identified by the *FileNumber* argument. *RecordNumber* specifies the record to be read, and *Variable* is the variable used to receive input from the file.

IF...THEN...ELSE *Statements*

Syntax 1:
IF *BooleanExpression* THEN *ThenStatment* [ELSE *ElseStatement*]

Syntax 2:   IF *BooleanExpression* THEN

.
.
.

[ELSEIF *BooleanExpression* THEN]

.
.
.

[ELSE]

.

.

.

END IF

Description: Allows program control to vary depending on the conditions set by one or more Boolean expressions. Statements following the THEN clause are executed only when the Boolean expression that precedes them is true. Statements following the optional ELSE clause are executed only if none of the preceding Boolean expressions is true.

INKEY$ Function

Syntax: INKEY$

Description: Uses the keyboard buffer in memory to return a one- or two-byte string that identifies the key or key combination that has been pressed. If no character is waiting in the buffer, the null string is returned.

INPUT$ Function

Syntax: INPUT$ (*n*[, [#]*Filenumber*])

Description: Returns the next *n* characters from the specified file. If no file number is given, the characters are returned from the keyboard.

INPUT Statement

Syntax: INPUT[;][*"PromptString"* {; | ,}]*VariableList*

Description: Pauses program execution to receive input from the keyboard after displaying the optional prompt string. The input value(s) is (are) assigned to the variable(s) in the variable list. If a semicolon separates the prompt string from the variable list, a question mark is added to the prompt. If a comma is used, no question mark appears.

INPUT # Statement

Syntax: INPUT #*FileNumber*, *VariableList*

Description: Reads data items from the specified file to the variables in the variable list. Individual items in the file must be separated by appropriate delimiters.

INSTR Function

Syntax: INSTR([*Start,*]*SearchInString*, *SearchForString*)

Description: Returns an integer value that identifies the position of the first occurrence of the *SearchForString* argument in the *SearchInString* argument. The optional *Start* argument gives a position for starting the search.

INT Function

Syntax: INT(*NumericExpression*)

Description: Returns the largest integer value less than or equal to the numeric expression given in the argument.

KILL Statement

Syntax: KILL *FileSpecification*

Description: Removes the specified file from your disk. The file specification argument must be a string expression.

LCASE$ Function

Syntax: LCASE$(*StringExpression*)

Description: Converts all letters in the string expression to lowercase and returns the converted string.

LEFT$ Function

Syntax: LEFT$(*StringExpression*, *n*)

Description: Returns the first *n* characters in the *StringExpression* argument.

LEN Function

Syntax 1:   LEN(*StringExpression*)

Syntax 2:   LEN(*VariableName*)

Description: If the argument given is a string expression, LEN returns the number of characters in the string. If the argument given is a variable, LEN returns the number of bytes required by that variable.

LET Statement

Syntax: [LET] *VariableName* = *Expression*

Description: Sets the named variable equal to the expression.

LINE Statement

Syntax:
LINE [[STEP](*x1,y1*)] – [STEP](*x2,y2*)[,[*Color*][,[B[F]][,*Style*]]]

Description: A graphics statement used for drawing lines or boxes. The endpoints of the line can be given as absolute values by using coordinates, or in reference to the most recently plotted point by using the STEP clause. The *Color* argument determines the color of the line or box. The B argument draws an outlined box, using the two points to determine the position of diagonally opposite corners, while BF draws a filled in box of the same dimensions.

LINE INPUT Statement

Syntax: LINE INPUT[;]["*PromptString*";]*StringVariable*

Description: Causes program execution to pause for keyboard input. An entire line of input characters (up to 255) is assigned to the specified string variable. (This line can include delimiters such as commas, which cannot be included when a simple INPUT statement is used.)

LINE INPUT # Statement

Syntax: LINE INPUT #*FileNumber*, *StringVariable*

Description: Reads an entire line of data from a sequential file. Individual lines of data are delimited by a Carriage Return/Line Feed (CR-LF).

LOCATE Statement

Syntax: LOCATE [*Row*][,[*Column*][,[*Cursor*][,[*Start,Stop*]]]]

Description: Positions the cursor at the specified row and column. The position of the upper left-hand corner is 1,1. If you omit a row or column argument, LOCATE uses the most recent cursor position for that value. The *Cursor* argument controls whether the cursor is visible, and *Start* and *Stop* control its size on the screen.

LOF Function

Syntax: LOF(*Filenumber*)

Description: Returns an integer value that gives the length of the specified file in bytes.

LTRIM$ Function

Syntax: LTRIM$(*StringExpression*)

Description: Trims any leading spaces from a string expression and then returns the trimmed expression.

MID$ Function

Syntax: MID$(*StringExpression, Start* [,*Length*])

Description: Returns the portion of a string expression that starts at the position given by the *Start* argument. If the *Length* argument is included, the returned value begins at the start position and continues for the number of characters specified by *Length*.

MKDIR Statement

Syntax: MKDIR *PathName*

Description: Creates a new directory with the name given in the argument. *PathName* must be given as a string expression.

ON ERROR Statement

Syntax: ON ERROR GOTO *LineLabel*

Description: Enables error-trapping so that a program can handle run-time errors without an interruption of program execution. When an error occurs after the ON ERROR statement has been executed, program control is transferred to the line given in the *LineLabel* argument.

OPEN Statement

Syntax:
OPEN *FileName* [FOR *Mode*] AS [#]*FileNumber*[LEN = *RecordLength*]

Description: Opens the specified file for input and/or output. The file name must be given as a string expression. *Mode* can be: OUTPUT, INPUT, APPEND, RANDOM, or BINARY. (Additional clauses can be added to an open statement to control access to the open file. Refer to the online index for more information.)

PLAY Statement

Syntax: PLAY *CommandString*

Description: Plays musical notes determined by the command string. Command string elements include: A–G for specifying pitch, O*n* for setting octaves, L*n* for setting note length, and T*n* for set-ting tempo.

PRESET Statement

Syntax: PRESET [STEP] (*x,y*) [*Color*]

Description: A graphics statement that draws a point at the specified location. If no color argument is given, PSET uses the current background color, erasing any previous point drawn at that location. Refer to PSET for more information about statement syntax.

PRINT Statement

Syntax: PRINT [*Expression1*][{, | ;}*Expression2*]...

Description: Sends output to the monitor screen. Commas cause output to be placed in 14-character-wide columns. Semicolons cause items to be placed immediately after the previously displayed item. If no argument is given, PRINT results in a blank line.

PRINT # Statement

Syntax: PRINT #*FileNumber*, [*Expression1*][{, | ;}*Expression2*]...

Description: Writes data to a sequential file specified by the *FileNumber* argument. Commas cause output to be written in 14-character-wide columns. Semicolons cause items to be written immediately after the previously displayed item.

PRINT USING Statement

Syntax: PRINT USING *FormatString*; *ExpressionList*

Description: Displays strings or numbers on screen using a format determined by the *FormatString* argument.

PRINT # USING Statement

Syntax: PRINT #*FileNumber* USING *FormatString*; *ExpressionList*

Description: Writes data to the specified sequential file, using a format determined by the *FormatString* argument.

PSET Statement

Syntax: PSET [STEP](x,y)[,*Color*]

Description: A graphics statement that places a point at the specified location. If no STEP clause is included, x and y measure horizontal and vertical distance from the upper left-hand corner of the screen. If the STEP clause is used, x and y measure distances from the most recently plotted point. If no *Color* argument is used, PSET uses the current foreground color.

PUT Statement

Syntax: PUT [#]*FileNumber*[,[*RecordNumber*][,*VariableName*]]

Description: Writes data from the specified variable to a random-access file at a position in that file controlled by the record number.

RANDOMIZE Statement

Syntax: RANDOMIZE [*NumericExpression*]

Description: Reseeds the random number generator. Using different values for the argument in a RANDOMIZE statement makes subsequent RND statements produce varying lists of random values each time a program runs.

READ Statement

Syntax: READ *VariableList*

Description: Reads data values from a DATA statement to the variables in the variable list.

REM Statement

Syntax 1:   REM *RemarkStatement*

Syntax 2:   '*RemarkStatement*

Description: Allows you to include explanatory statements in your program that have no effect on program execution. Apostrophes can also be used to mark remark statements that follow program code on the same line. If REM is not the first statement on a line, it must be preceded by a colon.

RESET Statement

Syntax: RESET

Description: Closes all open files.

RESTORE Statement

Syntax: RESTORE [{*LineNumber* | *LineLabel*}]

Description: Causes subsequent READ statements to read data starting with the first item in the first DATA statement. If a line label is given, data is read from the first DATA statement following that line label.

RESUME *Statement*

Syntax: RESUME [0]
RESUME NEXT
RESUME {*LineNumber* | *LineLabel*}

Description: Directs program flow to the next line to be executed after completion of an error-handling routine. RESUME causes the program to return to the line at which the error occurred. RESUME NEXT causes the program to return to the line immediately following the one at which the error occurred. RESUME followed by a line identifier causes program execution to continue with the identified line.

RIGHT$ *Function*

Syntax: RIGHT$(*StringExpression,n*)

Description: Returns the last *n* characters in a string expression.

RMDIR *Statement*

Syntax: RMDIR *PathName*

Description: Removes the directory with the name given in the argument. *PathName* must be given as a string expression.

RND *Function*

Syntax: RND

Description: Returns a single-precision random number between zero and one (noninclusive).

RTRIM$ *Function*

Syntax: RTRIM$(*StringExpression*)

Description: Trims any trailing spaces from a string expression and then returns the trimmed expression.

SCREEN *Statement*

Syntax: SCREEN [Mode]

Description: A graphics statement that sets a display screen mode. A graphics screen mode must be selected before graphics statements can be used in a program. (Additional arguments can be used with the SCREEN statement. Refer to the online index for more information.)

SELECT CASE Statement

Syntax: SELECT CASE *Expression*
     CASE *ExpressionList1*

       .
       .
       .

     [CASE ExpressionList2]

       .
       .
       .

     [CASE ELSE]

       .
       .
       .

     END SELECT

Description: A branching control structure that matches the item given in the *Expression* argument with the items given in the expression lists. When these two items match, the statement block under the appropriate CASE statement is executed. If a CASE ELSE clause is used, the statement block beneath this clause is executed if no match is found.

SGN Function

Syntax: SGN(*NumericExpression*)

Description: Returns 1 if the numeric expression is positive, 0 if the expression is equal to zero, and − 1 if the expression is negative.

SHARED Statement

Syntax:
SHARED *Variable1* [AS *DataType*][, *Variable2* [AS *DataType*]]

Description: Declares the listed variables to be SHARED between the module-level code and the SUB and FUNCTION procedures of a program module. Can also be used to establish the data type of SHARED variables.

SHELL Statement

Syntax: SHELL [*CommandString*]

Description: Temporarily exits a program to perform the DOS command given in the argument. If no argument is given, SHELL temporarily exits the program, and DOS prompts are repeatedly displayed, allowing a variety of DOS commands to be executed. Typing exit at a DOS prompt returns control to the program.

SIN Function

Syntax: SIN (*RadianAngleMeasure*)

Description: Returns the sine of the angle given in the argument. Angle measurements must be given in radians.

SLEEP Statement

Syntax: SLEEP [*IntegerValue*]

Description: Causes program execution to pause for the number of seconds given in the argument or until a key is pressed.

SOUND Statement

Syntax: SOUND *Frequency, Duration*

Description: Produces a sound from the computer's speaker using the specified values to establish frequency and duration.

SPACE$ Function

Syntax: SPACE$(*n*)

Description: Returns a string value containing *n* spaces.

SPC Function

Syntax: PRINT ... SPC(*n*) ...

Description: Produces *n* blank spaces between items being displayed with a PRINT statement.

SQR Function

Syntax: SQR(*NumericExpression*)

Description: Returns the square root of the numeric expression given in the argument.

STATIC Statement

Syntax: STATIC *VariableList*

Description: Makes simple variables local to the procedure that contains the STATIC statement and preserves the value of these variables between procedure calls.

STR$ Function

Syntax: STR$(*NumericExpression*)

Description: Converts the number given by the numeric expression to its string representation and returns that string expression.

STRING$ Function

Syntax 1: STRING$(*n,ASCIICodeNumber*)

Syntax 2: STRING$(*n,StringExpression*)

Description: Returns a string containing a string character (or characters) repeated *n* times. The repeated character or characters is determined by the second argument. This can be given using the ASCII code number for a display character, or by using a string expression.

SUB Statements

Syntax: SUB *ProcedureName* [*ParameterList*] [STATIC]
.
.
.
ProcedureName = *Expression*
.
.
.
END SUB

Description: SUB and END SUB statements enclose a block of statements that can be invoked by a CALL statement. Procedure names are global and cannot be used to define variables or procedures elsewhere in the same program. Variables within a procedure are local to that procedure unless otherwise specified. The items in the parameter list receive values from a list of items of the same data-type(s) used as arguments in the CALL statement that invokes the procedure.

SWAP Statement

Syntax: SWAP *Variable1*, *Variable2*

Description: Exchanges the values of the two variables given as arguments. The two variables must be the same data-type.

TAB Function

Syntax: PRINT ... TAB(*IntegerValue*)...

Description: Used within a PRINT statement, the TAB function moves subsequent screen display to the column indicated in the argument.

TAN Function

Syntax: TAN (*RadianAngleMeasure*)

Description: Returns the tangent of the angle given in the argument. Angle measurements must be given in radians.

TIME$ Function

Syntax: TIME$

Description: Returns the current operating system time as a string value.

TIME$ Statement

Syntax: TIME$ = *StringExpression*

Description: Sets the string expression equal to the current operating system time.

TIMER Function

Syntax: TIMER

Description: Returns the number of seconds that have elapsed since midnight, according to the operating system clock. This is a single-precision number by default. TIMER can also be used with integer or double-precision variables, in which case the value returned uses the data-type of the variable it is assigned to.

TYPE Statement

Syntax: TYPE *UserDataType*
        Element1 AS *DataType*
        Element2 AS *DataType*

        .

        .

      END TYPE

Description: TYPE structures are used to define composite data-types. Each element in the composite type is defined as having one of the five QuickBASIC data-types (or a composite type previously defined by the user). String elements must also be assigned a character length as follows, where n equals the length of the string element:

        Element AS STRING * n

UCASE$ Function

Syntax: UCASE$(*StringExpression*)

Description: Converts all letters in the string expression to uppercase and returns the converted string.

VAL Function

Syntax: VAL(*StringExpression*)

Description: Converts a string of digits into the numeric value they represent and returns that value.

VIEW Statement

Syntax: VIEW [[SCREEN](*x1,y1*) – (*x2,y2*)[,[*Color*][,*Border*]]]

Description: A graphics statement that defines screen limits for graphics output. The coordinates define diagonally opposite corners of the graphics viewport. Using SCREEN means that the coordinates of subsequent graphics statements will be absolute to the screen. When SCREEN is omitted, the coordinates of subsequent graphics statements are plotted relative to the viewport. The *Color* argument gives the color used to fill the viewport; if it is omitted, the area is not filled. Any numeric value in the *Border* argument position draws a line around the viewport.

VIEW PRINT *Statement*

Syntax: VIEW PRINT [*TopLine* TO *BottomLine*]

Description: Defines limits for text output. *TopLine* gives the upper limit for subsequent text output, and *BottomLine* gives the lower limit. Subsequent CLS, LOCATE, and PRINT statements operate within these boundaries. When no argument is used, the text viewport occupies the entire screen.

WINDOW *Statement*

Syntax: WINDOW [[SCREEN](*x1,y1*) − (*x2,y2*)]

Description: Redefines the coordinate grid used for graphics output. (*x1,y1*) and (*x2,y2*) give new coordinates for the corners of the viewport. If no arguments are included, the viewport is reset to the default coordinates for the screen mode being used. Using SCREEN inverts the direction of the y axis, making it go from smaller to larger values as you move from the top of the screen toward the bottom.

WRITE *Statement*

Syntax: WRITE [*ExpressionList*]

Description: Displays output on the monitor screen. Items in the expression list can be string or numeric values and must be separated by commas. If no argument is given, a blank line is displayed. Each item displayed is separated by a comma. String items are also enclosed in double quotation marks. No leading or trailing spaces are placed around numeric output.

WRITE # *Statement*

Syntax: WRITE #*FileNumber*, [*ExpressionList*]

Description: Writes the data in the expression list to a sequential-access data file. Items in the expression list can be string or numeric values and must be separated by commas. If no argument is given, a blank line is written to the file. Commas are written to the file as delimiters between each item on the list. String items are also enclosed in double quotation marks.

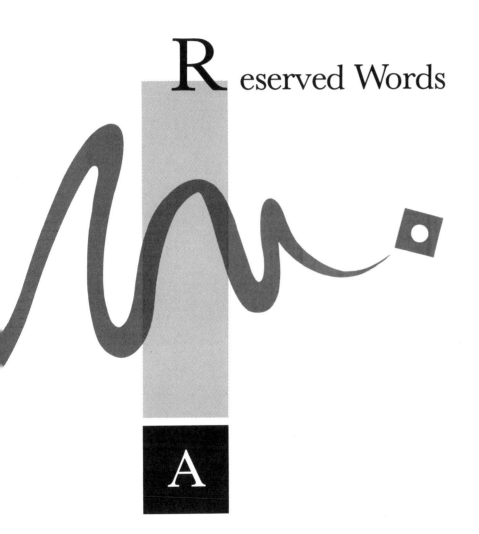

Reserved Words

A

APPENDIX *A*

THE FOLLOWING WORDS MAKE UP THE QUICKBASIC command language and cannot be used as line identifiers, variable names, or procedure names in your programs.

ABS	CHDIR	CVSMBF
ACCESS	CHR$	DATA
ALIAS	CINT	DATE$
AND	CIRCLE	DECLARE
ANY	CLEAR	DEF
APPEND	CLNG	DEFDBL
AS	CLOSE	DEFINT
ASAVE	CLS	DEFLNG
ASC	COLOR	DEFSNG
ATN	COM	DEFSTR
BASE	COMMAND$	DIM
BEEP	COMMON	DO
BINARY	CONST	DOUBLE
BLOAD	COS	DRAW
BYVAL	CSNG	ELSE
CALL	CSRLIN	ELSEIF
CALLS	CVD	END
CASE	CVDMBF	ENDIF
CDBL	CVI	ENVIRON
CDECL	CVL	ENVIRON$
CHAIN	CVS	EOF

EQV	INTEGER	MKDMBF$
ERASE	IOCTL	MKI$
ERDEV$	IOCTL$	MKL$
ERL	IS	MKS$
ERR	KEY	MKSMBF$
ERROR	KILL	MOD
EXIT	LBOUND	NAME
EXP	LCASE$	NEXT
FIELD	LEFT$	NOT
FILEATTR	LEN	OCT$
FILES	LET	OFF
FIX	LINE	ON
FOR	LIST	OPEN
FRE	LOC	OPTION
FREEFILE	LOCAL	OR
FUNCTION	LOCATE	OUT
GET	LOCK	OUTPUT
GOSUB	LOF	PAINT
GOTO	LOG	PALETTE
HEX$	LONG	PCOPY
IF	LOOP	PEEK
IMP	LPOS	PEN
INKEY$	LPRINT	PLAY
INP	LSET	PMAP
INPUT	LTRIM$	POINT
INPUT$	MID$	POKE
INSTR	MKD$	POS
INT	MKDIR	PRESET

PRINT	SHARED	TIMER
PSET	SHELL	TO
PUT	SIGNAL	TROFF
RANDOM	SIN	TRON
RANDOMIZE	SINGLE	TYPE
READ	SLEEP	UBOUND
REDIM	SOUND	UCASE$
REM	SPACE$	UEVENT
RESET	SPC	UNLOCK
RESTORE	SQR	UNTIL
RESUME	STATIC	USING
RETURN	STEP	VAL
RIGHT$	STICK	VARPTR
RMDIR	STOP	VARPTR$
RND	STR$	VARSEG
RSET	STRIG	VIEW
RTRIM$	STRING	WAIT
RUN	STRING$	WEND
SADD	SUB	WHILE
SCREEN	SWAP	WIDTH
SEEK	SYSTEM	WINDOW
SEG	TAB	WRITE
SELECT	TAN	XOR
SETMEM	THEN	
SGN	TIME$	

U sing QuickBASIC with a Floppy-Drive System

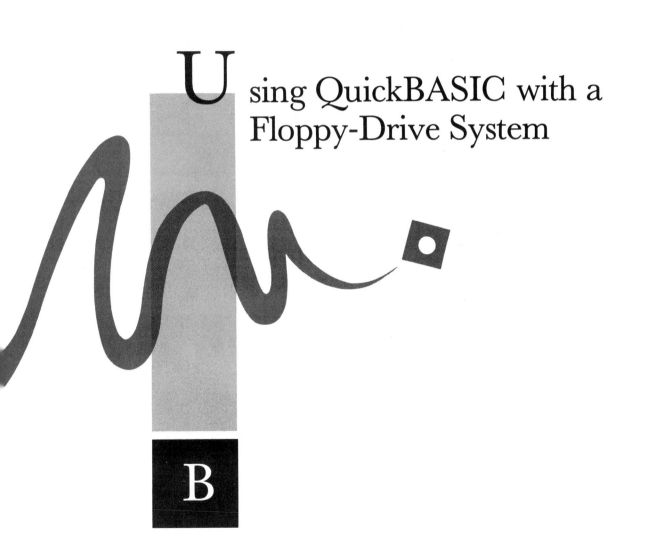

B

APPENDIX **B**

THIS APPENDIX DESCRIBES TECHNIQUES FOR USING
QuickBASIC on a system with two floppy drives using standard
5¼-inch 360K disks. Before starting, it is advisable to place write-
protect tabs on each of the five distribution diskettes that came with
your distribution package and make duplicate copies of these disks
with the DOS DISKCOPY command. Use these duplicates to create
the working diskettes described in the following sections.

The five distribution disks are listed and described here:

- **Setup/Express**: This disk contains a program for installing
  QuickBASIC on a hard disk, and a variety of sample BASIC
  programs.

- **Program**: This disk contains the QuickBASIC program file
  (QB.EXE) and one of the three files used to provide on-line
  help (QB45QCK.HLP).

- **Utilities 1**: This disk contains files you will need in order to
  make .EXE programs which can be run directly from the
  operating system.

- **Utilities 2**: This disk includes one of the three help files
  (QB45ENER.HLP). Two of the utilities programs included
  are MOUSE.COM, which you must run before you can use
  a mouse with your system, and MSHERC.COM, which
  you must run before you can run graphics programs in a system using a Hercules graphics card. This disk also contains
  two text files: README.DOC, which includes information
  about using QuickBASIC, and PACKING.LST, which
  describes all the files on each of the distribution diskettes.

- **Advisor**: This disk includes the third QuickBASIC help file
  (QB45ADVR.HLP) and a variety of sample programs.

PREPARING A
WORKING PROGRAM DISK

QuickBASIC is easiest to use if you copy the program file to a working disk that you can also use to start up your system. Create a working program disk as follows:

1. Place your operating system disk in A, and a new disk in B, and format the new disk with the command

   FORMAT B: /S

   (Using the /S option makes this a "Bootable" disk—one that you can use to start up your system.)

2. Place the *Program* distribution disk in drive A and copy the QuickBASIC program to the formatted disk in drive B with this command:

   COPY QB.EXE B:

3. Label this disk "QuickBASIC/Program & System."

STARTING QUICKBASIC

To get started with QuickBASIC:

1. Place the *QuickBASIC/Program & System* disk you just created in drive A.

2. Place a blank, formatted disk in drive B. This disk will be used to store your program files.

3. At the DOS prompt, type

   qb ↵

   You will see the QuickBASIC Welcome box.

4. Press Esc to clear this box and get started with QuickBASIC.

See Chapter 15 for more information about the QuickBASIC display options.

In order to avoid inadvertently saving your programs on this program disk, you might want to place a write-protect tab on it. However, if you want to change display options using the Options menu, you should first remove this tab. You can replace it after you have made your changes and exited to the operating system.

SAVING A PROGRAM

To save a program to the disk in drive B:

1. Press Alt to activate the Menu bar.

2. Press ⏎ to open the Files menu. (Pressing **F** will also open the menu.)

3. Highlight *Save As* and press ⏎ to select this command. (Pressing **A** will also select this command.)

4. The Save As dialog box will open, and the cursor will be in the *File Name:* input area. Type

   B:*Filename*

   replacing *Filename* with the name you are giving to the program you want to save.

5. Press ⏎ to close the dialog box and complete the save command.

OPENING A FILE

To open a file that has been saved to the B drive:

1. Press Alt to activate the Menu bar.

2. Press ⏎ or **F** to open the File menu.

3. Highlight *Open Program* and press ⏎ (or press **O**) to activate the Open Program command.

4. The Open Program dialog box will appear, with **.BAS* visible in the *File Name:* input area and the current directory identified as *A:* just below this input area. Type

   B: ⏎

When you first
move the cursor to
the *Files* list box, it will be
positioned under the
name of the first file on
the list. However, this file
is not selected until you
press the ↓ key. Pressing
the ↓ key the first time
highlights the first file on
the list.

to change to the B drive. The current drive will change to
B:, and the programs on the disk in the drive will be listed in
the *Files* list box.

5. Press Tab to move the cursor to the *Files* list box.

6. Use the cursor-control keys to highlight the file you want to
    open, and press ◄─┘ to open this file.

USING ONLINE HELP

To use QuickBASIC's online help features, you need to have
access to three separate help files. If you attempt to use an online help
feature with a disk that does not include the necessary help file, you
will see a message on screen identifying the missing file, followed by
instructions telling you to put the floppy disk with this file into
the drive.

The *QuickBASIC/Program & System* disk you are using contains no
help files, nor is there sufficient disk space to add any of these files to
the disk. One solution is to create special disks to use when you want
to work with online help. You will need two blank, formatted disks for
this purpose.

To prepare the first disk:

1. Place the distribution disk labeled *Program* into drive A and
    one of the blank, formatted disks in drive B.

2. Copy the QB45QCK.HLP file to your disk using this
    command:

    ```
    COPY A:QB45QCK.HLP B:
    ```

3. Remove the *Program* disk from drive A and replace it with the
    Utilities 2 disk. Copy the QB45ENER.HLP file to your disk
    using this command:

    ```
    COPY A:QB45ENER.HLP B:
    ```

4. After you have copied the two files to your disk, label it
    "HELP 1/QB45QCK.HLP & QB45ENER.HLP."

To prepare the second help disk:

1. Place the distribution disk labeled *Advisor* in drive A and the second blank, formatted disk in drive B.

2. Copy the QB45ADVR.HLP file to your disk using this command:

   `COPY A:QB45ADVR.HLP B:`

3. Label this disk "HELP 2/QB45ADVR.HLP."

Keep these two HELP disks handy when you want to use the online help. When you see a dialog box identifying a missing help file, replace the program disk in drive A with the HELP disk containing that file and press ↵.

CREATING .EXE PROGRAMS

You will need the distribution disk labeled *Utilities 1* in order to create .EXE files. The directions that follow explain how to make a file that does not include debug code and must be run on a disk that also includes the BRUN45.EXE file.

1. Copy the BRUN45.EXE file from the *Utilities 1* disk to the disk you are using for your program files.

2. Load QuickBASIC. Use the Options menu to select *Full Menus*. (Refer to Chapter 15 for more information about the Options menu.)

3. When the program you are working with is completed and running correctly, save it to the program disk in drive B.

4. Open the Run menu and select the *Make EXE File* command. Check to be sure that the *Produce Debug Code* option is not marked and that the *EXE Requiring BRUN45.EXE* choice is selected.

5. Be sure that the cursor is in the *EXE File Name* input box. Press the Home key and type *B:* to edit your .EXE file name so that it will be saved to drive B.

6. Press ◄─┘. The message "Cannot find file (BC.EXE). Input path:" will appear on screen.

7. When you see the missing file message, replace your program disk (in Drive A) with the *Utilities 1* disk and press ◄─┘. The compiling process will begin. Once it is complete, you will see the message "Cannot find file (QB.EXE). Input path:"

8. When you see the missing file message, replace the *Utilities 1* disk with your program disk and press ◄─┘. You will be returned to the QuickBASIC Work screen.

To run the executable file you just created, exit from QuickBASIC and change to drive B. Check the directory listing to be sure that both the BRUN45.EXE file and the .EXE file you just created are present. Type in the name of the file you created—leaving off the .EXE extension—and then press ◄─┘ to run the program.

A SCII Character Codes

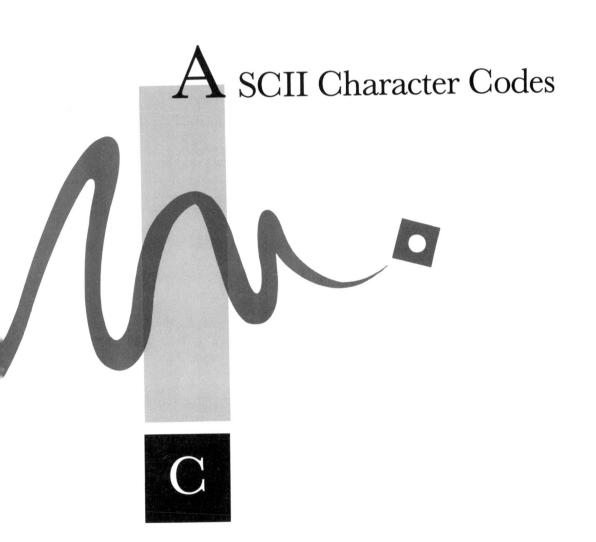

APPENDIX C

ASCII TABLE

ASCII VALUE	CHARACTER	CONTROL CHARACTER	ASCII VALUE	CHARACTER	CONTROL CHARACTER
000	(null)	NUL	016	►	DLE
001	☺	SOH	017	◄	DC1
002	●	STX	018	↕	DC2
003	♥	ETX	019	‼	DC3
004	♦	EOT	020	¶	DC4
005	♣	ENQ	021	§	NAK
006	♠	ACK	022	▬	SYN
007	(beep)	BEL	023	↨	ETB
008	◘	BS	024	↑	CAN
009	(tab)	HT	025	↓	EM
010	(line feed)	LF	026	→	SUB
011	(home)	VT	027	←	ESC
012	(form feed)	FF	028	(cursor right)	FS
013	(carriage return)	CR	029	(cursor left)	GS
014	♫	SO	030	(cursor up)	RS
015	☼	SI	031	(cursor down)	US

This table was reprinted by permission from *IBM PC Basic Manual* ©1984 by International Business Machines Corporation.

ASCII VALUE	CHARACTER	ASCII VALUE	CHARACTER
032	(space)	070	F
033	!	071	G
034	"	072	H
035	#	073	I
036	$	074	J
037	%	075	K
038	&	076	L
039	'	077	M
040	(	078	N
041	)	079	O
042	*	080	P
043	+	081	Q
044	,	082	R
045	-	083	S
046	.	084	T
047	/	085	U
048	0	086	V
049	1	087	W
050	2	088	X
051	3	089	Y
052	4	090	Z
053	5	091	[
054	6	092	\
055	7	093	]
056	8	094	∧
057	9	095	—
058	:	096	`
059	;	097	a
060	<	098	b
061	=	099	c
062	>	100	d
063	?	101	e
064	@	102	f
065	A	103	g
066	B	104	h
067	C	105	i
068	D	106	j
069	E	107	k

ASCII VALUE	CHARACTER	ASCII VALUE	CHARACTER
108	l	146	Æ
109	m	147	ô
110	n	148	ö
111	o	149	ò
112	p	150	û
113	q	151	ù
114	r	152	ÿ
115	s	153	Ö
116	t	154	Ü
117	u	155	¢
118	v	156	£
119	w	157	¥
120	x	158	Pt
121	y	159	ƒ
122	z	160	á
123	{	161	í
124	¦	162	ó
125	}	163	ú
126	~	164	ñ
127	△	165	Ñ
128	Ç	166	ª
129	ü	167	º
130	é	168	¿
131	â	169	⌐
132	ä	170	¬
133	à	171	½
134	å	172	¼
135	ç	173	¡
136	ê	174	«
137	ë	175	»
138	è	176	░
139	ï	177	▒
140	î	178	▓
141	ì	179	│
142	Ä	180	┤
143	Å	181	╡
144	É	182	╢
145	æ	183	╖

ASCII VALUE	CHARACTER	ASCII VALUE	CHARACTER
184	⌐	220	▀
185	╣	221	▌
186	║	222	▐
187	╗	223	▀
188	╝	224	α
189	╜	225	β
190	╛	226	Γ
191	┐	227	π
192	└	228	Σ
193	┴	229	σ
194	┬	230	μ
195	├	231	τ
196	─	232	Φ
197	┼	233	Θ
198	╞	234	Ω
199	╟	235	δ
200	╚	236	∞
201	╔	237	$\varnothing$
202	╩	238	ϵ
203	╦	239	$\cap$
204	╠	240	$\equiv$
205	═	241	$\pm$
206	╬	242	$\geq$
207	╧	243	$\leq$
208	╨	244	$\lceil$
209	╤	245	J
210	╥	246	$\div$
211	╙	247	$\approx$
212	╘	248	$\circ$
213	╒	249	•
214	╓	250	·
215	╫	251	$\sqrt{}$
216	╪	252	n
217	┘	253	^{2}
218	┌	254	■
219	█	255	(blank 'FF')

R un-Time Error Codes

D

APPENDIX *D*

CODE	DESCRIPTION
2	Syntax error
3	RETURN without GOSUB
4	Out of DATA
5	Illegal Function call
6	Overflow
7	Out of memory
9	Subscript out of range
10	Duplicate definition
11	Division by zero
13	Type mismatch
14	Out of string space
16	String formula too complex
19	No RESUME
20	RESUME without error
24	Device timeout
25	Device fault
27	Out of paper
39	CASE ELSE expected
40	Variable required
50	FIELD overflow

51	Internal error
52	Bad file name or number
53	File not found
54	Bad file mode
55	File already open
56	FIELD statement active
57	Device I/O error
58	File already exists
59	Bad record length
61	Disk full
62	Input past end of file
63	Bad record number
64	Bad file name
67	Too many files
68	Device unavailable
69	Communication-buffer overflow
70	Permission denied
71	Disk not ready
72	Disk-media error
73	Advanced feature unavailable
74	Rename across disks
75	Path/File access error
76	Path not found

INDEX

TO JOIN THE SYBEX MAILING LIST OR ORDER BOOKS
PLEASE COMPLETE THIS FORM

NAME _____ COMPANY _____

STREET _____ CITY _____

STATE _____ ZIP _____

☐ PLEASE MAIL ME MORE INFORMATION ABOUT **SYBEX** TITLES

ORDER FORM (There is no obligation to order)

PLEASE SEND ME THE FOLLOWING:

TITLE	QTY	PRICE
_____	____	____
_____	____	____
_____	____	____
_____	____	____

TOTAL BOOK ORDER   ____ $____

CUSTOMER SIGNATURE _____

SHIPPING AND HANDLING PLEASE ADD $2.00
PER BOOK VIA UPS   _____

FOR OVERSEAS SURFACE ADD $5.25 PER
BOOK PLUS $4.40 REGISTRATION FEE   _____

FOR OVERSEAS AIRMAIL ADD $18.25 PER
BOOK PLUS $4.40 REGISTRATION FEE   _____

CALIFORNIA RESIDENTS PLEASE ADD
APPLICABLE SALES TAX   _____

TOTAL AMOUNT PAYABLE   _____

☐ CHECK ENCLOSED   ☐ VISA
☐ MASTERCARD   ☐ AMERICAN EXPRESS

ACCOUNT NUMBER _____

EXPIR. DATE _____ DAYTIME PHONE _____

CHECK AREA OF COMPUTER INTEREST:

☐ BUSINESS SOFTWARE

☐ TECHNICAL PROGRAMMING

☐ OTHER: _____

THE FACTOR THAT WAS MOST IMPORTANT IN
YOUR SELECTION:

☐ THE SYBEX NAME

☐ QUALITY

☐ PRICE

☐ EXTRA FEATURES

☐ COMPREHENSIVENESS

☐ CLEAR WRITING

☐ OTHER _____

OTHER COMPUTER TITLES YOU WOULD LIKE
TO SEE IN PRINT:

_____

_____

OCCUPATION

☐ PROGRAMMER   ☐ TEACHER

☐ SENIOR EXECUTIVE   ☐ HOMEMAKER

☐ COMPUTER CONSULTANT   ☐ RETIRED

☐ SUPERVISOR   ☐ STUDENT

☐ MIDDLE MANAGEMENT   ☐ OTHER:

☐ ENGINEER/TECHNICAL   _____

☐ CLERICAL/SERVICE

☐ BUSINESS OWNER/SELF EMPLOYED

CHECK YOUR LEVEL OF COMPUTER USE

☐ NEW TO COMPUTERS

☐ INFREQUENT COMPUTER USER

☐ FREQUENT USER OF ONE SOFTWARE

PACKAGE:

NAME _____

☐ FREQUENT USER OF MANY SOFTWARE

PACKAGES

☐ PROFESSIONAL PROGRAMMER

OTHER COMMENTS:

_____

_____

_____

_____

_____

_____

_____

PLEASE FOLD, SEAL, AND MAIL TO SYBEX

SYBEX, INC.
2021 CHALLENGER DR. #100
ALAMEDA, CALIFORNIA USA
94501

SEAL

SYBEX Computer Books are different.

Here is why . . .

At SYBEX, each book is designed with you in mind. Every manuscript is carefully selected and supervised by our editors, who are themselves computer experts. We publish the best authors, whose technical expertise is matched by an ability to write clearly and to communicate effectively. Programs are thoroughly tested for accuracy by our technical staff. Our computerized production department goes to great lengths to make sure that each book is well-designed.

In the pursuit of timeliness, SYBEX has achieved many publishing firsts. SYBEX was among the first to integrate personal computers used by authors and staff into the publishing process. SYBEX was the first to publish books on the CP/M operating system, microprocessor interfacing techniques, word processing, and many more topics.

Expertise in computers and dedication to the highest quality product have made SYBEX a world leader in computer book publishing. Translated into fourteen languages, SYBEX books have helped millions of people around the world to get the most from their computers. We hope we have helped you, too.

For a complete catalog of our publications:

SYBEX, Inc. 2021 Challenger Drive, #100, Alameda, CA 94501
Tel: (415) 523-8233/(800) 227-2346 Telex: 336311
Fax: (415) 523-2373

THE QUICKBASIC FULL MENUS: A COMMAND SUMMARY

The page number in the right column indicates where in Chapter 15 the command is summarized.
Commands followed by three dots (. . .) call up dialog boxes.

	Shortcut Key Alternatives	Page
The File Menu		
New Program		350
Open Program . . .		351
Merge . . .		352
Save		352
Save As . . .		353
Save All		354
Create File . . .		354
Load File . . .		355
Unload File . . .		355
Print . . .		355
DOS Shell		356
Exit		356
The Edit Menu		
Undo	Alt +Backspace	358
Cut	Shift +Del	358
Copy	Ctrl +Ins	359
Paste	Shift +Ins	359
Clear	Del	360
New SUB . . .		360
New FUNCTION . . .		360
The View Menu		
SUBs . . .	F2	361
Next SUB	Shift +F2	361
Split		362
Next Statement		362
Output Screen	F4	363
Included File		363
Included Lines		363
The Search Menu		
Find . . .		364
Selected Text	Ctrl +\	365
Repeat Last Find	F3	365
Change . . .		365
Label . . .		367